People-Reading

People-Reading

How We Control Others, How They Control Us

Dr. Ernst G. Beier and Evans G. Valens

 STEIN AND DAY/*Publishers*/New York

First published in 1975
Copyright © 1975 by Ernst G. Beier and Evans G. Valens
All rights reserved
Designed by Ed Kaplin
Printed in the United States of America
Stein and Day/*Publishers*/Scarborough House, Briarcliff Manor, New York 10510

Library of Congress Cataloging in Publication Data

Beier, Ernst Gunter.
People-reading.

   1. Control (Psychology)   2.   Persuasion (Psychology)
3. Nonverbal communication.   4.   Personality, Disorders
of. I. Valens, Evans G., joint author. II.   Title.
BF632.5.B44   153.8′52   74-26977
ISBN 0-8128-1781-8

For Frances and Win

ACKNOWLEDGMENTS

We wish to acknowledge our indebtedness to the scientists and scholars who helped us formulate our work on communication; to members of the Communication Research Group, who made important contributions to much of the research on which the present work is based, especially to Kent Burns, Steve Donoviel, Marie Griffin, Kim Korner, Don Miller, Dale Miller, Dan Sternberg, Peter Robinson, David Young, and Alex Zantra; to our students, who kept us on our toes; and to friends and patients who have allowed us to gain insight into our life-styles. We want to express special thanks to Wendy Smith who, with ever-friendly smiles, helped us with the many drafts of the manuscript. We thank Abigail Van Buren for permission to quote from "Dear Abby." We owe a particular debt to Hanna M. Beier, a wonderful woman who is still the artist at her advanced age. And to Mary Solberg, our editor, who has made a unique contribution to this book. Her blunt queries forced us to rework many of our explanations, and her spirit repeatedly informed our style.

Contents

Preface

Nobody knows what man thought of himself when he first became self-conscious, but for a long while after that he seems to have seen himself as some kind of marionette controlled by gods, spirits, and demons who could perhaps be placated. Ordinary men took counsel with their shamans and wise men and over the centuries produced prayers, dances, and rituals, and sacrificial rites, all for the purpose of influencing man's fate.

More familiar to us today is the rational model of the human animal, which has been particularly popular in North America ever since the McGuffey's Readers and Horatio Alger. It could as well be called the Abe Lincoln model because it assumes that anyone can become president, or just about anything else, if he will just plan ahead and work hard enough at it.

This model defines man as a perfectible machine, predictable, trainable, rational, manageable, and capable of self-control through the application of will power. Being both moralistic and mechanistic, it serves alike for Boy Scouts and Marxists. It assumes that men can be directly guided to or programmed for almost any desired goal.

Unfortunately, this model of human behavior is idealized and inaccurate. It assumes that people strive naturally for the traditional virtues—to be good, helpful, friendly, sociable, successful, well liked, happy, and sexually attractive. This assumption touches only part of man's motivational structure—the fully conscious part with which we all like to delude ourselves.

The virtues make good reading. We talk about them a lot since the very voicing of such desires is traditionally rewarded by approval. The virtues are also, by definition, what we all strive to promote in others or in "mankind."

But as for ourselves, personally, we have our own way of doing things. We are driven by our own private motivations, aware and unaware, sweet and sour, and in this area we do not settle for generalities. The aim is not to be proper and "good" but simply to get people to believe that we are.

Sigmund Freud was aware that the advice-givers of his time were not doing anything for people with serious psychological problems, and he approached human behavior scientifically rather than moralistically. He tried to observe the actual consequences of various behaviors instead of making value judgments, and the result was an entirely new concept—the psychoanalytic model of man. This revolutionary approach to individual psychology did not offer advice, but rather looked into the patient's past for the roots of his current problem.

Freud assumed that we do *not* know what we really want. He discovered that we find direction in our lives by organizing our motivations, *unconscious* as well as conscious, and he searched for them in childhood experiences, particularly in those experiences that had left emotional scars. He soon realized that analysis of the past was not enough. The disturbing emotions must also be transferred onto some present focus such as the analyst himself in order to work them through and allow them to become current and tangible.

Psychoanalysis has been criticized for its preoccupation with the past. One of the most articulate critics is Carl Rogers, who developed an alternate model of human behavior, based on a phenomenological approach to current experience. He believes that the past is a dead issue and that a person will change for the better if, in the nonthreatening setting of a client-centered therapy, he learns to consider alternative ways of perceiving his own behavior. Gaining perspective in this way allows him to explore new possibilities.

Rogers endows man with a natural motivation toward a better life (his "growth principle"), which he believes will assert itself as long as the individual is given a chance to come to grips with it. The great value of Rogers' unduly optimistic model of man lies in his realization that our unconscious motivations are clearly reflected in current behavior and do not need to be searched for in the past.

Rogers is one of the stalwarts of the humanistic tradition in psychology, strongly opposed to the "technocracy" of B. F. Skinner and others. Encounter groups also follow this tradition, stressing group experience and rapport. In an encounter group, the individual finds himself in a situation where he is encouraged to speak openly and to act out his fears and other hang-ups. Group pressure challenges him to do so, and group support helps him resolve his difficulties.

Skinner's basic work, which led to the therapeutic approach of *behavior modification,* assumes that personality can be made to order and implies a "modular" model of man, a squared-off creature made from thousands of unrelated little response modules loosely glued together. Successful in certain limited settings, it has a high failure rate in complex situations.

Behavior modification has a formidable advantage over other models in that it spells out rather precisely the goals of therapeutic effort.

If you know how many words per minute a child reads, then, after the proper conditioning effort, you can measure to what extent your intervention was a success. This is very different from the more general psychotherapies where the goal is personality reorganization rather than the removal of the problem or the symptom. A person might overcome unhappiness or hopelessness, but unfortunately hope and happiness do not come in measurable units.

A very different model is that of "interactional man," which holds that human interaction is a fundamental principle of behavior. *Interactional analysis* (Eric Berne, J. Haley, and others) assumes that we can do very little about an individual's behavior if we study him in isolation.

A major implication of this popular new approach is that a man with behavioral difficulties cannot maintain his maladjustments without the active and consistent support of people who are close to him. One speaks not of a maladjusted individual but of a maladjusted interaction pattern, and the problem of accurate interpersonal communication becomes crucial. For example, whereas *we* might try to help a "maladjusted" member of a family, the interactionalist would hold that we do not have a problem individual; we have a disturbed family.

The model on which this book is based is a "communication analysis" model. The label refers to the recognition that subtle cues exist that are not commonly thought to be communications at all. These cues are delivered without awareness and they account for man's astounding ability to influence and control others without even trying.

The model follows Berne's view of man as a product of human interaction and, along with Rogers, looks to the present rather than to the past for evidence of hidden problems. It embraces Freud's discovery that conflicting motivations operate at an unconscious level and that behavior can be altered by current experience. It also relies on Skinner, in that it utilizes concepts of reinforcement and reward.

Five assumptions implicit in this model point up the significance of the unaware aspect of communicative behavior and suggest a way in which we might catch sight of our ingeniously camouflaged maneuverings:

1. We need to be involved with other people and we will go to great lengths to bring this about; we prefer the involvement of love, but if that escapes us, hate will do.
2. It is usually easier to elicit responses of hate than of love.
3. We crave certainty and are prepared to sacrifice a great deal to make people close to us behave predictably.
4. Our attempts to involve others and to make them predictable—that is, our manipulations—are maintained only insofar as they continue to fulfill these functions.

5. Our most cherished motivations tend to be hidden; we don't care to be made aware of them, and we often find ourselves working diligently for goals we claim we do not want.

A central ingredient of this model derives from the fact that language is the reinforcer par excellence. A person's characteristic behavior—including all his successful manipulations—is reinforced whenever he receives the expected, or "social," response. The key to changing his characteristic behavior lies in delivering an unexpected, "*a*social" response in the right way at the right time.

Usually, when a man says, "I hate my boss," he can count on a familiar response. His wife might say, "Yes, he's an s.o.b." The boss's secretary might put up a stiff argument. In either case, he has without thinking launched himself into a familiar routine.

In psychoanalysis, the same statement might draw the response, "He is like your father." Rogers might respond with no more than "You feel angry." The behavior modifier might set up a program to reward only noncomplaining remarks. In each of these "therapeutic" responses, the therapist produces a surprising reaction and refuses to take sides. This helps to extinguish the client's usual expectation and leads him to accept responsibility for his own feelings and statements rather than looking for a scapegoat.

Our own model is based on the observation that people need to be involved with others and that such involvement is achieved mainly by way of one's ability to communicate, to deliver telling messages. Each of us creates a unique social-emotional style, a special way of prompting desired responses in others. This style is far from perfect, but we come to rely on it because we like to live in a predictable world—even if this world is a predictably uncomfortable one.

How can this style be changed, if there is reason to change it? It will never change if it continues to work; in fact, we won't even notice it. But if there is a malfunction, it suddenly becomes very important. We notice it, we question it, and we *do* something about it.

In other words, an individual's behavior changes when it draws an unexpected response. Therefore, we should be able to change another person's behavior by responding to him in an unexpected manner. When such a response is given with hostility (as it was when the Queen of Hearts responded to Alice's reasonable statement by screaming, "Off with her head!"), it tends to produce a sense of danger and uncertainty. But if an unexpected response is given without rancor (as when a friend says, "I really can't sympathize with you, but I do know how you feel"), then there is a possibility of a positive reaction to it.

Unaware communication is a powerful aspect of our communication process and it is uniquely applicable to influencing human behavior. It accounts for our style with people—the characteristic ways, verbal and nonverbal, in which we approach them and subtly bend their responses in our direction. It therefore accounts for our ability to control without seeming to control and explains why we can deliver messages quite beyond the literal sense of our words.

Since we have learned a lot from Dr. Skinner, and since we are here saddled with many of the terms he legitimately uses in his own ways, a word of clarification is in order. We shall be talking about modifying behavior but not about *behavior modification,* which is a particular attempt to construct a "science" of human behavior and a technology for manipulating it; its basic technique is to reward or to punish certain behavior.

Whether we like it or not, there *is* a "science" of influencing others. The most successful by-products of this science are the minor arts of propagandizing, advertising, and political maneuvering. These by-products are significant for the two important contributions they have made to our lives: they are now worth a great deal of money to their practitioners, and the rest of us have acquired an absolutely desperate need to discover an effective technique for depropagandizing, for discriminating the kernels of truth that do exist in the chaff of advertising, and for establishing some principles of political credibility so that we may regain our smothered freedom of informed decision and choice. We feel that a discipline that has made possible such intrusive minor arts should be held responsible for offering, in addition, a defense against them.

This book is both theoretical and practical. It is concerned with the question of why we behave as we do and with the further question of just what kind of information we have to look for and work with in order to change behavior—other people's and our own as well. We do not change someone by training him to jump through *our* hoops; rather, we lead him to explore a current circumstance and choose for himself a more satisfying alternative, one which is compatible with his personal style. The aim is not simply to teach a new skill in communication but to examine and improve the whole fabric of an unsettling relationship. The procedure results in changed attitudes and thus provides for more than superficial solutions to interpersonal problems.

1

Controlling and Being Controlled: How Do We Do It?

Imagine that we are each implanted with electrodes that can deliver selected radio pulses to selected points in the brain. By pushing the appropriate buttons on a convenient, portable radio transmitter, other people (friends, enemies, teachers, press agents) can trigger us to respond in certain preselected ways: docile, angry, affectionate, sexy, defensive, aggressive. Or cause us to act out a specific role on demand, such as the stereotype of "parent" or "lover" or "boss" or "dependable friend" or "romantic" or "realist." Such is the depressing portrait that presumably depicts the automated common citizen of an Orwellian future: a plastic peasant, implanted, imprinted, psychologically imprisoned, an object to be manipulated.

The uneasy truth is that all of this is already true. We are all "implanted" and we all respond much of the time to the button-pushing of the people around us—particularly of those who know us well, although politicians and advertisers have their own consoles tied into us, too.

For we are all psychologically prefabricated, implanted with marvelously efficient electrochemical circuits (the nervous system, modified by experience), which can be triggered by subtle, nonliteral signals and cues from outside. Each of us has embedded in him a large number of thoroughly learned response patterns that can be set off at any time by an appropriate stimulus. We can be pacified, enraged, estranged, or seduced almost at will by anyone who knows the code.

Even if we know nothing at all about changing and controlling other people, we still change and control them, although somewhat blindly. And we ourselves are forever subject to control we don't know about from at least three different sources: 1) our best friends and enemies, who control us without knowing it; 2) advertisers, promoters, politicians, and other professional behavior-changers who control us deliberately and often underhandedly; and 3) the culture's traditional institutions and authority figures, which by definition are dedicated to educating us for adjustment and conformity.

All three sources endanger the individual's freedom, and the less the individual knows about it, the more he is endangered. The ideal answer would be for everyone to become personally responsible for determining and carrying out whatever changes are to be made in his own unconscious behavior. It is a matter of self-government on an essential, personal level.

Without knowledge of how behavior can be changed, we are helpless under the fingers of a skilled button-pusher. We know these people well (except in our own case, of course), for they are the dependable cat's-paws and go-fetchers, the marionettes who have become bendable, foldable, spindleable, and Skinnerable because they have allowed their options to be programmed out of them.

In other words, we are all the time being grossly manipulated insofar as we permit it. And we permit it insofar as we are unaware of what's going on.

We always choose what we do, but the choice is usually by default; rather than making a conscious choice, we are pushed into choosing without being aware of it. The only way out of such serfdom is to become aware of the ways in which the push-buttons work, to strip the cover off the mechanism so we can see what's really going on inside this mysterious black box of unconscious motivation and guillibility.

To survive in the wilds, an animal must be able to cope with its environment. This means the immediate world must make sense to it and must be in some measure controllable. Making sense of the environment may be as simple as knowing that the snapping of a twig means danger. Control means skills such as foraging for food and escaping from predators. A gazelle with a broken leg cannot cope and neither can a blind hawk or a coyote without a sense of smell.

Psychological survival is something else—a heavy challenge for people but not an obvious problem for most other animals. To survive in the wilds of civilization, a human being must be able to cope with his environment—to understand it, predict it, and in some measure control it.

The obvious way to control the immediate environment is to rely on *open communication.* The obvious way to predict is to look at precedents, or to analyze the pressures operating in some current situation, and to extrapolate from that. A stranger in a strange land has no way of doing either.

The kind of communication that serves to control and predict routine demands and the more concrete events in life is fairly straightforward.

But suppose what we need is love. How do we manage *that?* What if we desperately need to know that we are respected for ourselves alone? What if we need only a sympathetic ear, yet people flee when they see us coming?

The ordinary, conscious skills we use in control and prediction lead nowhere when it comes to our deep needs and subtler desires, so we look for other means. We cannot *command* a generous response, but there are ways to *engineer* it. The technique has many names—conning, snowing, sweet-talking, brainwashing, beguiling—and all of them are forms of conscious, but hidden, communication, which means that the true purpose of the communication is hidden from the receiver.

Both these conscious techniques for controlling other people—either overt pressuring and bargaining or deliberately camouflaged engineering—are sharply limited in their effectiveness. We can only push our friends so far and we can only fool some of the people some of the time. Isn't there some other way, some better way, to communicate our needs and control our circumstances?

Suppose we are jammed inside an elevator, straining for elbow room against the pressure of all those other elbows. We *ask* the people behind us to move back, and then we punctuate the request with our own elbows. Nothing happens. So we try an old line: "Please. I'm four months pregnant." But our pleas and ploys won't work, and of course we don't dare relax for fear the others will crowd in upon us. What can we do? Not a thing, apparently.

But consider a woman in the elevator who suddenly, involuntarily, gasps for breath and develops a case of the dry heaves. Magically, a space is cleared around her. The woman is not sick and she is not putting us on. In fact she is very much embarrassed. "What happened, lady? What's the matter?" She doesn't know. She is bewildered and just a bit worried, but by the time we reach the street floor she has recovered.

Now why should a healthy young woman have a violent seizure at a time like this? Behavior serves some function—physiological, social, or psychological—and if we know what the behavior accomplishes we have a clue to its "meaning" or "purpose." In this case, the woman's behavior caused her physical distress and deep embarrassment, but it doesn't seem likely that she would have had a seizure just to become uncomfortable.

There was another consequence, a remarkable one: inside this hot, sweaty cage packed with short-tempered shoppers, this woman suddenly became the one person with plenty of room to breathe freely.

Her behavior illustrates a third way of coping with the environment and controlling other people: *communication that is hidden and unaware.* As in deliberately disguised manipulation, the other passengers are not aware of the woman's motivation; but in this case, neither is the woman herself. The controller has no idea that she is controlling.

Getting Our Way

The nature of unaware control becomes clearer when it is compared with conscious manipulation in terms of the techniques and goals of the manipulator and the defenses available to the "victim."

Conscious overt control consists of changing the behavior of others by direct measures ("Shape up or get out!"). Techniques include asking, demanding, threatening, buying, forcing, and persuading. The goals are known to everyone. Defenses can be adequate; since both techniques and goals are out in the open, the manipulation can be accurately assessed and dealt with by familiar means such as argument, avoidance, direct resistance—or acceptance.

Conscious but hidden control consists of consciously influencing behavior by indirect or hidden means. The manipulator knows precisely what he wants but is careful to hide this goal from his victim. His techniques include any available subterfuge, and he is particularly careful to disguise the fact that he is controlling ("I have two starving children at home, ma'am, and if I don't sell my quota of subscriptions by the end of the month . . . ").

The goals are clear to the manipulator but are unknown, or misknown, to the victim. They are not necessarily "bad" or "good," for they may be designed to save a frightened victim's life or otherwise to help him in spite of himself. But since the victim does not realize he is being controlled, he does not understand what is happening and he has few, if any, defense measures available to him.

Unaware control is the most effective and powerful form of control, for it can seldom be identified or mitigated. Since the "manipulator" honestly does not know he is manipulating, he is perfectly convincing, and he escapes all responsibility for the outcome.

Techniques are vastly detailed and subtle. They involve the transmission of unconscious cues that plant suggestions, establish moods, and set up the "target" person to act in a manner that rewards the manipulator in some way. The cues are often nonverbal and appear to be trivial, innocuous, and devoid of information.

Unaware control is of course hidden. It reminds us of *conscious* hidden control insofar as the "target" person, or "victim," is not aware of what is happening. However, its distinguishing feature is that *the manipulator himself is also not aware* of what is happening—which accounts for the great power of the technique and for the dogged persistence of the problems generated by it.

The goals of unaware control are latent—strongly motivated goals of which we are not aware. They are complex and relatively unspecific but of tremendous significance to the controller, although he neither recognizes nor acknowledges them. The hidden cues are designed to attract broadly gratifying responses, and the payoffs may appear inexplicable to an outsider; the reward may emerge as an angry reaction on the part of the "target" person, or as failure, or even as a very painful hurt.

Almost any kind of involvement with another human being, even if it is consciously rejected, is better than indifference. Endless bickering or repeated violence may be the only dependable form of involvement that some people are able to achieve.

There is no defense against unaware control unless we have learned how to identify hidden cues and unmask them. We strongly influence others and they strongly influence us, yet ordinarily we cannot say how or why, and our attempts to explain it or to counteract it are commonly irrelevant and misleading. Even the manipulator is helpless. He may be destroying a relationship and not know how to stop; he may be hurting himself and know that something is wrong but have no idea what it is or what to do about it.

Controlling others is a primary means of coping with a naturally indifferent or hostile environment. This means it is regularly used for "selfish" ends, survival being the most selfish of all. It is admired when it takes the form of ingenuity or leadership or open persuasion, and frowned upon when its purpose is seen as deceitful.

We believe that manipulating is legitimate as long as its ends and means are clearly communicated and openly perceived, and that it is detrimental and potentially dangerous insofar as it operates in the dark, hidden from those affected by it. The manipulator himself is always to be counted among those affected; he may in fact be more insidiously and profoundly affected than any of his "victims."

People consciously control their friends and enemies all the time, and we all know it. Our particular interest here lies in analyzing how we provoke responses by *unconscious* means. We surely carry out more manipulations each day without awareness than a good con man could handle consciously in a year, and our lives are gravely affected by it.

All of us do this. We shape the immediate emotional environment to our own unconscious ends. We rely upon the subtle coercions we have mastered as a result of the billions of little lifelong experiments we play out just below the surface of awareness.

There is nothing intrinsically evil about this, and when it is good it can be very, very good. When it is bad, however, it is likely to be rigid, frustrating, self-destructive, and—because controlling others is a voracious consumer of energy—exhausting. We draw rewards from those close to us, often boxing them in so there is no chance of their wriggling away without paying mightily for their freedom. Our unaware manipulations usually conflict with the conscious messages we deliver at the same time, and the resulting discord can be painful, intractable, and permanently damaging.

Frustrations caused by these unconscious efforts to control others sabotage our understanding of one another; they often create chronic stress, and sometimes they lead to precipitous solutions such as divorce or even homicide.

Is there a way out? Traditional schemes for changing behavior prove to be unworkable in this area. Advice may be reassuring but it doesn't lead anywhere. An individual's "understanding" of his problem is not likely to help him solve it and indeed may even make it more difficult for him. Analysis of the past may be interesting as personal history, but it contributes little to a solution. So what can we do?

The purpose of this book is to discover *how unaware control works,* how it can be identified, and how we may fruitfully intervene when it appears to threaten the healthy growth of a relationship. The focus is on *unaware* aspects of behavior which we ordinarily do not consider.

Our own behavior can be changed. As a result, the behavior of people involved in our lives can also be changed, and the changes may greatly increase the probability of their behaving in ways that are to our mutual advantage.

We cannot remake anyone's character to order, but we can surely dissolve some of the frustrations and misperceptions that have disturbed or diminished our closest relationships. We can also learn to label our behavior in a far more realistic manner than we are accustomed to—in terms of our own hopes and fears, intentions, and inner defenses.

Hidden Manipulators

Unaware control is spectacular for several reasons. It is not only more common than conscious manipulation; it is also extremely effective. Since it does not arouse suspicion, it can mobilize all kinds of feelings and energies in the service of a motivation nobody is aware of.

It is concerned with complex realities such as warmth, trust, sexuality, security, intelligence, and unacknowledged needs. It is so subtle that it can be used again and again with the same effect, unchecked and uncheckable. It leaves the perpetrator blameless. It is reliable because it triggers automatic, predictable responses. A very simple example is the frail child who regularly becomes sick to her stomach on mornings when she hasn't done her homework.

This skill may demand considerable courage when it involves committing ourselves to a painful or embarrassing role. It often calls upon a great range of emotion and bodily expression, and it sometimes involves real illness or even suicide. Most of the time, however, we use very subtle cues which are achieved by perfectly familiar means—by our choice of words, facial expression, eye contact, hand and finger and head movements, breathing mannerisms, and the ways in which we use such features as setting, context, mood, and dress. Sweaty palms or an unconsciously clenched fist deliver a stronger message than the polite declaration that goes along with it. A clear, convincing statement of goals means nothing if the overall impression is "This guy feels like a phony."

Controlling people unconsciously is neither an evil practice nor the refuge of hypocrites. It cannot be used as a tool by cynical manipulators, for it cannot be consciously controlled. Nor is it something reserved for special endeavors such as job-hunting or seduction. Rather, it is a common, nonstop part of our continual effort to keep from being sucked down into the quicksand of everyday life. It is sometimes essential if we are to get through the day with our dignity intact.

The process of unaware control can be seen in anyone at any time if we know how to look. We could even find it in ourselves—in the hunch of our shoulders and the turn of our lips, in the way we whisper and cry, in the light or dark that shows in our eyes. It is embedded in everything we do and cannot be separated from who we are. We use it against our enemies now and then, against ourselves often, and with our friends all the time.

It always works in some degree, but sometimes it backfires. An attractive young woman seeks therapeutic help because men of all sorts have been accosting her. She demands to know why. "Why should a nice girl like me be besieged by mashers all the time? I keep telling them to leave me alone. I go out of my way to avoid them. But they still keep moving in on me."

There seems to be no reasonable explanation. The woman has a stern voice and a forbidding countenance and is conservatively dressed. The therapist notices in himself, however, an impulse to move closer to her and to sympathize and pat her reassuringly. This prompts him to look for a specific cause, and he quickly realizes she is behaving in a subtly provocative manner wholly out of keeping with her words and the serious tone of her voice.

Her hands seem restless, and during the first ten minutes of the interview she manages—"accidentally" and without being aware of it—to pull the hem of her skirt, inch by inch, from just above the knee to well above midthigh. When this is pointed out to her, she is incensed by the implication that it could have anything to do with her complaint. "I just happen to have a skirt that rides up," she says, pulling the hem down in a way that makes it difficult for a man not to rivet his eyes on it—and still unaware that her behavior is in any way provocative.

The effectiveness of unaware control is partly due to the fact that it is not thought to be a "channel of communication" at all, so our guard is not up. An overt request such as "Please leave me alone!" is clearly understood as a communication, but a nervous woman adjusting her skirt can easily be dismissed as an empty or trivial event.

A second glance shows that it might well be just the other way around. "Communication" implies that a message is not only transmitted but also received and responded to. Therefore, a verbal command ("Leave me alone!") is not truly an act of communication unless it leads to some perceptible effect. A woman's fingers idly moving on her own thigh may be a medium far more powerful than language for delivering a message and eliciting a tangible response.

The woman in the elevator and the woman who inches up her skirt are simple instances of unaware control or, to put it less technically, of that part of everyday communication that affects others but that we do not ordinarily recognize for its communicative value.

This unaware aspect of communication is difficult to spot because it tends to be sophisticated and diffuse and it is often interwoven with the elements of conscious behavior. Typically, it takes the form of subtle cues that accompany conscious behavior bearing a very different message.

It is possible, for example, to say, "We'd love to have you stay with us again," in such a way that we believe we have delivered a sincere invitation to these dreadful people, while at the same time they feel so uncomfortable that they wouldn't dream of calling. We have been polite and generous—at least to our own satisfaction—and still have achieved our underlying, unadmitted goal.

Our unaware communications are so deeply embedded in everything we do that it is impossible to clearly distinguish our "conscious" acts from those of which we are unaware. The labels are clear enough, but events are not often built to fit them neatly. Almost any event has both aware and unaware aspects, and an accurate description would account for that fact and allow for it.

For example, we may be aware that we annoy people by not bathing but unaware of the fact that the negative reaction of the well-scrubbed is highly significant and rewarding to us; it appears to confirm our integrity and our freedom from cultural stereotyping.

The aware aspect of behavior has to do with conscious assessment of oneself and of the outside world; it is the logical mode we use when explaining, planning, or arguing. The unaware aspect has to do with the confirmation of feelings and the satisfaction of chronic needs, whether they be inevitable human needs or neurotic ones.

Learning Control

The problem of how to change unconscious behavior cannot even be stated realistically unless we understand something about early learning. How did we first learn to influence and control other people without knowing it?

We probably learned to manipulate in the same way we learned to stand or grasp a toy—by a series of tiny actions, a few of which we repeated because they brought results. The "simple" task (standing, grasping) is incredibly difficult for the undifferentiated nervous system of an infant, and its mastery takes him a long way toward later refinements such as skiing and dancing, or developing the touch of a sculptor, a violinist, or a lover.

A newborn child soon learns to associate certain sounds with a particular response from the environment. His early, limited "vocabulary" of repeatable noises is partially inborn and partially acquired, and it literally controls the behavior of concerned adults in the vicinity.

His communications become more discriminating as specific cries become associated with certain pleasures or with the relief of certain distresses. The child learns to make emergency noises that usually bring immediate attention, and he learns how to elicit friendly responses.

At the same time, he learns very early that he can be misunderstood. He may let go with a cry he assumes will bring food, but all it produces is a change of diapers. So, in a very vague sense, he learns about deception, how to pretend distress in order to gain certain comforts. He learns to play with sounds and he may try out new ones just to see what happens.

As soon as he appears to be "teachable," he is likely to be overwhelmed by overt instruction, which he loves. He is taught all the social games his parents can think of and he learns the great power of sounds like "please" and the limited power of sounds like "gimme."

He also discovers that the words alone are not as important as the way they are delivered and the circumstances that surround the message. The word "Potty!" is far more effective if it is said while dancing up and down with hands clasped between one's legs. Peripheral, nonverbal skills become increasingly important as the growing child discovers that asking for things directly doesn't work as well as it did when his parents were excited by each new word he mastered—particularly if there is now a new baby in the house.

By the age of three or four, he faces the sad fact that he knows of no perfectly reliable technique for getting what he wants, aside from displaying brute strength, which he doesn't have, or presenting an obviously legitimate and urgent plea (it is not every time that he can say, "But look, it's *bleeding!*").

Some children are so overwhelmed by the uncertainty of the world that they give up and withdraw, but most keep working at it and eventually find that a lot of things come their way when the emotional climate is right. Slowly, and without much awareness, the average child learns that his own behavior has a great deal to do with creating such an emotional climate in the people who mean something to him.

He develops a style that matches the expectations and demands and weaknesses of his family and at the same time evokes feelings that are to his advantage in one way or another. He learns, without knowing it, how to lead his family in his direction, how to suggest and prompt and seduce and coerce so that the odds are in favor of his getting his full share of attention and other satisfactions. He is well on the road to establishing his own characteristic style, a unique and automatic pattern of coping behavior that helps make his immediate world predictable and brings it under his personal control to some degree.

The variety of unaware manipulative behaviors displayed by children is always a surprise. By unconscious imitation and experiment, they seem to master nearly all of the effective tools for levering other people to respond in emotionally important ways—pathos, seduction, fright, pain, generosity, pity, anger, hate, cynicism, love.

In his perpetual struggle for emotional survival, the child soon learns that certain things are not easily available to him. A sense of insecurity is inevitable, for example, when he makes a bid for affection, only to find his parents totally absorbed in the antics of his baby sister. He becomes acutely sensitive to the failure of his efforts to attract attention and promote affectionate responses, and he casts about for a better way of coping with the situation.

Since there is no ideal answer, he is forced to resort to a compromise of some sort. There is no conscious plan, but he does experiment with other strategies, perhaps imitating something he has observed in other people, perhaps reverting to behavior that worked for him a year or two earlier.

The likely outcome is that he will regain some of the lost attention and affection—but at a price. He may develop stomach cramps and he may not eat at all unless coaxed. Or he may settle for concern instead of loving attention; he may start wetting his bed or "failing" in kindergarten or throwing temper tantrums or accidentally breaking a dish or two at every meal.

Despite the penalties attached, the child no longer feels helpless when his parents' love or attention is diverted to someone else. He knows how to avoid the pain of being ignored, and the price he pays is apparently the best bargain available. He embraces the compromise behavior as part of his evolving style.

This brief look at how unconscious control is learned suggests that unconscious behavior is not an applied technique that can be conditioned away or neatly cut out from the surrounding emotional tissue. It is a behavior deeply anchored in the complex fabric of daily activities and responses. Such behavior can be changed only if we can find a way of motivating the manipulator to make the change himself, to discover a more appropriate compromise behavior and put it into effect.

The main difficulty we face is that the very behavior we wish to have him change is something neither we nor he is aware of. How are we supposed to see the invisible and hear the inaudible? If we can nevertheless learn to do this, *then* we are ready for the final question: How do we go about grappling with an intangible manipulation?

2

How to Listen

Can we really change human behavior, you and I? Can we change people who coerce us unconsciously in ways we don't understand?

The answer is yes—if we can manage to locate the unaware behavior in the other person and react, with our new knowledge, in a way that forces him to take action. Attacking him directly is no solution, and neither is presenting him with a logical analysis, for we are dealing with the illogical and the invisible.

Other tools are available: they have to do with listening in a new way and responding to manipulation in a new way. The listening has to come first, and it requires some discipline since it involves getting in touch with motivations that are effective precisely because they elude detection.

The problem is, How do we perceive imperceptible maneuverings and tune in to the sounds of our own silences? The solution hinges on the central mechanism of unaware control, namely, the communication of a constant barrage of seemingly innocuous cues that are so subtle that we control others and are ourselves controlled without knowing it.

Essentially we are listening for subliminal sounds. The harder we try, the more superfluous noise we generate. It is rather like touching a snowflake in the hope of discovering its shape; our obvious, everyday senses are not fine enough. We have to find some way of sensing beneath the surface.

The art of listening is possibly the most important and certainly the most underrated of the social arts. It is the key to rapport, understanding, and mutual trust and an honest and convincing way of showing concern. It is also a prerequisite for anyone who hopes to influence another person's unaware behavior.

Listening as an art has to do with discovering, firsthand, what exists. It really involves all the senses. It is what happens when a child pries up a rock in the woods to see what's underneath or crouches by a thicket, listening for a sound that has just caught his ear.

The trick is to listen with more than ears, for vital information is flowing constantly from the other person's eyes and shoulders and face and fingers and pores; to listen for what he is showing, demanding, offering, crying out for. If he knows us well, his message will be of considerable strength and subtlety, custom built, keyed to our peculiar weaknesses, proclivities, and vulnerabilities.

We are not accustomed to listening directly to another person in this way. Most of our listening is second- or thirdhand. That is, we listen *through* someone rather than *to* him. We listen to reports *about* something that has happened at some previous time in some other place.

These reports are necessarily filtered, altered, and adulterated in the process of passing through one or more rather sloppy translations that often deliver more of the translator than of the purported subject matter. They are not going to tell us much about the other person's hidden motives or the strategies he uses in his unconscious attempts to follow them.

Firsthand listening for another person's unconscious messages calls for several techniques that require more than willingness to sit back and let sensations impinge upon us. It requires 1) disengagement; 2) mastery of the uncommon art of listening for consequences; 3) awareness of our own emotional reactions; 4) an ear for patterns as well as for single, sharp acts; 5) the ability to discriminate between pertinent information and the bright noise of diversion and camouflage; and 6) an understanding of the overriding function of compromise.

Disengagement: Listening Like a Child

We will be listening between the lines and under the lines and behind the lines, and we cannot catch the subtleties unless we extricate ourselves from our own immediate involvement. So we cool it: stop, look around, and prepare to commit our total attention to the task of listening, of staying with what is actually going on moment by moment. That is, we *disengage.*

To be disengaged means to have nothing to prove—to stop caring about one's own stake in what is going on. Some people listen for what they want to hear and are deaf to all the rest. Some listen for what will confirm their fears. Some attend only to the signals that trigger familiar reactions.

To listen without engagement, on the other hand, is an art that requires the aware detachment of a film critic, looking for whatever there is to be seen. The listener must learn to table his own hopes and fears. He must give up looking for compliments or bristling at insults. He must in a sense look on the present moment in the manner of a child watching a pair of ants struggling with a dead grasshopper, wondering what they will do next, engrossed but not interfering.

The listener must not judge or compare or interpret. Since the aim is simply to gather accurate information, he must learn to listen without fearing or expecting, without planning anything, without worrying about consistency or morality or justice. He must not expect to discover enough facts to draw a valid conclusion, for a human being is too complex to be easily explained and is a different person at different times or in different circumstances.

Niels Bohr's principle of complementarity applies here: the observer and the subject are an inseparable whole and the subject changes if the experimental environment changes. All views are partial, and they all complement one another, however contradictory they may appear to be. The temptation always is to listen to the literal meaning of what another person says about himself and overlook the fact that the subject is right here, now, directly visible and not in need of "interpretation."

Furthermore, the listener will have to give up his everyday need for reasonable explanations. Unaware behavior is broadly consistent within itself, but it is not responsive to the same rationality that rules our conscious activities. What the manipulator wants from us may be only faintly related to what he is overtly asking; if we ask for a reasonable explanation, we will be treated to a reasonable rationalization designed, like the noisy flight of a mother pheasant, to lead us away from the nest.

It is difficult not to become engaged, particularly if we like or dislike the other person and most particularly if we are afraid or if we want something of him. We commonly listen for what we expect to find, or we get absorbed in the subject of a conversation and forget to pay attention to what can be learned firsthand about the speaker. Many of us project our own motives onto the other so lavishly that we hear only a replay of our own tapes. Or we already know just what to expect and we find excuses for him or, in another mood, condemn him.

Accurate perception is impossible if we listen through filters that reduce the noise of reality and suppress selected frequencies. Inevitably, we propel ourselves toward the circumstance of the abandoned woman who cries, "But he told me he loved me!" Obviously, she has been hearing only what she wanted to hear.

Listening for Effects

How can anyone locate a hidden communication that nobody is aware of? By way of its *effects*. Like sunlight in empty space, its existence remains unsuspected until it strikes something. We recognize sunlight only by the way an otherwise dark object responds to it. To locate and decipher an unconscious message, then, we must look not for the message itself but for its reflection in the object that intercepts it.

In other words, the clue to our friend's unaware behavior lies in our own behavior—in the response he typically elicits from us. We don't know why he's doing it or how he manages it, but the design of his unseen technique reveals itself in what we do when we are with him. Like the Invisible Man, it is transparent but it still leaves footprints.

For example, a mother says to her daughter, "I want you to go back outside, young lady, and I want you to come into the house *quietly.*" Apparently, the only message involved here is the obvious one contained in the mother's request. But if we watch the daughter we may notice that she at once sits on her hands and assumes a prim and rigid posture.

This response reveals the nature of the mother's unadmitted and unaware manipulation. The girl has just burst in from school and she feels put down; her mood shifts quickly from exuberance to petulance, which gives the mother "every reason in the world" to become angry at the daughter's disobedience and lack of appreciation.

Unfortunately, the mother is not fully aware of her own hidden message, the controlling message against which the daughter of course rebels. The mother is hurt and puzzled to find the relationship turning sour, as it has many previous afternoons under very similar circumstances. At the same time, the daughter is bewildered by her inability to understand what motivates her mother.

The consequences of an unaware communication provide us with a clue that can lead to understanding both the motivations and the strategies of the sender. The message in this case was unconsciously designed to elicit a rebellious response, while appearing to be perfectly reasonable; the outcome gives the mother ample proof for her contention that her struggles to raise a well-mannered child are both uncomfortable and unappreciated. The strategy works (otherwise it would have been discarded long ago), and the consequences are a reliable indication that an unaware message has been effectively communicated.

This story incidentally illustrates the enigmatic fact that it is perfectly possible for an individual to make a choice without being aware of it. The woman had many options available to her when her daughter burst gleefully into the kitchen, letting the screen door bang behind her. Without giving the matter any conscious thought, the mother chose an action that had in the past led to satisfying confrontations and feelings of righteous anger.

When we first begin to listen for unconscious messages, we are easily put off by the obvious, literal meanings of the other person's statements. What he actually says is not very helpful unless we listen for what he is trying to accomplish.

We should ask not what a word means (according to a dictionary) but what happens when it is used. How do we feel when someone says, "You old bastard" . . . "Now just one minute, sweetie" . . . "My friend here has a problem" . . . "But it's only because I love you" . . . ?

Profanity is used for a definite purpose that is not often related to the literal meaning of the words. So are phrases of endearment. Words of sympathy are regularly used as constraints. Words and actions commonly defined as "loving" or "caring" or "concerned" are often used to control other people; they are ideal for the purpose because they demand and usually receive compliance, love, or support, and are nevertheless identified by most of us as expressions of "generosity" and "thoughtfulness."

Erotic statements may of course be used for erotic ends, but often they are used for nonsexual purposes. For example, an adolescent may indulge in intimately sexy conversation just to prove to a parent or friend that he is independent or that he has no respect for standards being forced upon him. And it is still tritely true that some women rely upon bedroom language as an aid to attaining emotional or financial security. By the same token, nonsexual conversation is often employed for seductive ends.

Another thing that can mislead us in our attempt to listen for unconscious messages is the tendency to apply stereotypical labels to certain common mannerisms. Nonverbal cues and unconscious gestures are different for each person and cannot be cataloged according to some universal "meaning." The unconscious tilt of a listener's head may mean "I don't believe a word you're saying"—or it may mean any of a hundred other things when the speaker, the mood, or the context is different. Moreover, single gestures may be of no significance in themselves. An unaware need will usually set in motion a complex sequence of interwoven cues; one gesture in isolation doesn't mean very much.

In general, there is no need to "analyze" behavior in order to understand what the real message is. It may appear in the form of sweet talk, bitching, or depression, but we don't have to label it or understand how the message gets to us or why it works. We need only know what happens as a result.

For example, a man says passionately, "I love you, I love you," and the woman responds with a desperate, "All right, I know! And I love you!" Let's look at what is really being communicated here. Is his message truly a message of love? And is hers?

He is pleading insistently for her time, support, affection, and attention, which she gives with considerable reluctance. She feels smothered and frightened. She is cornered because she feels guilty about hurting him when he professes such great love for her.

So she responds with words of love but in a voice of desperation which communicates the powerful message "Let me out of here!" This is precisely the response that he has elicited many times during the past few weeks, and it explains his hidden goal, which is to make her get out of his life without having to initiate the break himself.

In a similar case, a husband was about to leave his wife, complaining that, "for no good reason," she refused to sleep with him. He loved her very much, he told his friends. But further information revealed that the wife's physical withdrawal had occurred gradually, apparently as a result of his constant complaints about fatigue. It became evident that he had been thoroughly bored with the marriage for a year and that his feeling "dead tired" at about nine o'clock every night had been going on nearly as long.

His fatigue had been serving a purpose he had never admitted to himself: it caused his wife to withdraw, which provided him with a socially "valid" excuse for leaving her. His claim that he loved her had less to do with his real feelings than it had to do with the fact that he did not want to accept responsibility for splitting.

This man's technique is akin to that of the "injustice-collector," the person who sets up his friends in such a way that they are bound to respond in a manner he considers unjust; they deliver fewer favors than he expects or they fail to live up to all the promises he has drawn from them.

This appears to load him with unhappiness, but its main function is to provide him with a "valid" excuse for cutting down on his own giving and for making the vehement complaints he finds so satisfying. He now has someone to blame, and his sufferings earn him the "right" to do so. His ego thrives because he communicates clearly to himself that he deserves better than he is getting, and he also avoids any assumption of responsibility for his own unhappy fate.

The consequences that flow from this kind of control are geared to the immediate present. The anguished cry, "I never want to see you again!" does not refer to the future; the woman doesn't mean she is never going to want to see you again. Her hidden message is that right now she wants you to do something you predictably do whenever you are chastised or are fearful of losing her.

The same goes for past history. "I knew what you were really after the very first time I met you!" is not a reliable historical report; it is an attempt to satisfy some immediate need by punishing the other person.

The consequence of an unconscious behavior may even be dismal failure. We may wonder why anyone would, consciously or unconsciously, engineer a failure for himself—particularly since it is not always easy to do so. What fun is there in falling on your face? The answer is that there may be fringe benefits more important than the job itself.

A young man appears to pay almost no attention to his fiancée in public, although he is most affectionate in private. She is very annoyed, and he claims he ignores her only because she becomes demanding whenever he acknowledges her. Then he further claims that he can't help it because that just happens to be the kind of guy he is. Both statements are smoke screens hiding a truth he isn't at all ready to look at.

When we ask what the observable results of his inattentiveness are, and why he keeps generating these results again and again, we may discover that he is not at all sure he did the right thing when he proposed to her and that he really craves the freedom to reconsider the alternatives. It might be better just to hang loose for a while, and besides, Linda and Joan and Ruth are now back in town.

In all such cases, the first step toward understanding is learning to listen for the *consequences* rather than for the logic of the words exchanged.

Listening for Our Own Response

If we are being controlled in some hidden way by someone, the obvious place to listen for the consequences of his unaware behavior is in ourselves. He is creating a subtle emotional climate that leads us to respond in ways that are to his benefit, so we now have to listen to how we behave in his presence if we are to discover what he really wants from us.

We have to ignore the literal meaning of his words and pay attention to how we feel when he says them—or when he says nothing at all, for inattentiveness is an effective means of soliciting certain responses. If we are upset when he fails to pay attention, it is very possible that he is trying—unconsciously—to upset us. So we listen not for the sound of him but for the sounds *we* make, responding: for the hmms, cries, groans, purrs, moans, sighs, and disbelieving grunts.

What actions are we prompted to take? What happens to us? Do we, without apparent reason, become angry? Amused? Sentimental? Sympathetic? Whatever we do or feel is a clue to the meaning of his behavior and may constitute the real purpose of his message, for it may be a response he has ingeniously, although unconsciously, engineered. The literal meaning of his statements may be incidental to the real message. We are the instrument that makes his subsonic vibrations audible.

The objection may be raised that we are not just instruments for amplifying other people's skills in controlling us, but that we also feel emotions in our own right and have our own reasons for behaving as we do. For example, a teacher may have had a stomach upset, and when he goes to class he feels sour and ill. To what extent are the students responsible if they now elicit a sour and ill response from him?

The answer is that we know very little indeed if we have observed only one single episode. But if we have observed with reasonable frequency that, day after day, the students do repeatedly elicit this kind of response from the teacher, we would argue that they must have learned what information to send out in order to produce the sour response. The teacher, under these circumstances, has been their instrument.

Suppose a friend has lost his job and is depressed. Is his dour countenance an expression of the hurt he has suffered? Probably, but the only good clue we really have is our own reaction to him. Our reactions tell us what rewards his glum sighs are bringing him. What do we do about it? Do we pay attention to him, sympathize with him, reassure him and express our affection? Probably. At least we feel like doing so.

His depression, then, may be not only a symptom of hurting but also a remarkably successful technique for alleviating it. We must remember that even though he may feel unhappy about his job, he does not have to look unhappy. In fact, he could be flippant or hopeful (about another job prospect) or indifferent. This man's strategy, however, is to present himself as a depressed victim of fate; his style is to elicit sympathy and concern by making unhappy noises.

To understand what's going on here, we have to listen objectively to our own responses and at the same time disengage both from the subject matter (concern about depression) and from the feeling he is trying to arouse in us (sympathy and guilt).

If we are fortunate enough to be the subject of our friend's conversation as well as the object of control, our chances of hearing the inaudible should be much improved. In this case, our friend has chosen to zero in on us, and every phrase and every inflection is loaded with information about his unacknowledged goals regarding us.

If we take it personally and act out our response, we fall right into his trap. But if we merely take note of how we feel and think of this in terms of what he may hope to gain from the encounter, we will discover a wealth of information about his unconscious wishes. All we have to remember is that what he says about us reflects *his* wishes.

When a manipulator talks about himself, the distortion is even more profound. We won't learn much about his objective self from the literal content of his self-report, but we can learn a great deal about him by looking at the feelings his report manages to arouse in us. His logic is pretty good: his purposes, as he describes them, are laudable, the reasons he gives for what he does are convincing, and his excuses are understandable.

However, his needs and the nature of his relationship with us make it impossible for him to give an objective description of himself. His explanation is itself an instance of further coping behavior unconsciously designed to draw the response he wants from us. His purposes may be quite unrelated to the labels he chooses to paste on them.

For example, he may paint a picture of himself that makes us feel like giving him more room or more respect or more concern than we normally would. He has many available means for controlling us aside from talking directly about himself, but self-descriptions are probably the most obvious.

The effects show in our own behavior: every time we soft-pedal something when he's around, every time we walk about on tiptoe, every time we are careful about what we say, we can be sure that we have been drawn into a cooperative exchange that is of considerable benefit to him. Which is to say, we have been manipulated.

The manipulator may have the best of conscious intentions, and it is not easy to dismiss them and look bluntly at the real consequences. His intended expressions of feeling are often quite out of phase with the expressions he actually, and unconsciously, portrays.

In a recent experiment at the University of Utah (E. G. Beier's Communication Laboratory), we asked several students to act out six different moods on videotape—anger, fear, seductivity, indifference, happiness, and sadness. Then we let them review their own portrayals of the emotions and eliminate any they felt were unrepresentative. The chosen portrayals were emotionally authentic in the eyes of their creators.

When we played the videotapes of these mood expressions to large audiences of "judges," we discovered that the judges could decode the intended moods with an accuracy of only about 50 per cent. In other words, all of our "actors" apparently sent out discordant information. Their portrayals failed about half of the time to represent their intentions.

One young woman, who tried like everyone else to appear angry, fearful, seductive, indifferent, happy, and sad—and who subsequently edited her own performance for authenticity—appeared to her judges as angry in every case. Another young woman demonstrated a similar one-dimensionality, but in her case, whatever else she thought she was doing, she invariably impressed her judges as seductive. Even when she wanted to be angry, men whistled at her.

It was as if she wanted to communicate two discordant feelings at the same time and therefore compromised. While maintaining the self-image of a person who wanted to show anger, she nevertheless communicated seductivity.

Listening for Patterns

Having an ear for patterns means being aware of the fine structure of behavior rather than focusing on a highly specific goal.

We are so accustomed to describing goals and desires in simple, "target" terms that we come to believe the goal is all there is to it: if we attain it, that's all that matters. All we want, we confidently announce, is to win the game, land the contract, make a million—and we imagine that the best thing that could happen would be to be handed the prize —*now*—on a silver platter.

The truth is that our joy would be short-lived if it were handled that way. If winning were all that counted, we should be happy to sit down to a game of chess with a very weak player and achieve checkmate in two minutes. But in real life, if the game gets too easy, we cheat by making mistakes in order to keep it going. Getting there is more than half the fun.

A person with an ear for fine structural patterns will be interested in the whole fabric of the exchange in which the target behavior happens to be embedded, alert to the rewards, challenges, risks, ego traps, and ego trips to be found along the way. If he is not tone-deaf, he will quickly come to appreciate the network of pleasures and payoffs that accompany certain repetitive behaviors but usually escape attention.

People talk about simple rewards, but what hooks them is the entire pattern of actions that leads to the "reward" and follows it. For example, a wife blames her husband's drinking for everything that has gone wrong with their marriage. "If he'd only stop drinking!" Obviously, she is not perceiving the network of minor satisfactions and relaxations that make alcohol attractive to him, and she has never considered the very pertinent question, "And what are *you* doing to keep him in his cups?"

This is not to say that astute listening is an unmitigated blessing, for listening is itself an *act* and can be very threatening unless handled with restraint. If the listener is still emotionally engaged—if he is still concerned with proving something to himself—he may turn the art of paying close attention into an offensive game. It is most disturbing to feel that your every move is being studiously recorded.

Returning to our example of the woman who was shocked to find herself pursued by mashers, we might easily conclude that the purpose of her provocative behavior was simply to bolster her ego by getting men to make passes at her, prim though she imagined herself to be. Such a clear and singular purpose makes sense to us and seems to explain her conduct—but it does not explain why she had tremendous difficulty changing her manner.

Actually, her unconscious purpose involved a multitude of subtle goals, all interwoven and interdependent and variously rewarding. Eventually she came to see how effective her "inadvertent" behavior was in confirming her own sour opinion of the male animal, while at the same time providing the pleasure of being sought after without (to her own knowledge) having solicited such attention. There were also fringe benefits such as the assurance that she was attractive, although proper, and the immediate prospect of being comforted (by a male therapist) in her role of innocent ingenue put upon by callous males.

What motivated this woman was not a single wish but a number of conflicting needs. The reward she coveted was not one discrete prize but a whole basketful of goodies. The behavior she engaged in was not a simple, directed act but a long, complicated pattern of fixed, predictable actions that provided continuing excitement and satisfaction as it unfolded: her own enigmatic, cold-but-coy acting, for example, or the man's changing and sometimes baffled response; the experience of being able (albeit unconsciously) to control the situation and predict the outcome; the drama of confrontation; the pleasure of voicing a harsh but "justified" complaint to others; and the comfort of their sympathetic reaction.

She never indulged in just the simple, isolated act of pulling up her skirt; rather, she went through a long and involved fixed action pattern, and there is no easy label that could possibly do justice to this experience.

It is always convenient to find a label for a problem because labeling something feels very much like understanding it. The best thing about a label is that it allows us to identify the visible part of the iceberg without worrying about the great bulk beneath the surface which supports the part we pin the label on. We imagine that all we have to do to get rid of it is to destroy that clearly labeled part that juts up from the sea. If we actually do focus our efforts and destroy this part (by melting or chopping or bombarding it, for example), we shall of course be overwhelmed to discover that there is still an iceberg there.

The lesson to be derived from the iceberg image is that we cannot possibly change a situation or solve a significant problem if we look only at the most visible fragment of it. Something more is keeping it afloat. We may be able to get rid of the fragment, but for reasons we cannot comprehend, the problem remains.

If we hope to discover what is truly important to another person, we shall have to give much more attention to his route than to his avowed destination.

Listening for Discord

A fifth technique for tuning in on another person's unaware messages is to distinguish diversionary tactics from pertinent communication. The difficulty is that his hidden behavior is at least as important as his overt (and largely verbal) behavior; both together represent his true style.

Everyone holds in his own head a model of himself, his self-image. It is of great significance, for it is what gives him his conscious identity and the feeling that he is of some consequence. He supports this model in many ways: with self-descriptions, explanations, posturings, and commitments, for example. He tries overtly to project himself as he wishes to be seen, which entails concealing thoughts and feelings that don't fit the image.

The image may be noble or rebellious or wise or helpless or sweet or ruthless, depending upon where he imagines he wants to go and who his heroes are. In all cases, the instrument commonly employed to check out a self-image is the mirror.

Other needs are hidden, embodied in subtler behaviors that project a powerful but diffuse emotional image. This emotional field of force impels other people as if by magic, surreptitiously shaping their responses. It works like the field of a magnet held beneath a table sprinkled with iron filings—an unseen force that attracts and repels, a force whose shape cannot be viewed directly but may be inferred from the intricately patterned response of the iron filings.

Whereas the self-image is acted out and deliberately projected for the world to see, the emotional image is projected unconsciously and cannot be recognized by looking in a mirror; it can only be positively identified by the way in which others respond to it.

This hidden emotional image is relatively independent of the self-image and often at odds with it. It might be described as the way a person unconsciously sets up other people to behave in a consistent, predictable manner. It includes the way we approach friends and strangers, whether we are quiet or talkative, and what we pretend to be interested in. It includes such common but emotionally loaded items as where we live, what we wear, where we work, and what we eat, drink, and otherwise ingest.

Our emotional image may be diverse and eclectic or it may have some dominant implied theme such as "I'll be nice if you cooperate," or "I dare you!" or "Look how I work my fingers to the bone and nobody cares," or "I think I'm Beautiful People, don't you?" or just "Help!"

The emotional pressures we bring to bear are largely unconscious and are typically determined by hidden motivations we don't want to face. Our self-image, on the other hand, is determined by the needs we consciously ascribe to ourselves. Both together—self-image and the latent emotional image—determine our style.

Occasionally we may run into that graceful person whose style is such that his manifest self-image and his latent emotional image support each other most of the time. His hidden messages are easy to read because they are compatible with his overt communications and support a similar motive. His overall behavior is concordant. His declared intentions, which are part of his self-image, do not differ from or conflict with the demands he unconsciously makes on other people. Both are fairly reflected in the overall way in which he operates, that is, in his style.

Discordance, or dissonance, is more familiar to most of us. It is the reformed alcoholic telling his grocer, "I never even *think* about booze anymore. Give me a dozen eggs and a fifth of milk." It occurs when a person's self-image is grossly incompatible with his emotional image as perceived by others. It reflects disparity between an individual's hidden motivations and the needs he talks about.

The display of such discordance is often harder on the discordant individual than it is on his friends because it supports their view of his style while he—being unaware that his style is discordant—has no way of understanding their negative responses. If a woman claims she is angry at a man but at the same time sends out seductive information by way of cues she doesn't realize she is delivering, she is setting up a conflict for herself. Her sensual behavior is satisfying but not conscious; at the same time, her conscious anger reassures her and she never suspects that she herself might be the author—or at least the co-author—of the responses she is collecting.

A man is in love with the idea of love. His style is to talk his way through life. He is courting a woman who initially accepts his advances but has since drawn back from him. He brings her gifts, writes her love letters, and tells her repeatedly how much he loves her. Finally he complains bitterly that she must be cold and unable to respond to being loved.

The fact is that she is unusually responsive to being loved but not at all responsive to being *told* she is loved. She cannot explain herself except to say, "But why do you have to keep *telling* me, then? It's like making promises all the time. If you just loved me, I'd know it without your doing a thing."

He has no way of understanding what she is trying to tell him. His self-image is that of a romantic lover, extremely loving and beloved, and he cannot afford to admit that he might not be loving at all in her sense of the word. His style is to engineer an apparently loving response by declarations and flattery, an approach that has apparently worked for him in the past.

The woman in this case is all too aware of his discordant style and is turned off by it. The man himself is honestly blind to the fact that his style includes behaviors that alienate the woman he says he loves.

Compromise: When a Problem Is Really a Solution

Discordance—that is, the disparity between our intentions and the emotional reality of our behavior, as expressed in our style—sounds like a symptom of illness or imbalance. At least it seems like a problem that ought to be cleaned up.

Discordant behavior is in fact not a sign of illness; it serves, rather, as a *compromise,* embracing a number of conflicting needs and motivations. It is therefore not a problem at all but a solution, a subtly devised arrangement that serves to resolve some earlier conflict.

The smoker who says, "I hate smoking but I can't stop," doesn't even know what his problem is. His friends see clearly that he doesn't hate smoking at all; his complaints are themselves a part of his rather successful solution to the earlier problem of how to keep smoking and at the same time keep his conscience relatively clear.

Compromise behavior includes a lot of uncomfortable items and it may not make us very happy, but it produces some order and predictability in our all too fluid world. It is a big package that contains one or more things we very much want, plus the garbage we had to buy along with it. The garbage part is what we see as our "problem," but we cannot dump it without dumping the entire package.

The reason the "problem" persists is that we don't want to let go of the compromise. We need to experience the rewards the compromise brings us, and we long to experience them in peace. We want the compromise to continue because it is the most satisfying one we have been able to devise. It may be grossly inadequate, but it is nonetheless a hidden way of having most of our cake and eating it too.

For example, a founding member of an organization devoted to supporting good causes is constantly critical of the fund-raising programs. His self-image tells him his own ideas are vastly superior, but whenever he is invited to carry out one of them, he finds himself in a bind. A rough business problem has just come up, or his asthma has taken a turn for the worse, or he's tied up straightening out a relative's estate. So his friends let him off the hook.

The fact is that he is not at all certain his own ideas are workable. His compromise behavior is that he postpones the day of reckoning and keeps intact his dream of superiority. He even avoids responsibility for chickening out by prompting his friends to suggest the postponement because they feel sorry for him.

Compromise behavior also serves as a rough and imperfect solution to the problem of handling painful emotions from the past. It is related to what Freud called repression, the act of burying or hiding or otherwise avoiding the recall of traumatic experiences. According to Freud, the repression of painful memories serves to allay anxiety and defend the ego from attack and injury. But repression occurs within a single individual, whereas compromise behavior necessarily involves interaction with others.

Both are protective devices; compromise behavior is typically used when someone feels vulnerable and needs to guard against risk or reproach. By acting out the compromise, he can coerce others into behaving in safe, familiar ways without having to acknowledge responsibility for doing so.

For example, a young woman's father dislikes her fiancé, but she claims she is in no way concerned about her father's opinion. Nevertheless, she becomes critical and antagonistic with her boy friend, and he breaks the engagement. She is devastated, even though it was her own behavior that drove him away.

Unable to choose between father and lover, she felt compelled to combine her conflicting needs. Her discordant messages—aware and unaware—achieved a compromise. She is not aware that she engineered a compromise and she is not happy with it, but it does save her from facing a showdown with her father and it saves her from taking responsibility for the broken engagement.

The attendant frustrations appear to be among the inevitable ironies of human existence, for there is no way of getting a grip on the situation as long as its source remains unconscious. The inexplicable feeling of inner discord leaves the manipulator insecure, and this malaise is maintained because there is no known cause or cure. The poor manipulator has victimized himself along with the others; he complains bitterly and blames the others since he feels that someone is responsible, and obviously it isn't himself.

In summary, to tune in on unaware behavior and hear the real message communicated by a discordant style, we have to disengage from emotional involvement and we then have to listen for the consequences of the other person's behavior; in particular, we should look for such consequences in ourselves; we need to develop an ear for patterns and learn to discriminate pertinent information from attractive diversions; and we must understand the rewarding function of even the most painful compromise behaviors.

These six points are not difficult to understand intellectually, but they may be extremely difficult to carry out in practice, because we have good reason to subvert them and have become skillful at doing so. It is more comfortable to hear only what we choose to hear. Also, we know how to amplify such information to the point where it drowns out the subtle cues we need if we are going to actually change anyone's behavior. So we shall now consider several seductive kinds of information that we do *not* wish to listen to.

3

How Not to Listen

There are three important ways in which the effort of listening can easily be wasted: logical listening, emotional listening, and passive listening. These three are closely related, and they form the substance of this chapter and the following chapter:

Listening to words: why not to listen with a logical ear.

Listening to feelings: why not to weep at all his sad tales.

Listening as an act: why passive listening won't work.

The first two are concerned with what the other person does to keep us from hearing accurately, the third with what *we* do to keep us from hearing accurately.

Let the Listener Beware

The listener, like the buyer, is often on the receiving end of a sales pitch. The speaker doesn't want him listening in on the conversation as a critical outsider. He wants the listener to follow the words and buy the argument. His most familiar technique is to act as a self-interpreter, to give the listener a secondhand report that is more convincing than the real thing.

Secondhand listening is a skill peculiar to people. It is the ability to interpret symbols that refer to events, ideas, and experiences removed from the listener in space and time. It is what allows us to learn most of what we learn in school and everything we learn from books and newspapers. We know it is not as reliable or as exciting as firsthand experience, and sometimes we wish we could have been present at some great moment in history or perhaps be there now on the other side of the globe.

Ironically, we don't often take advantage of firsthand listening when we have the chance. Even when we *are* there, the secondhand habit persists. In our most immediate personal encounters we commonly stand before someone important to us and attend less to his behavior than to his reports about his behavior. We listen to his echoes and reflections and take lightly our own direct perceptions. It is like talking with a reporter who has just interviewed himself and is now giving us a simple, encapsulated analysis of who he is. We accept this easy-to-take, predigested description. We listen to what he wants us to hear.

What he wants us to hear are his words (his *reports about* what he does, perceives, believes) and his moods or feelings (his public display of the sensitivities he would like the world to notice). His words and his feelings occur spontaneously for the most part, but both are often used in the service of nonrational needs he does not dare admit or openly express. There is a need unspoken behind his rational explanation. There is a motive unrecognized behind his anger.

In the previous chapter we were listening for the effects of subtle cues to discover the hidden motivations that allow someone to control others without realizing what he is doing. Now we are concerned with spotting these same cues so that we, as listeners, will not be stuck with our old listening patterns.

An oversimplified example of such a cue is the statement, "I don't want to sound impatient. . . ." Our accustomed listening response is to believe him. What the man probably means is, "I very well do mean to sound impatient. It's the only way I know to get you off the dime." Actually he is giving a double message, which is, "I want to sound impatient without sounding impatient"—that is, without paying the price of being consciously perceived as an impatient person.

Whenever we are involved in such a communication as a listener, we have the unique privilege of witnessing a production staged for our specific benefit. The production is designed, consciously or unconsciously, to prompt certain behavior on our part by projecting a particular image. It is also designed to convince us—and possibly the subject himself—that this projection is how it really *is*. Whether the image is negative or positive, helpless or enthusiastic, wise or foolish, we may assume it will be presented with conviction and confidence.

Even though the speaker is not aware of the fact, his experience has been that when he is in need, he can count on his unconscious manipulative talents. His logic can bring us to accept just about anything for which he needs our acceptance, and his emotions smooth the way. He is a master of countless techniques and persuasive tricks, and if we get sucked into his logic, or if we accept his apparent emotions at face value, we will simply be repeating and reinforcing an old pattern.

For example, a wife weeps and says, "I was so hurt by your wanting to move away from all our friends just because of that job, I cried all night. It would be traumatic for the children to change schools again, after all they've been through. We lose all those hours we put in on our garden. . . . It makes *no sense!*" The husband capitulates and turns down an interesting job offer in another city, and his wife knows more surely than ever that when she is hurt things happen her way, especially if she backs up her feelings with a good argument.

As astute listeners, we dare not be seduced by the literal meaning of the narrative being played out for us, that is, by what the other person is consciously presenting on his personal stage. Much of it is accurate, much is not, and common sense cannot often tell the difference.

We want to avoid colluding in his artful drama, but we do want to know how things are with him behind the scenes. What is he angling for? What is the performance accomplishing for him? What responses is it designed to elicit from us?

Listening to Words: Why We Shouldn't Listen with a Logical Ear

Words are powerful manipulators of human behavior. Witness the effectiveness of GO BACK . . . EAT . . . STOP . . . WOMEN . . . EXIT. We make full use of all the overt communications we know will work, plus a few that don't such as, "John, no!" Direct commands and prohibitions are limited, however, because people are sensitive about being told what to do.

Words are especially powerful when used to deliver a logical argument. Logic is not truth but it has the ring of truth, which of course makes it the first refuge of a scoundrel. To be convincing, an argument does not have to be accurate, it only has to make good sense. And the speaker is already one up on us if he can con us into accepting his choice of weapons—*his* kind of logic played according to *his* rules.

An obliging salesman calls on a housewife, peddling an excellent, reasonably priced encyclopedia. The woman listens to his several suggestions and questions but limits her answer to a single response: a quiet, definitive *no.*

"Do you care about your children's education?"

"No."

"You must be kidding. Why not?"

"No reason."

Of course the question she hears—and answers—is the real question: Do you care about your children's education enough to buy another encyclopedia from me? The salesman soon abandons his pitch and tells the woman she has given him the one and only response he cannot handle. What he needs from her is any reason whatever for not going along with his offer; this he can turn neatly to his advantage. He doesn't care, he says, whether she argues against him or with him; he only cares that she become involved in *his* argument in some way.

Words are particularly misleading when they claim to represent "unbiased logic" or "objective truth." In either case, they do not deliver reliable information when the content carries an emotional load. A "perfectly objective" classroom lecture on the history of Europe is not likely to come out the same in England as it does in France or Russia. And when we are entangled in personal relationships *The Truth* is far more malleable than this. The unschooled brain, interested only in psychological survival, does not ask, "What is the truth?" It asks, "Can the truth do anything for me?"

In such endeavors as downhill racing or scientific investigation, the truth, in the form of accurate perception, is sought and treasured. In such endeavors as the pursuit of unconscious needs within a personal relationship, the truth may be a matter of indifference, or it may be something to be avoided at all costs.

If we hope to gain perspective on a relationship, we had better look beyond the other person's logically convincing argument. What, behind the logic of it, is his purpose? Why is he piling this particular information on us at this particular moment?

Verbal Shields: Hiding Behind Words

The unvarnished truth is hard to handle. It's risky. It tends to be crude, inconsistent, and not exactly honorable. There is too much at stake to let it all hang out, so the average person has learned to shield himself. He softens the blow, deflects it, stops it cold if he can. And this he does largely by masking truth with logic. He retouches it just enough so that he can live with it, and he adds a few colors of his own. The tardy husband says, "Yes, as a matter of fact, I had an early supper with Charlotte, but you know I couldn't finish those reports without something in my stomach."

Of necessity, he has become an expert at filtering reality. He deftly applies his personalized psychological spot remover. He changes the model in his head without having to do anything uncomfortable about the actual circumstances the model is supposed to represent. He alters the map without having to mess with the terrain. He becomes right in retrospect. He justifies the fiasco that has just happened or is about to happen. He throws up rational defenses and invents tenable excuses that enable him to escape responsibility. In short, although he cannot literally go back and change reality, he can do a beautiful job of doctoring the tapes.

We should not listen too seriously, therefore, to the immediate surface logic of the other person's explanation of things important to him. We can be certain that it will be presented in such a way that it clearly does "make sense" and that the sense it makes will be precisely the sense the speaker wants it to make.

The subject's own excuses, apologies, self-corrections, and explanations are surefire warnings to the firsthand listener. We cannot afford to take him seriously when he begins, "What I really meant was. . . ." What he really means is precisely what he does do and what he does say, *particularly* the "slips" and "mistakes" and "accidents."

He himself is stuck with his own excuses and explanations since he wants to believe them and therefore cannot see beyond them. We, fortunately, are not stuck, and this is what gives us the opportunity to see what is usually hidden behind the bright façade of "good excuses."

We can also be of direct help by not asking for a rational accounting of what we hear. Unschooled listeners are in the habit of putting great pressure on the speaker to give a logical reason for everything he says. "Why? It doesn't make sense! Give me one good reason!" They demand that everything appear to be rational, whether it is or not, and they make it very hard for anyone to be intuitive and at ease about his immediate nonrational feelings.

Direct rational analysis, as well as it may work with conscious, practical tasks, cannot do justice to manipulative behavior that is hidden and unconscious. What it does do in fact, when brought to bear on hidden motivations, is to camouflage the problem.

So we would do well not to listen for logic when there is passion in the air, be it anger or joy, hurt or triumph, or a desperate need. A raised voice, tears in the eyes, clenched fists, a heavy frown, flashing eyes ... these are clues that are trying to tell us: behind the rational analysis and the neat argument lie the needs and motivations that have to be uncovered before the real issue can be found and faced.

The way to listen to a logical presentation is to disregard the question of how reasonable the argument is and listen for what it is doing for the speaker. Is he justifying something he doesn't feel very good about? Why does this mean so much to him? What responsibilities will he avoid if we accept his presentation as fact? What does he want us to believe, and how important is it to him that we do believe it? Why? What arguments does he repeat—as if he were not quite sure that once was enough?

The information he feeds us is invaluable, even though his words are not to be taken literally. When he raises his verbal shield against what he sees as the slings and arrows of outrageous fortune, the gesture that protects his face also exposes some other vulnerable part of his anatomy, most likely an important need or fear.

A director tells his leading lady, "It wasn't *my* fault the show failed. You know perfectly well I'm the best director in the business, whatever the critics may think! But what can I do when I get half the budget I ask for, run into union problems at the last moment, and have to deal with a perfectionist like Walter who wants real live horses? How can I keep peace backstage when Walter blames everybody else for his own lack of foresight? People are going to think that *I'm* the one who didn't have the show together for the opening!"

If we accept his explanations, we learn nothing. If we argue against them, we are merely raining pointless blows upon his impervious shield. But if we relax and simply watch how he handles the shield, we may learn something. The tenacity with which he puts forth his arguments is a good indicator of how insecure he feels. If he has many unmet needs, he will be afraid we won't see what he wants us to see. Like the television commentator at a convention who insists upon telling us exactly what it is we are looking at, he assumes we won't get the proper message if we witness the raw event without his appended interpretation.

Through the filter of a private logic, he perceives selectively, so that what he tells us will support whatever conclusions he has come to have about himself. Without being aware of it, he gives us the chance to observe discrepancies that may exist between what he wants us to believe about his goals and what his behavior actually accomplishes.

"I'm really a terribly generous person," a friend says, looking us in the eye as he absentmindedly takes back half the tip he has just placed under the edge of his plate.

Verbal Cages: Locking Ourselves In

If an individual gets into the habit of setting up verbal shields between himself and the rest of the world, he soon completes the circle and finds himself enclosed in a cage. A few dozen logical defenses—a few thousand reasonable words—are woven together until they completely surround the weaver. The magic wall protects him and at the same time isolates him.

The foundation upon which verbal cages are built is the verb *to be*. The basic theorem is: "Whatever I say I am, that I must be." A man says, in public, "I am a vengeful rival," and from this time forward he feels bound to live up to his words. A woman says, "I am such a vulnerable person that I don't dare commit myself emotionally." Having said it —many times, in a variety of ways—she believes it; her life is then played out dodging commitments, even though she secretly may long to commit herself. In short, building a verbal cage is a classic way of consolidating a discordant style and putting oneself in a lasting bind.

This all-encompassing form of self-justification becomes a neatly closed circle for the lush who explains, while still in his cups, "Since I'm an alcoholic, I have to drink." If we accept the argument, we are suckers who thereby contribute to the problem and help perpetuate it.

Think of someone who is not willing to risk being seen exactly as he is. Imagine that he builds around himself a cage and that he covers the cage with silver screening upon which he can project—from inside— words and pictures that describe the self he is willing for the world to see. What he is and what he really wants are masked by the carefully edited slides he projects onto the screen. What nonrational need lies behind his reasonable words?

We cannot see in directly, but two strong clues are available. One is that we can observe how people outside the cage react to the pictures, which they assume to be the real thing. These outsiders *are* being taken in—in a way we hopefully are not—and their responses should reflect the behaviors the man in the cage wishes to encourage in them.

Commonly, they come to accept the cage as real, and the occupant thus is relieved of the need to examine his problem or change his behavior. "I am extraordinarily stupid" is a very handy cage; whatever the speaker may be accused of, he is obviously too stupid to know better. Other familiar cages are "I'm too old," "He's practically blind," and "We're too proud to consider anything like that."

The other clue is that we can see what the man really wants because what he really wants is what he has here so painstakingly built for himself: a cage that hides some vitally important part of his self, while projecting an image of the self he wants us to be influenced by. He may project a list of other "wants" on the cage wall, but his major need is what he already has: the cage itself, the compromise that provides him with illusions he can sustain and live with.

Anyone who volunteers an analysis of himself is going to be objectively inaccurate when it comes to the details that are most important to him. The reasons he discovers for his behavior—and projects onto the walls of his cage—are not the driving reasons. He has no particular need to be accurate, but he is powerfully motivated to assure himself and others that his treasured self-image is true.

A dead giveaway to anyone who listens with discrimination is the cage labeled: "But I can't help it. That's the way I am!" Of course it is the way he is. He made himself that way in order to get precisely the satisfactions he is getting, and he cannot change because he can't face giving them up. He put himself together the way he is for his own good reasons, and now he has built a little cage ("That's the way I am!") that keeps him from moving or even considering a move.

Another common cage is: "I really must do something about that." The message is that the speaker distinctly plans to do nothing whatever aside from declaring his good intentions.

A good way of spotting a verbal cage is to listen for descriptions of behavior that appear to give the speaker no choice. Behavior so described seems to be inevitable, and of course it is tremendously oversimplified—which is how reality comes out when filtered through a very needful brain.

Life in fact is inevitably whimsical, enigmatic, complex, unexpected, unjust, fluid, irrational, lecherous, and crammed with mixed blessings. But when we are insecure or hurting, we long for an excuse to avoid further uncertainty and we grab for anything familiar.

The irony of all these techniques for hiding uncomfortable personal truths from others is that the hider is most successful at hiding them from himself. Sooner or later he is going to wake up and cry out, "Why am I the last to know?" The reason he is the last to know is that he has clearly *chosen* to be the last to know.

A common example is the man who goes about making impressive noises. The message he gives himself is that he is impressing people. He has so much invested in this effort that he cannot afford to perceive the message the people are actually receiving when they whisper, "What the hell is this joker trying to prove?"

In order to gather the information we need to change another person's behavior, we have to learn not to listen uncritically to what people most want us to hear. The very best binoculars won't work if the subject is too close, and in a like manner things go out of focus whenever we lose our distance. We have to stay far enough away to resist being charmed by the other person's persuasiveness, sucked into his favorite game, or controlled by his private needs.

4

Listening to Feelings

Some children have an amazing ability to contract a case of the sniffles shortly before it's time to leave for school. They may beg to go anyway, but they are kept home. As soon as the school bus leaves, the child starts getting better.

This is no trick. He really feels stuffed up and sick at eight o'clock and blooming with health by lunch time. Without realizing it, he has delivered a double message, with the result that he gets to stay home from school without asking, without even admitting that he wanted to.

The lesson for us as listeners is: an individual often seems to be at the mercy of his feelings, but it may be that these feelings are very useful to him. People regularly marshal their feelings for their private purposes and often express only those that bring them rewarding responses.

Feelings thus are not only an effect of outside events but also a cause. If feeling blue happens to draw support from their friends, they may repeatedly choose—albeit unconsciously—to elicit sad and lonely symptoms from themselves.

A dramatic response to unpleasant news isn't just a response; it is also a statement to the world—about how sensitive and concerned the speaker is, perhaps, or about how tough he is. A dramatic response to something *we* have done or said is an emotional statement to us that leaves us feeling different—perhaps elated and open to his subsequent suggestions, perhaps only pressured in some way.

The reason we need to be aware of the unconscious manipulative uses of emotion is twofold. First, by listening to feelings as "behavior with a purpose," we gather precisely the information we need to change such behavior. Second, being aware of the active uses of emotion can save us from being taken in by the display.

"I Can't Help It": Emotion as an Excuse

Most people like to believe that feelings originate outside themselves. Something "happens" to them that "makes" them sad or happy or angry or lustful. These feelings in turn cause them to behave in unusual ways.

The assumption is convenient because it lets them off the hook. Behavior that otherwise would be unacceptable or suspect becomes "understandable" when an emotional state is seen as the cause. If they feel depressed enough, they can probably quit early, and if they are hopelessly in love they can get away with all kinds of weird performances.

When someone is driven to take his hostile feelings out on *us,* we suffer and we feel helpless. If we complain, we are told, "But I can't help it. That's how I *feel* about it." The speaker is giving us a double message: he wants us to know he doesn't like us, but he doesn't want us to hold him personally responsible. He cons us into sympathizing with his apparent, conscious dilemma. What can we do if the other guy is driven by feelings he can't control?

The answer is that we can do a great deal. The first step is to gather new information from the immediate situation. As listeners, we have much to learn from emotional displays, but we will miss most of it if we get entangled in the speaker's own theories about his own feelings.

What we need is a fresh point of view. We need to turn his cause-and-effect relationship upside down: instead of supposing that he does what he does because of his feelings, let us imagine that he has the feelings he has because of what they allow him to do. This changes our perspective and affects our hearing. Rather than searching for outside reasons to explain his actions, we listen for the inner origin of his feelings and for what he says and does in the name of these feelings.

Take a man who yells, "You make me so mad I could strangle you!" His anger gives him reason to do violence, to satisfy an aggressive urge he would never feel justified in following without the presence of the anger. And his anger is clearly the fault of the other person. He never says, "*I* make me so mad I could strangle you." If we listen for ways in which he might be profiting from the emotion, or even creating it, we may learn something. When the man says, "The more I think about it, the madder I get," it becomes pretty obvious who is generating the anger.

Nobody can be run by his feelings unless, at some level of his being, he wants to be run by his feelings. Or, to put it the other way around, anybody who wants to do something he normally finds unacceptable can generate an emotion that will, at least in his own eyes, "explain" and thus excuse the act.

Joanne says her husband's constant nagging makes her furious, and she stomps out of the house and spends the night with a friend. Later she explains, "That terrible nagging made me feel so angry that it drove me into the arms of another man." This may sound logical, but if it were true that nagging causes infidelity, it would then be true that all nagging husbands are cuckolds. Joanne actually had a broad spectrum of possible responses to choose from.

Her friend Alice counters excessive nagging by getting drunk and blames it on her husband. Sarah responds to nagging with aggressive indifference; Maggie takes a similar problem to a marriage counselor; Virginia arranges for her husband to take a short vacation alone. Joanne chooses to see anger as the cause of infidelity; it could be that a wish for infidelity was the cause of her anger.

Emotion is not necessarily displayed in order to allow or excuse out-of-the-ordinary behavior; but it may be, and none of us is immune. Pleasing and displeasing events occur every day in everyone's life, and each of us uses a selected few of these events for his own conscious and unconscious purposes. Anyone who wants to feel bad has a wide choice of events that can act as an understandable trigger.

Some people don't wait around for an event they can blame but manufacture their own trauma or joy. They behave in a way that nudges others into "doing something" to them, and they then respond with the emotion they are moved to display. The process reveals itself if we are listening on the appropriate wavelengths.

Anyone who habitually uses his feelings as an excuse for marginal or unacceptable behavior usually has a fine ear for events with emotional overtones. He listens selectively, sensitive to anything that might be serviceable in triggering feelings he is accustomed to expressing. For example, he will listen for offenses; he seems to be tuned exclusively to receive messages that bug him. In the presence of such a person we are inclined to whisper and go around on tiptoe. He is an obvious case of anger looking for something to be about.

In a way, this circumstance makes our task as listeners easier. We assume the other person has the feelings he has because they are bringing him some kind of reward, and we are listening for a clue as to what reward he is unconsciously soliciting. Since he repeats the same routine again and again, we have an endless opportunity to listen for the consequences of the emotions he keeps encouraging in himself.

Feelings That Control: Emotion as an Act

Feelings may erupt spontaneously regardless of whether or not anyone is around to notice. Or they may be felt without any outward display, as is often true of grief. But the innocent and heartfelt expression of one's feelings can also serve as a powerful means of influencing or controlling the behavior of other people—especially when any wish for control is honestly denied.

Granted that emotions are at times expressed without regard to their effect, let us nevertheless listen *as if* they were unconsciously designed to create a specific mood or bias in the other person. When we listen in this way, we are certain to hear things we would otherwise miss.

The reason we have to be wary of listening in the usual, social way is that such easy listening is precisely the kind of engagement the speaker has come to expect of us. The listener who responds in kind to the mood projected upon him is gullible, and he thus perpetuates an established pattern that is in some degree responsible for whatever problems he and the speaker are having.

A U.S. official in postwar Germany was hit with an unexpected crisis. His deputy, with whom he'd had crisis problems before, arrived at the office one minute late and was greeted volcanically: "Where have *you* been? We've got a two-month investigation to clean up and get on the courier plane by five o'clock. Now get your ass moving!" The deputy listened calmly and said, "Lou, I'm going out and get a haircut."

He had heard the message that the sky was falling but he refused to be stampeded. He also had heard the message that a difficult job had to be accomplished in a short time. He returned half an hour later and applied himself with quiet efficiency.

Apparently, we unconsciously choose precisely what feelings to show, feelings that are subtly tailored to fit the situation and the end in view. Would our expressed feelings be the same with a potential employer as with a potential lover? Or if we had no audience at all?

This goes for good feelings as well as for heavy ones. A happy person not only cooperates with the feeling but often initiates it. A chronically unhappy person is difficult to "help" because unhappiness is just what he chooses to display and he may be quite pleased about some of the responses that his "unhappiness" generates.

Any emotion can serve when displayed at the right moment, even a feeling as mild as expectation. An expectant child can make a lot of things happen simply by virtue of his very bright eyes. If the child is nevertheless ignored, he may "feel disappointed" and go into a sulk that predictably makes us feel guilty. We imagine we have "caused" his petulance by "hurting his feelings," and we overlook the use to which the scowling and pouting is being put.

If this strategy fails to make us pay attention, he may resort to the even more reliable technique of disruptive and destructive behavior—screaming, kicking, scratching, tearing the room apart. Being spanked is far better than being ignored, and there is security and satisfaction in his knowing that he is perfectly able to make it happen whenever he feels like it.

The technique is not by any means peculiar to the young. Parents often react aggressively when their devoted children withdraw as adolescents. The parents are lonely and they unconsciously search for ways to engage their children again. The child's indifference is at best annoying, and at worst it engenders profound insecurity. Any attention is better than none, and a parent will do what he can, which usually means he will complain about his offspring's dress or hairstyle or, if all else fails, about his friends.

The lesson here is not to be diverted by searching for the "cause" of hurt feelings or disappointment. Rather, we should listen for what changes are brought about in other people's behavior as a result of feelings being expressed. A child is "heartbroken" when told he cannot go on a camping trip, and he cries uncontrollably. Eventually, his mother gives in to him, and of course he stops crying at once.

We are not talking about pretense. To consciously take on a pained expression in order to gain sympathy or attention doesn't work very many times because the game is pretty obvious. But everyone knows from experience that when he is really hurt, honestly and truly, the odds are great that a rewarding response will soon be forthcoming from one place or another. He will have brought subtle pressure to bear and will at the same time remain blissfully ignorant of his own secret design.

If we happen to be the "victim" and feel pressure in some vague way, we don't need to waste time listening for dishonesty or fakery. The important message is probably coming to us by way of some perfectly honest feeling that has been made use of before in a similar manner.

There is seldom anything malevolent about using an emotion to influence or control behavior, and the feeling involved may be as un-remarkable as boredom. If we look at boredom as an active message rather than as a passive reaction, and if we attend to consequences rather than to causes, it becomes clear that we are dealing with the art of unconscious coercion.

Our host for the evening displays boredom, although we would be just as happy to stay around for another drink. He never consciously suggests that we leave, and yet we are soon asking for our coats; he never has to take responsibility for edging us out of the house. Boredom is a very effective feeling.

So is cowering fear. A strong sense of vulnerability and defenseless-ness is sometimes powerful enough to stop an attacker in his tracks. Some animals, when about to be attacked by a dominant animal of the same species, roll onto their backs with legs in the air. The attacker accepts the message and leaves them alone.

Among humans, the frightened cry, "I'm at your mercy!" is an attempt, often successful, to capitalize on an aggressor's sense of guilt or obligation or nobility. Feeling vulnerable and showing it is thus an act, an action, a signal, an unconscious way of engineering a nonthreatening response from another person.

Another unconscious coercer is a feeling of dejection expressed as a wish to kill oneself. People spring into action. Once a chronically un-happy person discovers how effective the technique is, he may be counted on to use it again. Even more convincing—because the subject remains blameless—is an emotion that expresses itself in the form of a psychosomatic symptom. The principle is the same, but no one can accuse the "victim" of malingering or of turning in false alarms. How can he turn off a rash or put away a headache?

The lesson here is simply: if we let our own emotions be pushbuttoned, and allow the other person's "hurt feelings" to trigger a familiar response pattern in us, the resulting involvement will render us incapable of listening for the real need that undoubtedly lies beneath the expressed hurt.

There are feelings directed only to oneself, and they too may be unconscious communications. If we (the listener) can identify the uses of such self-directed emotions in someone we know, we probably can gain insight into some of his persistent emotional patterns. Feelings of anxiety late in the afternoon may be used to "prove" the existence of an absolutely valid need for alcohol. Some of the most vehement explosions of anger are directed at hammers; the hammer stoically accepts responsibility and leaves the hammerer off the hook.

Having Your Cake and Trying to Eat It: Discordance as an Achievement

Emotions are most disturbing—and most revealing, if we care to follow the clue—when they are inconsistent or when they obviously clash with other behavior. What are we to make of a woman who says, between kisses, that she can't stand the sight of us?

Dissonant or discordant behavior involves conflicts and contradictions between what a person says and what he does, between his conscious and his unconscious activities, between what he believes he wants for himself and what he actually brings about.

An example is the angry woman who speaks sweetly and smiles a lot. She fully believes her own smile and sweet voice, and yet her companion becomes increasingly tense and displeased. The angry woman's behavior is discordant, and she is thereby doing just what she wishes to do: being perfectly pleasant and at the same time satisfying an unconscious motivation to express anger. She could, if she truly wished, learn that she is giving an angry message despite her sweet smile; but she also wishes to satisfy her conscious need to be, or at least to act, friendly at all times.

Psychological discordance of this sort is often uncomfortable, but it is not an error or an accident or a lapse. It is a discriminating compromise, unconsciously chosen, which delivers precisely the messages the subject wants to deliver.

Discordance allows him to preserve his beliefs and at the same time to experience satisfactions that may not be consistent with them. We all do this, for it is an everyday way of coping with hope and necessity. And it works. The trouble comes with the side effects, which sometimes build to a point of acute distress.

One of the side effects of discordance is distorted communication that brings frustration and pain to others. If we happen to be among the "victims" of such behavior, the discomfort may be great enough that we are driven to do something about it. Presumably, this is why we are interested in learning to listen in such a way that we may be able to bring about a constructive change in the behavior of good friends and enemies. Just as physical pain focuses our attention on a physical malfunction, psychological discordance can draw our attention to behavior that is not functioning in a very satisfactory manner.

An attractive woman is dating a distinguished widower and she accepts his advances with obvious pleasure. They thoroughly enjoy each other's company until he begins giving her strongly discordant messages. He says she is what he always dreamed of, adding that he is falling madly in love with her.

At the same time he begins having what he calls "little problems"— sharp anger about trivial matters, bouts of impotence, and whole evenings of stony silence. He finds reason after reason that seems to account for his difficulties, but nothing improves and the affair breaks up in a depressing and hostile way.

Had the woman known what to listen for in a discordant message, she might have been able to help him salvage the relationship. For one thing, the reasons he gave were no more than hopeful guesses. His underlying motivations were probably not ones he was comfortable with, so he was continually motivated to find an "easier" reason.

Months later, he was able to acknowledge that he probably had never been in love in the first place. However, he had always wanted to fall in love with just such a glamorous woman, and, once given the chance, he was determined not to blow it. It was precisely this determination that ruined an otherwise affectionate friendship.

Paradox: Listening for What's Not Being Said

What should we listen for when we suspect a discordant message? A good start is to keep an ear open for any unusually consistent and logical personal story, typically one that seems "almost too good to be true." This can alert us to messages delivered without the subject's awareness.

For example, a rigid but well-meaning grade school teacher recently embraced the concepts of individualized instruction and the open classroom in her traditional Central Valley school in California. To the surprise of her friends, she began to talk convincingly and with warm enthusiasm about the new freedom in the classroom; in practice, however, she followed an authoritarian set of rules she had written down to make sure *her* classroom would be properly "open."

Three kinds of information are available here if we know what to listen for. First, we have the teacher's own conscious, clearly reported belief that she is now a liberated, freewheeling teacher committed to the joys and rewards of the new education. Second, there is the message she is not aware of but which the children receive from her forever stern face, her sharp commands, and her insistence upon quiet in the room. Third, there is the message of the discordance itself: the discrepancy between her aware and unaware messages.

We learn from the discordance that she is a walking contradiction: she dictates freedom. She has two very strong needs—to be known as a "young" and freshly innovative teacher, and to control a rowdy group of third and fourth graders by the only means she knows will work. She manages both of these contradictory aims by means of her discordant and pathetic compromise.

We listen for descriptions as a clue, but what we are really interested in is the discrepancy itself. What is the *whole* message—the whole, self-contradictory message by which unconscious as well as conscious needs are being met—at least to some degree? The two aspects are both represented all the time in everything we do, and the discordance that results, while it may have uncomfortable or even devastating side effects, is first of all an achievement. It is an ingenious compromise that allows us to realize some wonderfully confusing satisfactions while leaving our neatly consistent self-image intact.

Whenever we hear a discordant message, we should ask what double or multiple ends it is accomplishing. The "cure," which we shall deal with in later chapters, does not lie in discouraging discordance per se but in reordering the priorities so that a more effective and rewarding compromise can be nurtured. It does not have to do with changing our means for getting what we assume we want; it has to do with changing our wants themselves.

Listening as an Act: Why Passive Listening Won't Work

When a message is distorted, most of us blame the speaker, and when it is clear and convincing, we give him all the credit. We overlook the fact that communication depends as much upon the receiver as it does upon the sender. Without a tuned-in listener, the message itself falls apart. In other words, firsthand listening is not a passive indulgence; it is an *act* of communication, a positive focusing of attention.

The listener has to be constantly alert, listening for what is wanted but not asked for, attending to the many messages given by tone, manner, and gesture, and scanning the environment to catch the consequences of what the speaker is saying. He also has to avoid the usual seductions, such as being talked into accepting rationalizations because they appear to be perfectly reasonable.

Finally, he must remember that the act of listening is itself a never-ending communication. The listener delivers a constant flow of messages, although he is rarely aware of doing so. Inattention, for example, may seem like no message at all, and yet it often communicates a feeling of unconcern or hypocrisy powerful enough to make the speaker explode with anger.

Many of us *try* to be good listeners, but trying defeats our purpose.

We are taught so much about speaking; we are taught almost nothing about listening, and the little we are taught is destructive. We are taught, by instruction and by example, to "help" the speaker, to agree with him, to "look interested," to keep murmuring encouragement. Nobody can keep a complicated act like this going and still have his faculties clear for the job of listening. Furthermore, it is no compliment, but rather a grave insult, to pretend interest or encouragement.

We normally go further than this, in the mistaken belief that we are demonstrating rapport. We jump to conclusions before the speaker himself gets there, we tell him again and again what the word is he's looking for, we toss in examples from our own experience (proof enough that we weren't really listening to *him*), and we assure him that we understand (he knows very well that we don't).

There is only one way to listen, to hear what is going on in the other person. That is to be quiet, in fact and in mind. To assume nothing, to draw no conclusions. To simply listen and do nothing else. To forget about analyzing what we hear and to forgo the pleasure of supplementing it from our own experience. There is no need to think or to answer the questions he asks of himself.

If we can be still in this way, we may find where it is the other person really wants to go. We will hear cleanly, without contamination from our own needs and problems. We will not only *hear* (perhaps for the first time), we will quite possibly find that all kinds of people tend to seek our company.

Being quiet does not have to mean silence. A good listener will point out discrepancies and will ask about things he does not understand. But he will truly *ask,* not suggest his own answers. He will interrupt a compulsive talker—repeatedly if necessary. It may be impolite to cut in on a compulsive talker, but it is certainly not an insult. It shows that we are really listening and that we care about what is bothering the speaker. Compulsive talkers go on incessantly about trivia because they are afraid of talking about what they really want to talk about. Their jabbering is just as distracting to themselves as it is to a listener.

Listening in this way—as opposed to the comfortable artifice of pretending to listen—makes some speakers uncomfortable because it is essentially an intimate act. Love has everything to do with true listening, with wanting to know where the other person is, what he needs, where he is going, and what he cares about once his fears are quieted.

Don't Listen for What You Hope to Hear

Anyone who listens to another through the filter of his own hopes and fears will automatically seize upon those fragments of the speaker's thought and feelings that confirm his own expectations: that is, he will be listening to his own echo. Not only that, but since there is something at stake for the listener, he will be vulnerable to all sorts of emotional triggering and persuasion.

A woman who considers herself plain and uninteresting is likely to remember every compliment her lover bestows upon other women and dismiss his positive comments about herself as "nothing but flattery." She may feel rejected whenever he criticizes her and may therefore go to great lengths to please him. Obviously her vision is clouded.

The most insidious distraction in this area occurs when we believe we already know how the other person will act. As long as we believe we understand him, we will listen for anything that confirms this belief and tend to distrust any evidence that doesn't fit our satisfying, prefabricated model of who he really is. (After all, it would make us wrong.)

If we can stay loose from what we want to hear and what we expect to hear, then our own relationship with the speaker will not greatly bias our perceptions. Ideally, we ought to notice whatever gives us an emotional kick—but without acting on it: notice—but without responding—that he is making us angry. We want to observe the consequences of his behavior but stay with our own feelings, the ones we brought with us.

If he attacks us verbally, we do not want to leap to our feet with a defensive argument; that would entail a complete loss of our ability to listen. We are really not interested now in justifying ourselves; we want to know what is really the matter with our friend and why he can't help attacking us. If we are afraid of loss or hurt or anger or rejection, we are in no position to listen. If we get defensive about a symptom such as anger, we lose the opportunity to discover what this anger is a symptom of.

A corollary of listening without expectation is not to take first impressions seriously. A first impression is very much like the cover of a book. It pretends to show us what the book is about but its real purpose is to sell the book. Whatever may be inside, the jacket is designed to make it appear attractive to us in a simple and memorable fashion.

As listeners, even as voyeurs, we are most vulnerable to deception when we first meet someone. Since this first impression is all we have to go on, we can't very well ask, "Is it true?" We can only ask, "Is it consistent? Is it convincing?" If we leave this first encounter with a distinct impression that makes good sense to us, we will assume the impression and the person are identical.

We imagine that we know the book even though we only know its cover. Since we now believe we know what it's about, we may not even bother to look into the next time we encounter it; our minds are set and it's a drag to go back and reexamine our own beliefs. Which is to say, first impressions are self-perpetuating.

First impressions are also likely to be inaccurate. The subject is adept at playing the role he wants us to see. The impression we get is also influenced by external circumstances. If a friend introduces us to "a really marvelous person," it's easy to ignore the negative characteristics. If we meet someone, fender to fender, in an intersection, it may be difficult to recognize his good points.

While a first impression is probably misleading, it is at the same time a mine of reliable information concerning the other person's self-image. Seldom will we again have the opportunity to see so clearly the image this person feels he must present to a new acquaintance. Once he knows us better, he will temper his image to our own taste, but at the moment his style with us is about as blunt and unsubtle as it will ever be, except in times of acute stress.

A first impression, then, is extremely useful. We only have to remember that it is the way he wants to be seen and may or may not have much to do with who he "really" is. A book cover usually tells more about the jacket designer than it does about the author.

At the same time, we as listeners cannot afford to analyze. We are not concerned with "explaining" the other person. We may hope to change him, however, and to do this we have to know what he is unconsciously trying to do and how important it is to him. If we analyze or interpret each fragment of behavior as we go along, we are left with a list of rational abstractions in place of unorganized but valid raw material.

Since we are dealing with nonrational behavior, the use of conscious analysis at this stage is rather like substituting the opinion of an uninvolved "expert witness" for firsthand testimony. The unaware cues by which our subject is unconsciously trying to control the current situation are the least obvious of his actions. They are far too subtle and sinuous to be caught or contained in the precise, regular mesh of which logical nets are made.

We are not referees or judges, trying to remain deaf to emotional outbursts as we decide whether a defendant has violated certain established, rational rules. Instead, we are asking: What effect does his behavior have on us and what effect does it have on himself? What is he, without being aware of it, trying to do? We are not concerned about the "goodness" or "badness" of his behavior. We are concerned that he may be pursuing valid unconscious needs in a manner that is costly to himself and to us.

5

Changing

Once we have listened intimately to the person who has been unconsciously manipulating us, and have thus discerned the nature of his style, we are in a position to change him—or, more accurately, to cause him to change himself.

The only way to influence behavior that the manipulator himself is not yet aware of is to feed back information along the same channel that he is using to influence us. This is the channel that carries his controlling messages to us and also carries back to him the message of our response. It is essentially a feedback circuit that lets him know at every stage of the game how effective his messages (unconscious and conscious) are.

Presumably, as a result of listening within ourselves for the consequences of his actions, we now have become aware of what he is trying to accomplish. *He* is not aware, however—quite the reverse of the usual, stereotypical plot wherein an "evil" manipulator knows full well what's going on but keeps his victim in the dark. We may not understand *how* he manages to manipulate us, but we have discovered what he is getting from it, and we are therefore in a position to *dis*manipulate him.

This is done, essentially, by refusing to reward his manipulation with the response he has come to expect. By allowing his manipulations to fail, we create a new effect, a new consequence. This consequence is so unexpected that it neutralizes him and causes him to search for a more appropriate, more consciously chosen alternative.

A possible difficulty arises from the fact that we, too, have to learn to handle our feelings and that we, too, are part of the process and cannot avoid being affected by it. Knowing in advance that we have the power to influence another human being's behavior, we should ask if the changes we are aiming for are those we really want. We are changing someone who is involved in our life in many intricately related ways, and a convincing change in even one message requires a new attitude on our part. To change the other person means to change the whole relationship between the two of us.

Cooling It

Assuming we have already listened well and know what it is we wish to change, three major steps are involved in changing another person's controlling behavior: disengagement, delivering a surprising response, and providing space for the change.

The first step is for us to disengage from our own automatic responses to the other person, to his subtle promptings and coercions. He has been tuning in on us for a long while, scanning our reactions and our preferences and our vulnerable and tender places, and he knows intuitively what kind of pressures and temptations will subvert our critical powers. Naturally, his efforts will be directed to areas in which he senses we are vulnerable, and he is not likely to tempt us with steak if he thinks we are vegetarians. If he is particularly canny, he may have discovered things about us that we don't know ourselves.

Neither of us is a pretender, for we know from experience that pretense is not convincing. When we are stimulated to react with hurt feelings, we really are hurt. When we frown with sympathy, we mean it. In order to disengage, we must recognize these as our real feelings but refrain from acting them out. Instead, we say to ourselves something like, "He makes me feel sad with his depressing talk and depressed face. Now, why would he want me to feel sad?"

As soon as we disengage from the familiar pattern, as soon as we become concerned with his needs rather than with our own, we cease to be predictable! No longer caught up in the emotional climate he has designed for us, we are free to respond to him or not, at will. At the same time, he himself, the manipulator, has now become predictable.

As soon as we recognize that a child's familiar bellyache only shows up on Monday mornings, we no longer have to worry about feeling responsible for his health. In fact, we now anticipate that whenever a weekend has been particularly exciting, his body is going to provide him with a good excuse for staying home from school.

The temptation is always there to slip back into the old emotional pattern, to respond again in the way we have been set up to respond. The simplest way to avoid this is to concentrate again and again on *listening*—listening without judging or concluding or interpreting, just listening for what is being communicated and for what the consequences are in our own feelings.

Disengagement is the crucial element which permits us, at the moment we respond, to do so in a new way. The other person has pushed a familiar button and, since we are disengaged, the expected response fails to come popping out of us. His most likely reaction will be to push the same button again, harder and longer. A child who is in the habit of getting his way by crying will now scream. Most button-pushers give up after a few consistent failures, but they may exert tremendous pressure the first time the button fails to produce.

The Element of Surprise: Unexpected Responses and How to Use Them

Almost any behavior can be temporarily changed by such gross means as violence or the threat of it, blackmail or bribery, the administration of drugs, electrical stimulation of the brain, and surgery. We have all been shoved, hit, threatened, conned, seduced, and influenced by alcohol or other drugs.

Depending upon the intensity of the stimulus, the effects are for the most part temporary, and behavior often reverts to its earlier state as soon as the pressure is relaxed. We do not willingly forsake the hardearned compromise behaviors that have been working for us, even though we may feel obliged to set them aside temporarily.

What is usually needed to initiate a decisive change in behavior is a strong shove, from either within or without. Internal motivation may come from a powerful personal experience such as religious conversion or perhaps even from falling desperately in love. External pressure often comes in the form of a dramatic feeling of failure or the backfiring of a previously reliable technique for controlling our social or physical environment. For example, the wife says, "I've had it! Goodbye!" or the boss says he appreciates all the extra work over the past twenty years but we really don't fit the company's new image and we can pick up our severance pay downstairs at five o'clock.

To take a more everyday example, we may feel "overmanipulated," pushed further than we are willing to be pushed; we may therefore react by disengaging and giving an "asocial" response, a behavior very different from the one being courted. Our young daughter threatens again and again to run away from home unless we play her favorite game with her, and one day we respond to this annoying threat by saying, "Fine. Let me help you pack your bags."

The manipulator experiences a resounding sense of failure, and his resulting uncertainty forces him to question his motivations and to look for a more effective strategy for influencing our behavior.

A supreme example of the asocial response was provided by the 1971 Los Angeles earthquake, which illustrates how a single experience may break a behavior pattern of long standing. A number of children were seen in a counseling center after the quake, and one child's problem was that he absolutely refused to close any door whatsoever. He had been told many times by his mother not to slam doors—a maneuver which had been very successful in gaining her attention.

The last time he had slammed a door, the earthquake struck and the ground began to shake beneath him. The habit of door-slamming was forever broken because the negative response was much greater than the child had bargained for. It was as if he had gone too far in his bid for attention, "overmanipulating" the environment, which then struck back with all its might.

A milder version of this "earthquake technique" is used in psychotherapy when the therapist refuses to deliver the usual, socially expectable response to his patient's covert cues, but gives an unexpected response instead. Therapists long ago learned—popular myth to the contrary—that they had no other lever but themselves, no other way of changing their patient's self-defeating behaviors. Their only power lies in using their own immediate behavior as a means for leaving the patient uncertain enough that he has to look around for a better way to satisfy his needs.

An effective unexpected response is one that avoids going along with what the patient anticipates but is not otherwise threatening. If the patient feels he is being backed toward a precipice, he may panic. But if he feels relatively secure and is not shocked into taking a defensive posture, he is usually able to explore alternatives.

A patient who has unconsciously perfected a means for making other people feel guilty may say to his therapist during an interview, "You really haven't done much for me, have you?" The expectable, or "social" response to this statement would be a somewhat guilty reaction and would likely involve a defensive or angry posture.

The therapist is trained not to strike at the bait, however. He remains disengaged and responds with a simple statement such as, "You had higher expectations." The patient's strategy isn't working. He is frustrated because his favorite style has failed him, but at the same time he does not feel threatened.

It doesn't require a therapist to make telling use of this technique. Any one of us can become the agent, or instrument, of change for a friend, or even for a constant enemy, by virtue of the fact that we are intimately involved. We can influence him by the way we respond to his strategies.

Suppose someone is levering us in some way—nothing obvious except that the result is uncomfortable and happens again and again. A friend calls us regularly, praises our abilities and good will, asks for help on his favorite community project, and makes us feel guilty if we don't comply. It is not clear how he is doing this or why, but we can safely assume that his behavior and our response to it mean something to him, for he has invested a great deal of energy and emotion in this submarine gambit.

If we deliberately withhold our usual response, his heretofore reliable technique is brought into serious question, his considerable efforts are wasted, and his anticipations are left dangling. He is forced to retreat and reprogram himself. The technique amounts to a form of psychological jujitsu, using the opponent's weight and strength against himself, redirecting his thrust so that it takes him to a place he had not intended to go to. The surprise awakens him to the discrepancy between what he had hoped to accomplish and the inappropriateness of the means he has been using to get there.

The unexpected, or asocial, response is always a surprise. It does not fit into the frame of our everyday world. We become alerted and uncertain. We try to understand where the surprise leaves us. Is it a surprise attack which we must guard against or a surprise gift presented by someone concerned about us? Once we are convinced the surprise will not harm us, we are able to relax our defenses and listen to the unexpected message it brings.

Sometimes this message holds immediate hope; sometimes it is uncomfortable and unrewarding and breaks the expected social stereotype, leaving the manipulator unable to predict and control. Even a friendly response may be asocial if the situation clearly calls for anger or distaste.

For example, a young man from India bicycled around the world, east to west, in 1972. In Chicago one evening a man with a gun stopped him and demanded his wallet. The cyclist said, "Why do you want my money, my brother?" The robber was startled and answered, "Why do you call me *brother?*"

"Because we are all brothers."

"What the hell are you? What are you doing?"

"I am bicycling around the world on twenty-three dollars."

"How do you get around the world on twenty-three dollars?"

"Because of people like you that help me out."

The robber shook his head, bewildered. Then he put his hand in his own pocket and said, "Can I help you, brother?"

The thief's expectations had been totally upset by the Indian's sincere, unexpected behavior. It is interesting to speculate about what would have happened to his career as thief if his next few victims had all responded in a similar manner.

Actually, in order to provide for a positive change, all unexpected responses should be given in a friendly atmosphere—that is, delivered without antagonism and without putting the other person down in any way. The response should be accompanied by a message to the effect that we are truly concerned for the other person. This type of response can range from an attentive "Hmm ... hmmm ... " to a real shocker that takes the wind out of the other person's sails.

For example, a young man is about to jump from the Golden Gate Bridge when a motorist stops beside him and says, "Hey, you! Before you jump, give me your wallet. You're not going to need it down there." In other situations a single unexpected response may not be dramatic enough to lead to a significant change; a whole series of unexpected behaviors may be needed to convince a person that his old technique no longer works.

Manipulative behavior is at best a compromise, and it persists only as long as it works. Since it has been tailored to a particular environment, a change in that environment means the manipulation is no longer going to work. The manipulator is then motivated to make some changes himself. The environment may be as intricately structured as an unruly kindergarten, but it often consists of no more nor less than the social and emotional reality of another human being—a "victim," for example.

A "victim" alters the environment whenever he responds in an unexpected manner. He can motivate the manipulator to change by allowing the customary manipulations to clearly fail. The manipulator's usual coping behavior then is no longer reliable, and he has to do something about it. The "victim" has interrupted his push-button routine and broken open his mind, leaving him free to search out new options.

Making His Prediction Come False

The classic example of the unexpected response is the strategy of passive resistance. The resister stops responding in the expected manner to the methods his oppressor has always depended upon for controlling him. The resister's unique power lies in his willingness to ignore traditional rewards and punishments and thereby confound the expectations and predictions of the "master."

To assume control of our own response, rather than reacting automatically or from fear or greed, is a decisive act that gives us an advantage over anyone who is subtly manipulating us, consciously or unconsciously. Previously, we were vulnerable because our response was predictable and could be controlled. Now the tables are turned. We cease to be predictable, since we are planning to dictate our own response.

At the same time we notice that the manipulator *is* predictable, and has been predictable all along if we had been astute enough to see it. Once he found a technique that worked, he carried it off in the same way every time. He had settled the problem of *us* and wasn't planning to open up that hornets' nest again.

Our power to change some key aspects of a relationship lies in the possibility that we can respond to the other person's predictable behavior in an unpredictable way. He has come to depend upon the fact that certain events (his own behaviors) are followed consistently by certain other events (our familiar responses).

As long as this pattern remains reliable, he knows what is going on in his world, what to expect, and what he could or could not do about it. Now, disoriented, he is unable to predict and therefore unable to protect himself or help himself or in any other way influence the events in which he is embroiled. He simply cannot go on as before.

He may try the old way again, hoping that some minor misunderstanding was to blame, and he may then redouble his efforts. But once he is sure that our changed response is for real, he has to act. If our response is hostile or threatening, he may even panic, for in this corner of his life, if not elsewhere, he has unaccountably lost his balance, his self-assurance, his strength.

Panic or a militantly defensive stance cannot lead to beneficial change, but both can be avoided if our unexpected response is supportive and meaningful. The response will have considerable shock value, but at the same time it can acknowledge the unspoken needs that prompted the manipulation in the first place.

If we have a sixteen-year-old daughter who periodically screams at us, we may be sure that our usual reaction serves to reinforce the screaming and to maintain the pattern. Perhaps we always sigh and say, "All right, stop screaming and I'll see what I can do." Her strategy for getting what we don't otherwise give is working perfectly.

Or perhaps we always punish her for screaming—send her to her room without supper, refuse to let her use the car this week. This may be just what she is unconsciously looking for—enough alienation to justify her angry bid for independence. Often there is additional fallout such as ill will between other members of the family.

In any case, changing *our* response will probably change *her* behavior. We might say with a shrug, "Screaming is good for your lungs," and accept the noise without either giving in or punishing. Or it may be that the girl feels neglected and is literally screaming for attention—which she gets in the form of our shouting back at her. In this case, we might react with a smile instead—a real smile in response to her need to make solid contact with us.

The girl may at first scream even louder, on the assumption that she hasn't really gotten to us yet, but her screaming technique is not likely to persist after it fails to elicit our anger several times in succession. If we weaken and do get angry, then she will have won the round, reassuring herself that she can indeed control and predict our response. Things will then go along as before.

Another meaningful response involves judicious bugging with a tape recorder. A typical argument is recorded, with the knowledge and consent of all those present. The tape may then be brought out on a calm day when parents and daughter are both willing to sit and listen to whatever is there to be heard, listening in particular for the message that comes through now as compared with the message that each of us *thought* was being transmitted at the time.

All of these antiscream techniques can be played just as well in the other direction if the problem is a daughter who has to deal with a screaming parent.

The unexpected response works at almost any age. Imagine a ten-year-old boy stopping a lifelong enemy in the street, shouting an insult and spinning him around. The "enemy" has been set up to respond in kind, but instead he relaxes and says, "Hi, Johnny. I like your shirt."

John's reaction can only be to ask himself: *What went wrong?* It is the first time in his life that his tried and true theory about how to pick a fight has failed. He is going to have to find a better way or change his expectations about who his "natural enemies" are.

The same kind of thing happens when a student refuses to go along with a teacher's negative expectations. If a teacher believes that certain pupils are no-good rebels, she will unconsciously prompt rebellious behavior by making them angry. She may accuse a child of making noise or taking things.

An imaginative student who finds himself in such a role can break this pattern by responding again and again with patience and friendliness. Accused of making too much noise, he says, "I'm sorry I bothered you." The teacher will likely intensify her anger since she is still convinced that this approach will prove the pupils she dislikes are rebellious.

But when the "rebellion button" still fails to produce the response she is looking for, she will most likely begin to apply the label "friendly" in place of "rebellious." If the student breaks before this point, however, and does indeed become rebellious, the teacher wins again and is thus encouraged to stick with her old pattern. It takes two to tangle and it is difficult to go on fighting if one is unable to drum up a fighting response.

This seems to be one of the most effective ways of getting a person to change both his motivation and his behavior—make his prediction come false. No one can live with unpredictability, and he will do whatever has to be done to restore his ability to assess and predict and therefore to act with assurance.

Sometimes the act of uninvolved but careful listening will in itself serve as an effective unexpected response. An unhappy friend who presents himself as a depressed victim of fate expects sympathy and an invitation to spend some time with us. But our new manner of listening communicates only a mild show of concern and no suggestion whatever of meeting again in the near future. This subverts his unconscious motivation (his unaware use of depression to obtain company), making him uncertain of his current style and leading him to seek a less discordant strategy.

At other times the offensive behavior may be so subtle that we can't even spot it. Suppose that every time a certain person shows up we find ourselves doing things we are sorry about later. We're glad to see him, and yet after ten or fifteen minutes we always fall into a big argument, and we leave feeling guilty.

We have reason to believe we are being manipulated in some way, but if we tell this person to knock it off he honestly won't know what we're talking about. Neither of us is aware of just what he is doing, and the only way of influencing his "invisible" action is to block our own impulse to respond in the usual way. He has set us up for this response and is waiting expectantly—but this time we listen attentively and remain silent. The new response renders his once reliable technique impotent. His steering wheel has come loose and he is forced to stop and make some repairs.

It might help to know what his motivations are, *why* he keeps doing this to us, but that information isn't essential. It is enough to be aware of the *consequences*. His technique would not persist unless it worked in some way, so we can assume there is some kind of reward in it for him.

The reward probably has to do with proving his ability to arouse our antagonism and subsequent guilt. That may not sound like much of a reward, but for him it may represent a personal involvement he doesn't know how to get in any other way.

Sabotaged by Need and Greed

An unexpected response that can always be relied upon is to refuse a proferred gift. Gifts of all kinds (presents, awards, rewards, compliments, friendly overtures), however well-meaning they may be, serve to obligate the receiver in some way. The slave who gratefully accepts a bonus from his "generous" master further enslaves himself. The housewife who at once returns the salesman's terribly friendly smile has already limited her options for resisting his sales pitch. The man who thrives on compliments is at the mercy of every accomplished flatterer. It is indeed better to give than to receive, for giving keeps the giver in control and keeps the receiver dependent and defensive.

Obviously, a receiver can change the giver's behavior by the simple strategy of refusing to accept the usual rewards that the encounter customarily brings him. For the slave, a quiet display of dignity may be an effective unexpected response. The besieged housewife can disarm a salesman with silence or by limiting her vocabulary to the single word *no* (a salesman cannot operate unless he can involve his potential customer, so he designs questions that are difficult to answer negatively: "Don't you think that every child should have his own Bible?") An insecure person could deprive his adversary of a most potent weapon simply by giving up his need for approval or his need for a proffered gift.

One particular form of the need for approval can be expressed as a fear of hurting other people's feelings—as in this plaintive letter to Abigail Van Buren:

Dear Abby:
A nervy couple we know drops by unexpectedly several times a week and always at dinnertime so we have to invite them to stay for dinner. They are breaking us in the food department. They finish off everything so we never have

any leftovers. Also they drink coffee (which isn't cheap) by the gallon. When one pot is empty the wife gets up and makes another pot just like she's in her own home.

They invited us to dinner at their place twice, and both times they served rice while they bragged that they had a whole cow in the freezer!

Don't suggest that we tell them we ate already when they come over. We tried that once and they said: "So did we," came in and sat until midnight and everybody's stomach was growling so loud we could hardly hear ourselves talk.

So how do we tell this couple not to come for dinner without hurting their feelings?

STUCK

The friendship and approval of this "nervy couple" is so important that the writer is willing to accept a compromise larded with major "inconveniences." At the same time, he cleverly gains himself a bonus (sympathy from others) by turning his nervy friends into tyrants, labeling them as such and abetting their "tyrannical" behavior.

Clearly, many people make others into tyrants and then complain about them, and this is particularly true in families, where it is very uncomfortable to directly confront the "tyrant." ("I can't go out with this guy because my mother would throw a fit if she knew I was going with an Indian from the reservation.")

In "Stuck's" case, the repeated invitations make it a problem for everyone concerned, and the question is, Why should he and his wife continue to invite this couple again and again if they feel taken advantage of? It appears that they invite their "friends" because of some hidden reward or advantage which they neither state nor admit, and then they claim to suffer.

Making an unexpected response work is an art, and a good way to learn is to begin by experimenting with small changes in our usual behavior, noticing what difference each change makes to the other person. We need to be consistent but remain flexible, to begin simply, and to save big problems until we feel at home with our new learning. Spectacular results are not common. Small changes achieved by unexpected responses are far more likely to be successful than a single dramatic episode.

The ability to deliver an appropriate unexpected response must be cultivated, for it certainly does not come naturally. We are too preoccupied with ourselves and our own hurts to listen well or to choose a fresh reaction. To make matters worse, the moment for responding is usually a moment of stress, and this tends to trigger a stereotypical defense reaction.

For example, Fred has cooked dinner for a friend, and later in the evening he turns down the lights. The woman moves uneasily and says,

"I've got to go." Fred is hurt. His immediate impulse is to say, as he has said in the past, "Aw, Joanie, *please.*" He hesitates, vaguely recalling that this plea hasn't been working very well. He desperately tries to think of a new ploy, a new response which will not elicit rejection. Nothing comes to mind. He is all hot and bothered, if not desperate. To relieve his frustration, he says, "Aw, Joanie, *please!*" Her answer is, "Oh, come off it, Fred," and she gets up to leave.

Fred's error? Not so much error as an inability to change in a time of stress. Let us go more deeply into this case. Fred had long ago programmed himself to flip into a "hurt" role when faced with disappointment, and Joan had gone along with him, sympathizing, as long as there was nothing much at stake; however, she had never done so when the issue was important.

A good programmer would have listened carefully and learned from his errors, but not Fred. Fred really believes—that is, he rationalizes—that allowing tears to come to his eyes is his only *honest* reaction. He continues to push the same old button, blind to what is clear to everyone around him: his appeals for pity are constraining, intimidating, and, before long, suffocating.

If he had listened to Joan instead of listening only to his own chagrin, he could have heard the tone of boredom or uneasiness and responded to *that* message . . . perhaps with something as simple as asking about her work and becoming a captivated audience. He also might have picked up the message that she has little respect for people who plead and whine.

Fred, however, has a hard time trying to change his stereotypical responses to unexpected ones. He is locked into the assumption that no woman could bear to leave him if she knew how unhappy he would be without her. He would reject as "manipulative" any deliberate change in his "natural," tearful reaction. "It would be artificial; it wouldn't be *me!*" he says—an ironic statement in view of the fact that he was already highly proficient in the manipulative art of portraying the outward signs of imminent grief.

His objection to making a change in his "natural" behavior is like objecting to the repair of a cleft palate because the operation would make an artificial change in the patient's speech and appearance. Fred's whining is deeply anchored in his behavior, and for him to try a different, unexpected response represents great daring, which is not likely to succeed when he is under severe stress.

From the outside, we can see that Fred would stand a far better chance of persuading Joan to stay if he were to stop relying on his old dramatic act and, instead, train himself to make small changes in his own behavior—such as eliminating the whining and self-pity.

Providing the Space to Change

The unexpected response and the resulting uncertainty are basic to any significant change in behavior. But in delivering this response, we do not *program* the person whose behavior is to be changed. We do not decide how he should act and then train him to act this way. We do not countermanipulate him or force him to go along in our own direction. All we can ever do is to *de*program him (via uncertainty)—with vivid results that stimulate him to *re*program himself.

Having helped motivate someone to explore new alternatives, we are now in the position of a gardener who has planted a seedling. We have to give it nourishment and room to grow. It must be protected from such "realities" as rabbits and gophers and weeds until its roots are established.

When the "seedling" is an individual's urge to change some aspect of his behavior, having room to grow means having the opportunity to experiment and practice in a nonthreatening place where there can be no potential "dire consequences" lurking in the shadows. One such place is an affectionate relationship that can accept the experimenting as playful experiences. Or it may be any kind of a relationship in which all parties are willing to treat the experimenting and practicing as a game. New strategies, wild or timid, can be tried out; everyone learns from the results, and a "failure" won't make the world come apart at the seams.

A church counselor is asked to work with a young man who would like very much to have him for an enemy. The young man says he drinks heavily, is on drugs, has a string of girls working for him and wouldn't think of changing his ways. He knows what to expect from the counselor—a disapproving lecture at the very least. And if this is what he gets (in a foolish attempt by the counselor himself to reprogram the young man's life), then the young man's belligerent bragging will be reinforced, and possibly the acts as well, if any of them are real.

If the young man's behavior stems from a feeling of rebellion, it may be very difficult for him to maintain this feeling if he is deprived of the big rewards such as being censured and misunderstood by "the establishment." Now let us assume the counselor reacts with concern but without censuring the young man's statements. By remaining disengaged, he will give the young man a sense of uncertainty about "authority figures," letting him know that not all adults have to be his enemies and thus planting the seed for a new attitude.

But for the sprouting seed to grow, the counselor will have to maintain a "game" setting. For a while, the young man will need to try out hundreds of his accustomed behaviors on the counselor, testing him against a range of old expectations. This is a game situation because it is like child's play; the player gains practice, but if he still plays poorly it doesn't matter very much. (If the young man, after only one session with the counselor, were left to test out new behaviors in real authority situations, he might well end up in court.)

Something similar occurs between good friends when they let their hair down. They offer each other a safe haven where it is possible to accept severe criticism without feeling challenged or rejected. They establish their own "game" setting, a psychological space in which they can stumble about and explore without having to worry about the consequences.

The approach is valid not only with good friends but also with "good" enemies—people one has to live with or work with in spite of heavy disagreements and antagonisms. The shock of an unexpected response makes the subject aware of what his behavior has been getting for him until now; being given the space to "play" allows him to look for less destructive ways of achieving the same thing. His unconscious motivation and his hidden purpose have been uncovered, and this new information permits him to deal with them more adequately.

The process of changing another person can best be seen as a matter of stacking the cards in favor of a significant change by arousing uncertainty in him. This uncertainty is bound to affect his unaware responses, but the outcome has to be reckoned in terms of probabilities; changes are not guaranteed but are strongly encouraged. What form this change will take is something that cannot be neatly controlled. Its direction can be influenced, however, by the peripheral feelings of the sender that accompany the conscious act of withholding the expected response.

A mother asks where her daughter is going and is told it's none of her business. This is nothing new, and it is typically followed by a wild scene full of accusations and, in the end, a tearful mother trying to make the girl feel sorry. This time the mother delivers an unexpected response. She says, "You're right. It's not my business at all. Have a lovely evening."

This behavior is way out of line, and the daughter is disturbed. She tries to retrieve the familiar old pattern by stepping up her aggression. She still thinks she can predict her mother's response, and she has to prove it to herself. She says, "You're damned right. You can just lay off me for a change. I'm sick of living under a dictatorship!"

Ordinarily, this response would have accelerated the mutual bitterness, but the mother doesn't give up so easily. She says, "I've been wrong, trying to run your life for you. I hope you have a ball tonight." The daughter is baffled and might remain totally disoriented were it not for the nonverbal cues accompanying the mother's statements.

The mother speaks without any overtones of sarcasm, complaint, or reproach, giving her daughter the information that she is concerned but has honestly come to realize how heavy-handed she has been about the whole thing. After the long silence, the daughter blurts out, "I'm going to the movies with Jim and I'll probably be home by midnight."

The example happens to be true, although it sounds almost too pat. It illustrates how the daughter's behavior was changed by uncertainty and how the direction of the change was clearly influenced by the mother's nonverbal cues, which gave the daughter the chance to choose her own way. Had the mother said the same words in a way that made her sound like a martyr, the direction of the change would certainly have been different.

Mothers ordinarily cannot disengage as fully and as quickly as this because they get too much satisfaction from replaying the old, familiar, predictable hassles week after week. The reason they often cling to them is that these harsh confrontations have been occasions in which there has been vivid contact. There is more to an unexpected response than meets the ear. A convincing change requires not only new words but a new attitude as well.

Interplay

Why does "dismanipulation" work? How can a simple change in our normal response stop a manipulator in his tracks and force him to reconsider his own behavior? The technique works only because we allowed ourselves to be manipulated in the first place. Only because we permitted it in the past are we able to control the situation now by withdrawing our permission.

For example, a friend has learned, consciously or unconsciously, how to get under our skin. It is a question of pushing the right button, and he knows all the right buttons. We, for our part, deliver a predictable response and thus become an essential link in the chain of events that sustains his manipulative behavior.

But suddenly, to his dismay, he pushes our anger button and we only shrug, or we give him a friendly hug; he pushes our purr button and we are no longer seduced. When this happens more than a few times, he becomes very uncertain about the cues he has always relied upon.

Our ability to assume control rests upon our willingness to give up the rewards (many of them subtle and hidden) that we are accustomed to. We gain the initiative because we have forfeited whatever advantages the relationship has been bringing us. This form of passive resistance generates an entirely new perspective and dissolves many of the automatic responses that have been running our lives. Also, it forces us to give up such hidden pleasures as punishing someone or nursing wounds or hoarding injustices. With passive resistance, neither insult nor promises have any leverage.

If we can say truthfully, "I don't care what you can give me," then we are free in that relationship, free to take it or leave it or, if we choose, to rebuild it. As a friend put it when he made this discovery, "Suddenly I can do what I want to do. The hell with anything I've done or anything I've stored up or earned or set up or invested in with this person. Life is free from here on, and if I'm not able to shove the entire past off the cliff when a shove is called for, then I've mortgaged my future and lost ownership of it."

To be so thoroughly disengaged is rare, and, although it can be reached voluntarily, it is in fact not a very practical answer to an unhappy engagement with others. There are simply too many anchors in most relationships. In fact, the real answer to the question of how to protect ourselves from being automatically engaged with others is that we already are protecting ourselves as much as we really want to at any given time.

Engagement cannot exist without a joint (though tacit) agreement between the "manipulator" and his so-called victim. We all control the environment to the best of our ability, but we soon reach a stalemate with some of the people we see regularly. All "controllers" or "manipulators" are "victims" as well, and all victims can also manipulate, so we are easily caught in a repeating pattern of mutual constraints. Some of these constraints are stabilizing, but others are destructive and painful and keep us from growing.

If we are anxious to make a stab at changing painful events, we often fail because we cannot let go of a compromise that is working, however unstable, in favor of a new one that we don't understand very well. We are up against the wall, psychologically constipated, often very much afraid to try anything new for fear of losing ground.

The way to break the stalemate is to initiate a change in our mutual pattern of subtle pressures and automatic responses; that is, to make an unexpected response that reflects a change we would like to see in the relationship and to maintain this new attitude. For most people locked into a mutual round of manipulating and countermanipulating, it never occurs to either of them that each has the power and the freedom to initiate and maintain a change; so they wait each other out and the marriage fails or the affair breaks up or the kids turn to whatever outside solace they can find. The essence of growth is finding the courage to explore new choices with patience.

6

Old Wine, New Labels

When anyone is stopped short by an unexpected response and has to explore new strategies for himself, his principal tool is *relabeling*. To discover a new label for an established behavior is not easy, but if the attempt is successful, it leads to a changed perception of it—a change in attitude and a reshuffling of priorities.

A new label always affects the people around us, and their new responses further modify the new label and give it a more permanent existence. For example, a person who labels his sexual behavior a "joy" affects others in a very different way from someone who labels it a "sin." The moment that a "terrible problem" becomes a "hairy game," a lot of tension dissolves.

This is not just a matter of *thinking* a different word; it has to do with *living* a different word. Life takes on a new odor when your most cherished problem suddenly becomes an intriguing game. The new label can be powerfully reflected in behavior. When we deal with "deep problems," we are concentrated and tense; when we deal with "games," we are imaginative and perhaps even enchanted.

What happens when we drop the label "loudmouth" and make it "spirited"? Clearly, every individual chooses a label that expresses his unique and peculiar attitudes at the moment. What if we stop thinking of ourselves as very "nice" (because we are friendly and sweet and never tell anyone what we really think of them) and consider the label "dishonest" or "scared to death that someone might not like me"? Are we really "lovable," or just "evasive"?

A very "nice" friend of ours was upset because a man she liked responded to her with total indifference one evening. However, she was perfectly cool about it. At their next—and last—meeting, the man apologized for his previous indifference; the woman merely shrugged and said, "Oh, that was nothing." She felt she had handled the situation thoughtfully and smoothly, and she later wondered why he did not call again. We said, without thinking, "Because you *lied.*" The woman turned with a look of sharp surprise at our relabeling effort. Then she said quietly, "Yes," and cried for some time.

It makes a difference whether we call a friend of the opposite sex a "love" or a "lover" or a "lay," and sometimes the mere switching of a label can change the quality of the relationship. Is it really "companionship" you're after, or is it "sex"? Is it really "sex" you're after, or is it "intimacy"? Labeling cannot be definitive, for it inevitably jams many different characteristics into a single pigeonhole. Relabeling implies a change in attitude: the willingness to see a given object in a different emotional light.

The Insidious Power of a Word or Two

Some people—parents, for example—are convinced that when they use certain labels they are speaking *The Truth*. Actually, they have chosen, according to their very personal needs, a few labels from among the thousands that are available.

"Well, what else can I possibly do? I can't let that selfish, infantile maniac go on screaming all day!" The only way out for such a parent is to learn to listen. True listening is difficult when we are angry, but it makes it clear that angry people use labels that generate even more anger. Only when we are able to disengage from the immediate emotion can we find other labels that may more fairly describe the child's behavior.

The power that can be generated by a single label is evident in a particular patient with severe depression. Asked if he knows what the cause might be, he says at once, "Because I'm a homosexual."

"Really?"

"Well, you certainly know what *that* means!"

"No. What does it mean?"

It develops that the patient's "sickness," as he calls it, is a one-shot affair that occupies an hour or so of his life once every few months. Why this behavior is newsworthy enough to demand a label, he never explains. Surely he has done a few thousand other and more important things during these months.

The relabeling of his behavior begins with his admission that he is at least not a "full-time" homosexual. He even goes on to relabel himself "bisexual," which leaves still other alternatives open. His problem is comparable to that of men who failed in business during the Depression and considered suicide because they labeled themselves "failures." In both cases, labeling is inaccurate, but people have a tendency to live up to their own labels once they have declared themselves. Labels always limit our options.

When we stimulate someone to change and give him the opportunity to do so in his own way, we are not offering advice or in any sense leading the way. To stimulate someone is to introduce new information not ordinarily available to him. When a man curses us and we say without sarcasm, "You have a right to be angry and you are very human," we are delivering a lot of new information: we are not letting him lay *his* label on us; we are not going to involve ourselves in the emotional climate he had prepared for us; we are strongly suggesting a new label for his own behavior ("You are very human"). The newly surfaced information provides him with the recognition that some of his current labels are profoundly unrealistic.

Let's look at the label for an emotional climate that is extremely easy to produce: anger. Most of us make the polite assumption that anger is "bad" except when directed at criminals, heretics, and enemies of the state. Otherwise, our goal is to remain cool, smooth, and unhassled, particularly when dealing with people we love and people we respect.

When anger breaks out between lovers or within a family, we are likely to label it "childish," "unsophisticated," "destructive," "vulgar," "coarse," "tasteless." But anger may also be defined as a valid emotion that communicates important interpersonal realities when clearly expressed. And to deny anger when it does exist is neither honest nor helpful; it leaves the other person ignorant of the true effect of his own behavior.

Is it really wrong to express anger when it first occurs? Is it better to bury it until it has built up explosive pressure from being bottled up? Or does expressing anger have something to do with integrity, with accurate communication, and with maintaining rapport and understanding?

People who will not or cannot express anger are slipping along the surface of reality with about as much purchase as a skater sockfoot on the ice. They may be labeling themselves "real nice guys" while their friends call them "hypocrites." By labeling anger "bad," we help create a situation which is likely to accumulate more anger and stockpile it. If we live by this label (anger = "bad"), our path can only lead from explosion to explosion. A different label would lead us into a different life-style. If we label anger a "valid experience," we may find life full of loud noises, but we will run into few real explosions.

One of us was once so taken with a comely friend that he showered her with attention and gifts and did everything he knew to make a positive impression on her—including withholding all the hostility he began to feel when she did not return his affection and attention in kind. When he asked why she was cool, she replied, "Because you're not real."

"That's ridiculous."

"Then why do I feel you're not leveling with me?"

"But I am."

"You can't be. You're never even angry with me. It would feel so good to have an honest fight."

He could not understand. He knew he suffered but he did not know how to restyle his behavior, or just which labels needed relabeling. What he labeled "nice," in his own approach to her, she called "inauthentic." He had no idea that he was using the label "nice" to deceive himself and to attract "injustices" and rejection.

When she finally rejected him, he wrote her a very angry letter. He knew this would seal her off from him forever, but the anger was important to him now. She telephoned him at once and said with much feeling, "I just read your letter. Thank you for your anger." This sudden information was experienced as a revelation and led eventually to a new way of labeling—and thus of handling—what he had been calling his "negative" emotions.

The Body Talks

Perhaps the most difficult experiences to relabel (because of the accompanying pain) are psychosomatic illnesses and the accidents of accident-prone individuals. We ask a patient who is seeking relief from migraine headaches why he has them. He is insulted by the question, for he clearly labels his pain "inevitable." We suggest that there is just a slight possibility that the attacks might come about because he *wants* them.

"You know nobody wants pain like that," he says.

"Perhaps. But let's play the game. It would help to know what it does for you."

"It nearly makes me die from the pain, that's what it does for me!"

"Maybe that's only a part of it. What else does it do? Try to recall, hour by hour, just what happened throughout your last attack."

The patient reports the following sequence of events. He knows the migraine is coming on, because he has felt the same "aura" before. Yes, he could have interrupted it at this point by stopping at once for an hour's rest, but he "couldn't afford the time." This is a curious excuse, in the light of what he knows about migraines, for the attack struck with full force some hours later and sent him to bed for four days.

During this time he did not work, and his mother-in-law (who normally did not help around the house) took care of him. We suggest that his migraines are paying off handsomely, that he has himself chosen to experience them, and that the same rewards might be achieved without a headache if he inquired into other means of taking time off from work and perhaps had a talk with his mother-in-law about sharing everyday domestic chores.

"Oh, I couldn't do that! My wife would accuse me of fighting with her mother, and then we'd be in a fight, and I don't like that at all."

The clue is that people often do things purposefully, even though they label the behavior "involuntary." The man accepted the pain he could have avoided in order to avoid facing his wife with a mother-in-law problem. The technique was painful and inefficient, but it bore the convincing label "There's no other way." This label had to be changed in order to make room for a less painful style.

Psychotherapy provides for such relabeling; the responses of the therapist make the client's old labels uncertain. Were the headaches really an "inevitable burden"? Or were they quite "profitable" in some ways? They were certainly "real"; but did they also function as a "technique" or even as a "manipulation" that brought rewards he had not been willing to go after in any other way?

The "aura," which once meant the "beginning of an attack," was relabeled as a "signal to retire" for an hour to reduce the probability of the attack. To talk with his mother-in-law was not "impossible"; it was "initially uncomfortable" but at the same time "warranted." What he risked with his wife was not a "destructive battle" but an "honest confrontation."

This type of relabeling is not usually labeled "relabeling," it is called "obtaining therapeutic help." The active relabeling occurs constantly through the give and take of the conversation. The man still recalled the same events after his "relabeling experience," but they no longer meant what they had meant before. Many of his customary ways of handling himself were no longer appropriate.

The big change came when he realized he had actually made a choice, opting for the "problem" of headaches and complaints in preference to more satisfying alternatives. Once he saw that the pain was part of a compromise he was freely choosing, his attitude changed almost at once. He worked out a new compromise that made life less edgy for all three of the principals.

The reward-winning migraine is incidentally an example of how we use our bodies to act out or at least to become part of a compromise to appease various pressures. Peptic ulcers, "nervous breakdowns," warts, infections, and perhaps even the common cold are other painful physical techniques we may use to save ourselves from having to face some other kinds of discomforts.

Another way to use one's body in the service of compromise is to become accident-prone. It is direct, and the "rewards" of the compromise are immediate. A man volunteers to help with a house his sister's family is building. It seems to be an excellent opportunity to talk at length with his sister, whom he has not seen for some years.

On the job, however, he finds himself tacking fiber glass insulation between the floor joists while his sister is off somewhere buying supplies. The sun is very hot, and fiber glass sticks to his sweat and is getting under his skin. He cannot express his resentment because he considers himself (or, as we say, labels himself) "above such feelings." He wants to quit, but he thinks of himself as "responsible," and responsible men do not renege on promises.

He is stuck with his labels, and there is no way out—until he accidentally loses his footing and falls through the insulation between the unfloored joists. The pain is what you might expect from a pair of broken ribs, but he is honorably discharged from his unpleasant job and has a long talk with his sister when she drives him to the hospital.

This man's misstep may have been an unmotivated accident, but it so happens that he had been involved in "rewarding" accidents on several previous occasions. Repeat performances are very convincing, and this time he tumbled to the fact that his accident had provided a very neat solution to an "insoluble" problem.

He could have had pretty much the same rewards by the remarkably simple expedient of stating clearly what he really wanted to do, but he had been just as convinced as the man with the migraine that he couldn't possibly do so.

7

Me, Myself, and I:
Can We Change Ourselves?*

"I have a problem. I keep messing up relationships and fighting with my boss. I want to change. I'm willing to sacrifice a lot. What can I do? Can I change myself?"

Not easily, and perhaps not at all. We are all victims of severe prejudice: we believe what we wish to believe about ourselves, and we bolster this self-image with carefully selected evidence and ingenious rationalizations. We are masters of subtle self-coercion and self-deceit.

The past as we recall it and the present as we sift the evidence moment by moment are not objective recordings, and we cannot accomplish change unless we begin with accurate data. We each see the world through self-colored glasses, and we like it that way.

We have spent our lives learning how to perceive people accurately, for we cannot cope with them unless we know more or less what they are about. With people we fiercely love or hate, we have difficulty because there is so much at stake for us that we cannot afford to admit good things about a hateful enemy or acknowledge negative qualities in someone we dearly love. Perceiving ourselves accurately is even more difficult because of the overwhelming importance of our own self-image, lovable or hateful, wise or wild.

Can't we still apply to ourselves the techniques for changing others—disengaging, listening for patterns and consequences, delivering an asocial response?

Mirror, Mirror, on the Wall

What we tell ourselves about ourselves and how we choose to see ourselves reflected provide both motivation and clear direction for potential change. But an accurate view is essential, and there is no way to see or hear ourselves objectively—that is, to disengage. If the view we

* Warning: this chapter may be injurious to your self-esteem.

have is illusory, we will squander our resources straining for a new way that is pointless or destructive.

It is easy to see that another person's view of himself is hopelessly biased, but we seldom perceive the prejudice in ourselves. We look in a mirror, take a deep breath, acknowledge ourselves with dignity, and believe that what we see is "how it really is." Other people, we believe, see in us what we see in the mirror. What we need to destroy this illusion is an irrefutable outside view—for example, a candid photograph of ourselves looking into the mirror. What we saw in the mirror was *beauty*, but what we see in the photograph of ourselves before the mirror is *vanity*.

Even in scientific experiments, what the observer sees depends upon how he sets up the experiment and what he hopes to see. The classic example, of course, is that light behaves like a wave when looked at in one way and like a sequence of particles when seen in another. Our perceptions and our actions are often determined by motivations we are not aware of; therefore, we have no way of changing them. We have chosen unconsciously, and we assume there are no options.

The idea of "unconscious choice" appears to be a contradiction of terms since choosing is commonly thought to be a deliberate act. As Freud pointed out, however, simple everyday behavior is full of unconscious choices that stem from unconscious motivations. We commit revealing "errors" and "slips" for valid reasons that our conscious minds refuse to accept.

When someone we dislike approaches in the distance, we "inadvertently" cross the street, even though we have not consciously recognized him. It may appear to be a matter of chance whether we take the high road or the low road, but if we just happen to take the high road every time, it is likely that we are unconsciously motivated to make this choice.

A businessman who is deeply troubled by insomnia asks a psychologist to give him a posthypnotic suggestion that will help him fall asleep at will. The psychologist says he has no particular faith in hypnosis as an aid to sleeping, but the patient still wants to try it. Somewhat to the psychologist's surprise, the posthypnotic suggestion works beautifully and the man is overjoyed: he sleeps well every night and always awakes feeling refreshed. Six weeks later the two happen to meet on the street and the psychologist asks the man if he is still sleeping well.

"I haven't had a decent night's sleep in weeks," the man replies. "It is ruining my work and I'm so irritable that my wife talks about walking out on me."

"How long since the posthypnotic suggestion stopped working?" the psychologist asks.

"Oh, it still works fine. It's just that when I'm tossing around unable to sleep, I never think of using it."

What the man really wants is what he repeatedly chooses. He could avoid insomnia, but unconsciously he chooses not to. Since he cannot admit to such an absurd act as choosing exactly what he wants to avoid, he perceives it as an act of forgetfulness. His discordant behavior (his actions belie his words) is a compromise he had made among various pressures in his life. His choice is painful to him but it must bring him rewards as well or he would not keep repeating it.

Sometimes it is possible to discover—by looking critically at the consequences—why such an "irrational" choice is made. The insomniac knew he hated his sleeplessness, but it gave him a socially acceptable excuse for doing poorly at work; it was also a covert way of encouraging his wife to leave him. If he had been willing to acknowledge the possibility of such "unacceptable" motives, he might well have found himself sleeping soundly every night, with or without posthypnotic suggestion.

Let's reverse the question at this point and ask if there is really such a thing as *conscious* choice. Is it possible to make a conscious choice for a good reason—and to know that this was indeed the real reason for the choice? Surely we can make a conscious choice for what we believe to be a good reason. But when unaware needs are not taken into consideration, the main function of the conscious choice often seems to be to supply a rational justification for an otherwise unaware, emotional choice.

Some of the most dramatic evidence of the existence of unconscious motivation comes from experiments in the areas of need perception, subliminal perception, and dreaming. The basic principle of need perception is that we strongly tend to see whatever it is we most need to see and that we perceive most readily those things that verify our beliefs and justify our actions.

A child recognizes words associated with food more easily when he is hungry. Poor children are likely to draw dimes bigger than rich children draw them. Adults and children alike spontaneously discover excellent reasons for doing what they like to do and tend to believe they are *right* simply because they don't think of any counterarguments.

Obviously, two people with differing needs cannot perceive a given event in the same way, and the ensuing argument may prove to be impossible to resolve. Charlie Chaplin was possessed by need perception in *The Gold Rush* when, starving in a snowbound cabin, he began to see his partner as an enormous chicken.

Subliminal perception made headlines in 1954 when experimenters flashed the word "Coca-Cola" on a movie theater screen for just one twenty-fourth of a second, too short a time for the audience to recognize it. During this experiment, more Coca-Cola was reportedly consumed than at any other time.

Psychologists have not been able to reproduce this experiment, but at least some research appears to verify the original results. We have investigated subliminal perception by displaying "shocking" words and emotionally "benign" words, exposing them for such a small fraction of a second that our subjects were not aware of them. The subjects responded to the shocking words with an increase in galvanic skin response and with a rise in the emotional tone of their speech. It appears that people respond physically and emotionally to events of which they are not aware.

One of Freud's central assumptions was that unconscious motivations can be understood by deciphering the hidden content of dreams. He believed that these motivations originated in early-childhood events and that they could also be uncovered by way of "free association," wherein an individual is encouraged to let his mind wander and say whatever occurs to him.

Dreaming does not provide scientific proof of unconscious motivation, but it provides convincing evidence of it to people who subscribe to psychoanalytic theory or who for other reasons have learned to take their dreams seriously. Often they are able to make valid deductions concerning basic motivations they were not aware of.

Do I Really Want What I Want to Want?

Unconscious motivation is the main reason that accurate self-listening is unlikely, if not impossible. Even if we could partly disengage from ourselves, we are still obsessed by specific conscious needs and fears, unable to perceive the complex pattern of which they are an inseparable part. It becomes a matter of misinforming ourselves about what we want.

We are usually concerned with some "target" that we define in simple, direct terms. "I want a happy weekend for a change." "I don't want to be frigid any longer." "I want to stop fighting with my daughter every afternoon." "I want to stop getting sick to my stomach whenever my boss asks me to take over the staff meeting." We see the target clearly and the request sounds reasonable enough.

What we do not see, and do not want to see, is the fixed-action pattern in which the target is embedded. We lift the target out of its context and try to deal with it alone. We go at it like the two Indonesian farmers who were found beating a tractor with whips because it had stalled and now refused to start. They had received the tractor, along with a maintenance handbook, through our old Point Four program. They had been shown how to use it in place of oxen, and now they wanted it to move and it refused.

As Americans, we can appreciate the complex mechanical context in which a single machine has to be treated if its behavior is to be changed. The farmers knew only that it was getting dark and starting to rain and they had a load of grain to get into the barn.

All of us, psychologically, are peasants working our own little plots. There is no way in which we can see beyond what looms directly between us and our immediate goal. But we really want a lot more than just to get the rice into the barn. We want to express our anger, for example, and we want to avoid the forbidding task of learning how to read a tractor manual.

What is most difficult to accept is that our current "distressing" behavior is something we have chosen because, for all its demerits, it was the best compromise we were able to work out. We have even come to treasure it because of the effort involved in maintaining the delicate balance that the compromise represents. If the behavior in question keeps bringing us what we claim we don't want, it may be that this is precisely what we *do* want: namely, the whole pattern of saying we want one thing, getting its opposite, and complaining about it.

When an inveterate smoker talks about quitting as he reaches for another cigarette, for example, he is doing just what he wants to do— talking about quitting while smoking. The complaint itself is usually an essential part of the pattern, but we never complain about the whole pattern since that includes a number of satisfactions. We fix on a single sharp corner of it and let this become our target, our goal, perhaps our inspiration.

The "I'll-quit-tomorrow" smoker doesn't want to drop the whole satisfying pattern of smoking, which includes the pleasures of anticipation, smelling, lighting up, relaxing after dinner, feeling the security of having an extra carton stashed in the hall closet. He just wants to cut out the part that puts tar on his lungs.

If he honestly wanted to give up the entire pattern, he would stop smoking at once, though perhaps with some pain. We cannot even give up something as "obviously unwanted" as tension headaches unless, at the same time, we want to give up the subtle rewards that go with them.

The rational mind does not want to agree with this analysis. It cannot understand why we can't just get rid of the specific habit or symptom that's troubling us and leave everything else alone. However, each of us knows unconsciously that the single item we're trying to jettison has roots in all kinds of other wishes and fears and routines. It cannot be neatly removed like a worn-out appendix. So we continue to do what we do despite our own protests and resolutions.

There is no way to change one isolated item of behavior if the item is significant and the change is to be a lasting one. We have to change the pattern of which it is a part. Perhaps this means we have to change our entire life-style, since all of our behaviors are intricately interlocked. This may be a lot more change than we are willing to undertake.

We Americans seem to be oriented more toward discrete targets than toward patterns. Our general approach to problem-solving is to isolate the specific part or function that seems to be "in trouble" and to "fix" it by means of a strongly focused effort. Then we put back, or reconnect, the repaired fragment. The method is highly successful with many problems, from open-heart surgery and kidney transplants to fixing broken toilets and automobiles.

Psychologists, for their part, in trying to make the study of human behavior more properly "scientific," tend to follow the ideal of the physical sciences: they investigate very small segments of behavior, where theories may be verified experimentally with reasonable certainty. We hear a lot about things like stimulus/response or the emotional correlates of EEG patterns. It is not surprising that we often think in terms of isolated "target" behaviors and of modifying such behaviors by means of direct reinforcement. We have almost lost sight of larger contexts such as an individual's overall life-style or the personal meaning of his existence.

The "small-segment," or pigeonhole, approach to behavior is reflected in the way we think about our motivations and choices. We are aware of one shiny facet of a situation and assume that the situation is not much larger than this visible fragment. We can say exactly why we like a certain musical selection (because of the lilt) or a particular house (because of the way it fits the lot); but we fail to notice the hundreds of other reasons, some of them far more significant, that account for our listening repeatedly to this music or actually buying the house. We are aware of having a "small sex problem" and we seek a simple solution when the real difficulty is that our life isn't working.

We lock ourselves into a word cage: having described our problem clearly and convincingly, we look only for solutions that fit the problem-as-we-have-defined-it. If the big drawback of our life is a debilitating, chronic stomachache, we go to great expense to cure it, only to have it replaced by a debilitating, chronic backache.

The worst thing about fixing on a single aspect of a problem is that we become dreadfully attached to this target (or to finding some way of eliminating it). It becomes the key to the happiness or success or dignity that we somehow have been denied. "If only that woman would say yes, my whole life would come together." "If only my son would sit down and talk it over with me" ... "If only I could stay with just one or two drinks" ...

Attachment to such a specific, singled-out goal is reinforced profoundly if we feel we are very close to attaining it. We have come to "need" it desperately and are therefore at its mercy.

Consequences

If there is any way at all of catching sight of our own patterned behavior and changing it in some way, it has to be based on strictly objective information about ourselves. What we need is an undoctored, uninterpreted, unexplained record of our own behavior. Since just about everything we say or think about ourselves is a doctored explanation, the significance of which we are careful to interpret for all listeners, we are obviously not our own best source. Our habit is to feed ourselves a constant commentary based on our conscious plans and best intentions.

This commentary, remarkably convincing, systematically discounts evidence of discordance and compromise.

If we describe ourselves as self-effacing, for example, we should not listen to this as a statement of fact (obviously we are not self-effacing, or we wouldn't boast about it). The description itself is a behavior that serves some purpose; the purpose will be reflected in the way others respond to it. If we describe ourselves as selfish, the claim may not have anything to do with whether or not we are selfish or by whose definition. These may simply be the words that always come out when we hope a friend will volunteer to tell us we are in reality remarkably generous. Or they may serve as a bulwark against being accused of selfishness, for it permits us to say, "Well, I warned you, didn't I?"

Asking others to describe us is not much more reliable than a self-description. It is said that only drunks and young children will give an honest description when asked, for only drunks and children have nothing at stake. What we can do, however, is turn around the techniques for listening to others. We can learn to read ourselves as others read us by listening very carefully to the consequences of our behavior in the responses of the people we are with.

Actions do speak louder than words, and our actions include all the subtle cues, overtones, undertones, gestures, and attitudes we use in the presence of others, usually without being aware of it. Most of them are nonverbal, but they speak with such authority that people often pay no attention to our words and very little to our private feelings and our declared intentions. It is difficult for us to see these actions since we are locked up "inside the machine." What we can see are the consequences of whatever it is we are doing.

The unsettling truth is that just about everything we do has meaning and that this meaning is usually revealed in the consequences. The only way to learn what we really communicate—what we are unconsciously trying to get for ourselves—is to believe the response that occurs. If we imagine we are "misunderstood" or if we look for a scapegoat, we forfeit the opportunity to see what we have really been doing.

We may be given a great variety of "reasons" for being fired from job after job, but the specific "reason" is incidental; the pertinent consequence is that we often set things up so that new employers fire us. A friend always gets asthma or stomach cramps when we visit him. A date is always bored or sleepy. A staff secretary usually gets to our letters last. A mother-in-law inevitably has an unavoidable accident when she does the dishes for us.

These misfortunes may appear to be accidents but they are in fact accurate personal revelations that make visible the other person's response to what we do when we are with him. *His* behavior becomes *our* best mirror.

Bootstrapping

If listening to oneself objectively is difficult, delivering an unexpected response to oneself is probably impossible. How can anyone ever catch himself by surprise? Even if he is able to predict the response in himself that he hopes for, how can he thwart this response and thus disappoint his own expectations? He cannot make his own manipulations fail in such a way that he is forced to change his strategies. He is somewhat in the position of a dentist trying to fill his own cavities.

But suppose we already know exactly what change we wish to make in our own behavior. Can't we then accomplish this change ourselves? Some individuals voluntarily give themselves an electric shock whenever they feel a desire to smoke. This is a manipulation designed to help them stop smoking. It now appears they may be putting themselves to a lot of pointless discomfort, since recent research in the general area of self-manipulating behavior is not promising.

For example, a pill has been developed that makes the pill-taker painfully sick if alcohol is ingested subsequently. And it works. The only trouble is that alcoholics stop taking the pill as soon as they are on their own. Even in hospitals, after voluntarily accepting the treatment, they will not take the pills if they can avoid it. The pill is a good crutch, a handy, made-to-order contingency; but who is going to supervise the crutches?

Listening to Me

Whenever we decide to improve ourselves, we create an intriguing problem: how can we tell that we do truly wish for this particular improvement? We say we want to stop smoking and we set up a situation to facilitate this goal. But when it comes right down to the next cigarette, we discover that we really do not want to give up smoking, and our efforts collapse.

The concept of self-control appears to be rational, but in fact it is essentially a discordant message. It always means, "I want to do what I don't want to do." It is—like the phrase "I should"—prime evidence of a discordant style. It splits the "self-controller" into two *I*'s with conflicting goals and demands. There is an illusion that someone else (who?) is controlling the "self." Not surprisingly, "self-control" is seldom effective.

Changing anyone's behavior has to do with recognizing the value of some other option. For example, a woman is wrestling with a pair of discordant messages: 1) I love to smoke, and 2) I'll live longer if I quit, and I sure want to live longer. She says quitting is more important than smoking, but she continues to smoke.

Despite what she tells us, she assigns first priority to no. 1. What she needs to make her reassign priorities is an effective unexpected response on the part of her body. Lung cancer, for example, and the loss of one lung. She still has the same pair of discordant messages, but now she gives priority to no. 2. The unexpected response worked, but it is not one she would have given herself voluntarily.

An unexpected response is important because we will not change without a compelling reason. But we cannot give ourselves a compelling enough reason. The only reasons we know are those we have already tried, and none of them was compelling enough to bring about a change.

A familiar question arises at this point. Why couldn't a friend help? Couldn't he do it *for* us, arrange an appropriate unexpected response that would leave us in a state of productive uncertainty? The answer is that a friend is likely to be of less help than a stranger.

Each of us sets up all of our friends to give us the answers we unconsciously desire, and we can't change this by telling them we want to be shoved or shocked into some new way of behaving. Sometimes, however, we may be lucky enough to find a friend who, at an appropriate time, will give us an unexpected response that directly addresses some underlying problem.

Two ski stories illustrate what such a friend can do. At the 1957 North American Ski Championships at Squaw Valley, U.S. downhill champion Linda Meyers appeared on the lodge porch displaying, with calculated nonchalance, her newly won Harriman Cup medal, a bronze *H*.

Her close friend Dick Buek, also an Olympic skier and national downhill champion, watched her, said nothing, but drove home to nearby Soda Springs for lunch. He reappeared at Squaw wearing every medal he had ever won—thirty-five of them, blanketing the front of his sweater from shoulders to waist. He walked around the lodge for ninety minutes, introducing himself to everyone, saying, "Good afternoon, I'm glad to make your acquaintance. My name is Linda Meyers." Miss Meyers' medal-wearing behavior subsequently changed.

The other story concerns Jill Kinmont, the national slalom champion who, at the age of eighteen, broke her neck in a pre-Olympic race in 1955. Two months after the accident she was visited by her friend the Olympic gold medalist Andrea Mead Lawrence. Jill was permanently paralyzed from the shoulders down and had no arm muscles except biceps.

She was lying on her back with her arms at the side of her head, and she said to Mrs. Lawrence, "Andy, could you put my arms down to my side?" Mrs. Lawrence returned Jill's glance bluntly and answered, "What's the matter with you? Have you tried to do it yourself?"

She did move Jill's arms, but later, alone, Jill tried for the first time since the accident to move her arms, something she had assumed was impossible. It wouldn't work at first, but after many attempts she discovered she could move them if she gave them a slight swinging start by thrusting violently with her shoulders.

Most people don't get this kind of support from their friends. The right kind of friend *can* happen to us, but it doesn't appear to be something that can be "arranged."

As a last resort, people who desperately want things to be different often ask if they can't simply make up their minds to try a lot harder. Many are willing to commit themselves to a tremendously energetic campaign. They cannot understand why there isn't a one-to-one correlation between effort expended and success achieved. The reason is that the experience of *trying* involves short-term surface changes. This is very different from the experience of *changing* as we discussed it in Chapter 5—changing in depth, changing one's whole style of coping with the immediate environment.

Although we cannot deliberately engineer a significant change in ourselves, we can allow for it or even invite it. And to allow oneself to change requires above all an easy, disengaged, listening attitude, and a willingness to accept new perceptions and new responses. The kind of deep change at stake here is a function of unconscious motivational states that do not respond to frontal attack.

Trying, on the other hand, is a matter of forcefully applying *more* of whatever it is we are already applying. The change is in quantity rather than in quality. This may work for the long distance runner and the weight lifter (it provides an effective, one-time surface change), but it doesn't work for the mother or the lover or the would-be peacemaker.

Trying is a focused, unrelaxing, unlistening process. People who are *really trying* do not open their minds or listen for their feelings as a *changing* person does. Instead, they clench their fists, clench their eyes, clench their ears, and clench their feelings. This is why a stalled relationship sometimes starts working the moment we stop trying.

The irony involved in wishing to change oneself is that the only deliberate changes we can count on are the trivial ones. The more significant or long-lasting the change, the more readily it evades conscious control and the more insidiously it does so. We can, of course, make any conscious choice we care to, but this change will have no staying power whatever if it is antagonistic to an established unconscious need.

We can easily switch brands or experiment with a new response or *try* to carry out some fine intention, but these are surface changes, outside changes. What we cannot do is design and execute a deep, inside change that involves our own compromise behaviors and unconscious motivations. We cannot deliberately reintegrate ourselves or resolve the discordance in our own style.

Having concluded that an unexpected response cannot be given to oneself, it may seem academic to ask if the final principle—that of not imposing a new program on the subject—can be self-administered. If we are in an uncertain, uncomfortable position, on the point of making some kind of change, could we allow ourselves the freedom to choose a new option, motivated by somewhat different pressures than we had been subject to before?

Perhaps we could, by forgetting the whole thing and allowing the search for a new solution to take care of itself. But this is not easy to do when the problem is and has been foremost on our minds most of the time. Being conscious of the problem, we are also conscious of how we would like to see it resolved—that is, we are already pressuring ourselves and probably trying to reapply an old, inadequate blueprint.

People do change, of course, and the right kind of friend may be what turns the trick for them. There are also sudden, inexplicable changes such as religious conversion or the spontaneous onset—or remission—of physical or psychological disorders—cancer or depression, for example. Certain unexpected social situations may serve as the motivating force: being rejected, being fired, being ostracized, being put unexpectedly in a position of grave responsibility.

Change may also result from meeting—in real life or in a book—some person or idea or circumstance that is profoundly impressive and makes us uncomfortable enough that we have to find a better way of handling familiar pressures. Finally, change can occur as the result of directed work with a therapist or teacher or religious counselor or even, in exceptional cases, with a wise friend.

Everything You Never Wanted to Know About Yourself and Were Afraid to Ask

We now have the answer to our original question. No, we cannot disengage ourselves; we cannot lift ourselves; we cannot give ourselves an unexpected response; there is no way we can consciously engineer a lasting change in ourselves. The only part of our technique for changing people that we can use on ourselves is listening for the consequences of behavior in the responses that immediately follow it. If there is anything at all we can do about ourselves, this is all we've got to do it with —listening.

The most valuable information about ourselves is what we don't have but can get if we choose to and if we can stand the reality of it. It is not only a matter of knowing where to look for the message; we have to really hear it—clearly and accurately, unsoftened, undoctored. It may then become painfully evident that we are in an untenable position with regard to some of our discordant behaviors. This we cannot live with, and a search for ways to change will probably begin without conscious effort.

Passive listening is not enough, however, when the performer *(I)* and the audience *(myself)* are one and the same person. We are both locked into the same body, and the view is too narrow. We commonly believe that we must get inside a problem in order to understand it, that we have to achieve some *in*sight about it.

This might suffice if we really knew the full nature and extent of our problem, which we don't. Insight only works within the frame or cage of what we already know. What we need is not *in*sight but what in German is called *"Um*sight," literally "aroundsight," or panorama—what's going on outside the cage on every side.

What we need in order to take charge of our own lives is listening that is active enough to greatly enhance the quantity and the accuracy of the information about ourselves that we gain by observing the consequences of our behavior. This we can do by deliberately changing the responses of the other person and noting what it takes, on our part, to achieve various different responses. The technique is a kind of psychological sonar, sending out messages of varied wavelengths and listening for the echoes that come back to us. Such echo-sounding makes the consequences of our behavior much clearer than inactive listening does.

Change cannot occur in a social vacuum, for interaction of some kind is required to consolidate it. We cannot give ourselves an unexpected response. However, we *can* give someone else an unexpected response, and this will be reflected in his subsequent behavior. Obviously, we don't know just what kind of message to give in order to prompt a specific new response in the other person, so we have to try out a number of different behaviors on him.

There is nothing new about the technique. Don Juans and other good salesmen apply it with regularity. As young children, we experimented constantly in order to find out what we could do to get attention and to encourage various responses on the part of parents or of other children. We made mistakes most of the time but were still delighted by the game. We felt free to pretend anything and free to fail repeatedly. From the results of this aggressive play we learned how to cope with our environment and in some degree to control other people.

Suppose we have a problem with a certain "friend" who is usually hostile to us despite our friendly intentions. Perhaps he is fundamentally a very hostile person. Or perhaps we manage in some unaware way to bring out hostility in him. We can test the question by changing our behavior—by being deliberately helpful and encouraging on one occasion and, on another, deliberately unfriendly. From our friend's response we can observe the effect of our various behaviors.

Or perhaps we are romantically inclined but our companion is always cool and removed. If we have been careful to be polite and obliging all the time, we might instead try being straightforward, saying what we really feel. We are likely to discover something about the unconscious purpose of our careful politeness; for example, our friend may be grateful rather than upset.

On every occasion we have an opportunity to measure the response we actually get against the response we expected to get. Conscious intent and unconscious design confront each other, and the discordance in our style becomes visible to us.

Seeing the discordance in our own behavior may be upsetting enough to drive us into uncertainty and thus into a search for a less divisive style. But we all have such a strong need for harmony and consistency that we avoid the sight of our own discords. We remain ignorant of them so we may continue to feel secure in whatever compromises we are tenaciously preserving. Our own discordance, in other words, is a secret we are careful to keep from ourselves. Rather, it is a closetful of secrets—quiet, low-key, powerful secrets that cannot be made use of until they are uncovered.

For example, imagine that we make a few casual remarks and our friends react with annoyance. We don't feel responsible because we know we aren't the kind that enjoys annoying people. Nevertheless it seems to happen again and again. We assume we must be the victim of an annoyed world. If we now take a few soundings by consciously changing the nature of whatever remarks we make, we may discover that our friends this time are warmed or delighted or amused.

The conclusion must be that our customary "casual remarks" are unconsciously designed to annoy our friends. But why should we wish to annoy our friends? The answer is unclear since we do not know what, in fact, we want out of life. It is probably something in the area of love or possessions or territory or certainty of some kind. By taking the consequences of our behavior seriously and by experimenting further with "behavioral sonar," we may find more specific clues.

A seventeen-year-old boy wears long wavy hair, bathes little, and uses hard-core slang around the house. He truly may not know these behaviors are offensive, yet he uses them again and again, always with the same response: lectures, complaints, threats. He detests this "uptight, unloving" behavior of his parents.

If he would try "sonar," he would quickly realize that different behaviors draw very different responses, and he might notice that he must have been motivated to elicit just the responses he did elicit. Why? Probably to give himself an excuse for looking down on his parents. And why should he do that? Perhaps to support his own shaky new philosophy in the face of harsh criticism, perhaps to test his own personal resources by rebelling.

Whatever his unrealized need, he can if he wishes discover the immediate goal served by his behavior. Then he has the option of appreciating the goal and staying with it or of changing his behavior, should the overall pattern prove to be distasteful to him or unproductive.

Getting off the Ground

What about totally *unconscious* behavior? The seventeen-year-old was not aware of the message he was giving his parents but he did know, of course, what he was literally doing. What about behavior so subtle that nobody notices it? The very subtle message may be at the same time ingenious and powerfully effective when it comes to getting another person to respond in a particular way again and again. How can we change, or experiment with, that part of our style of which we are not conscious?

One way this can be accomplished is simply by changing an attitude. We cannot do it deliberately, but we might be prompted to do so by a surprising challenge from outside. An attitude always makes itself known, often by way of slight physiological changes that are not consciously noticed.

A remarkable example of altering unconscious behavior occurred recently when a girl went backpacking in California with her boy friend and her dog. On the second day out, the dog appeared to be going progressively insane. It ran around in circles, howling. It tore holes in the boy's pack and chewed at his shoes. It knocked cooking pots into the fire, lunged at the girl, and at times cowered in the tent, whimpering. Nothing the girl said or did had the slightest effect on the dog's bizarre activities, which continued for several hours.

Finally it occurred to the girl that her friend might be somehow involved in the dog's behavior. She said, rather angrily, "You're the one who should do something!" The young man was surprised, but he took her seriously. He sat cross-legged on the ground, closed his eyes, and did what he called a "process" on the problem. He asked himself whether his own presence might have something to do with the dog's problem.

He had been assuming that he and the dog were on friendly terms, but he remembered his reaction when the girl had first told him she had to take the dog along. He had said to himself, as the dog came up to him, wagging its tail, "That dog's going to be a problem." He now realized that he must have proceeded—by means of a daylong sequence of subtle cues—to make his prediction come true.

As this became clearer to him, he noticed that his feelings about the dog were changing. When he stood up, the dog was fine ... and remained so throughout the trip.

The boy, in response to the girl's "accusation," had noticed that the dog's wild reaction might indeed be a reflection of something he was doing or feeling, and this new awareness had created a new emotional climate. In this changed interior setting, he was able to experience different feelings, which then betrayed themselves in unconscious communications between him and the dog.

Varying our own response and listening for its consequences helps us to relabel our behavior in terms of its real effects on others rather than in terms of our own hopes and fears and defenses. We *are* what we communicate. If we don't see clearly what it is we are communicating, we cannot have a very clear idea of who we are or what we want.

We cannot force change on ourselves. We can only increase the amount of meaningful information available and thus enhance the potential for seeing options we had never considered. Awareness of new options leads to uncertainty about some of our habitual patterns of behavior and makes new patterns possible. Change has to do with recognizing the value of options and with experiencing the fact that we are fully responsible for what we do choose.

The key to change lies in finding a way to break out of the walled city that constitutes our personal emotional world, for the answers to chronic psychological problems are only to be found outside the walls. Every possibility on the inside has already been investigated, and the most promising one has already been spoken for; it is the one we are using right now.

Friedrich Kekule's discovery of the structure of benzene is a familiar case in point. Everything Kekule knew about carbon chemistry indicated that the six carbon atoms in benzene should be linked in a linear sequence or Y of some kind. The problem persisted until he dreamed one night of a ring of snakes, each trying to devour the next snake's tail. Benzene proved indeed to be a ring-shaped molecule. Nothing in the known world of chemistry contained the key to this discovery.

If we stay within the original frame of a problem as we describe it to ourselves, the problem is likely to persist forever. A seemingly specific sexual problem may derive from a man's everyday habit of withholding the truth from himself and his friends. A writer who can't get started on his novel because he is broke and his mortgage payment is due finds that an unexpected inheritance pays off the mortgage but doesn't help the writing. His problem has nothing to do with money; it has to do with his style of confronting ambitious projects of any kind.

When the young man created a new emotional climate in regard to his assumptions about his girl's dog, he broke out of the frame of assuming that the dog must be sick and had to be cured. He, like Kekule, saw his entire problem in a completely new way.

Freedom and Dignity

Even though we cannot do very much about deliberately changing our own behavior, the issue of free choice is central to the problem of change, once we have been strongly motivated. If an individual knows that he *is* as he *is* and there's nothing significant he can ever do about it, then he will indeed be perfectly unable to do anything about it, even when shoved in the right direction. If he knows that he has real options in the real world and that there are ways of learning to choose among them, then he is at least open to the possibility of changing.

To change means to choose a behavior different from the one currently in use, to reassign priorities. Every step we take during the day, every act, every word, expresses our assignment of a priority. Any step could have been taken differently, but until we are driven to try new steps we are like a switch engine trying to make up trains in a marshaling yard where all the switches are frozen. A switch is by design an option machine; if we allow it to remain stuck in one position, we are thereby choosing to forfeit choice.

We still cannot very well act as our own dispatcher since we understand so little about the dual and dissonant nature of our own style. However, we certainly can prepare ourselves for change by experimenting with new roles and we can choose at any point either to ride with the old way or to accept change. As long as we remain ignorant of the unaware levels of our behavior, we are at the mercy of habit and are a setup for manipulation. Push the right button and we have to jump.

Anyone who learns that he can choose his own feelings and words and actions, on the other hand, is a free person and a powerful person. He knows that he shares responsibility for responses that assail him repeatedly, and he knows he can vary his own behavior in order to change these responses if he cares to. For example, although he may not be responsible for how the other person behaves toward him initially, when the same behavior is repeated time and again, he becomes responsible insofar as his cooperation is needed to maintain this repeating behavior. He therefore has the power to change the other person, to stop the repetition, if he chooses.

The idea that people have *chosen* to be what they are—albeit without awareness much of the time—is quite unacceptable to most of us because we cannot face that much responsibility. We need scapegoats on which to blame our weaknesses and we need concepts like "mistake" and "accident" and "unintentional" so we can excuse maneuvers that don't look so good in public.

The uncomfortable fact is, however, that most things we do we mean to do, and we choose to do them because they consistently lead to certain effects that are in some way to our advantage. When they stop working, we stop doing them. The reason it is much more difficult to change oneself than to change a friend is that we cannot afford, emotionally, to accept responsibility for our own slips of tongue and gesture.

People have far more choice about what they do than they are given credit for or than they themselves realize, and they exercise this choice constantly. They mean what they do. They mean what they say, even if what they say is false.

We are not helpless dolls that dance as we were built to dance every time someone winds us up. We do not behave as we behave by accident. Most of the time, we don't even have accidents by accident. We mean what we do—even if we do it unconsciously—because what we do brings certain predictable results and we prefer these results to others.

We may camouflage our covert communications with excuses or with "reasonable" labels, but it is really not these explanations that we most want to communicate. We *want* to be read in terms of the consequences of our behavior.

8

Blaming

"If you'd only stop nagging, we could be a happy family." "If the government weren't so wasteful, we wouldn't be in this predicament." "I could easily find a boy friend if I were only prettier."

All these statements attribute the cause of the speaker's unhappiness to some quality by which he feels victimized. If we listen closely to members of our family or to our neighbors, we can see that a substantial amount of time is devoted to blaming.

The wish to find fault is deeply ingrained in all of us because it serves a useful purpose. Whenever we blame, we believe that the cause to which we have attributed our troubles is the correct cause. The truth is, however, that we select this cause precisely because we have no intention of doing anything about the situation that is responsible for our problems.

If we were to devote our efforts to confronting adversity and correcting the true cause of our unhappiness, we would not be blamers. By the act of blaming, we choose to express our frustration rather than to correct our lives, and for this reason we invent causes we know we cannot do anything about.

Who can still a nagging wife, control a wasteful government, change a homely face? By choosing such blame targets, we become instant victims, helpless, wronged. We set up a situation that leaves us, the instant victims, no choice but to fire impotent barbs at an indomitable culprit.

Learning How

Blaming behavior is probably unique to man. It is hard to conceive of a dog blaming another dog for keeping him awake or to imagine an elephant pointing his trunk accusingly at another elephant. Only *Homo sapiens* appears to have the necessary tools and skills: a cerebral cortex capable of making complex associations, a sophisticated social history of cooperation and competition, and an extended infancy notable for its helplessness in childhood.

The child learns within the first year of life that he has to summon help in order to survive. In the absence of language at this early age, he can only transmit information by nonverbal means and, in this fumbling manner, "pray" for whatever help he needs. When help is not received and his nonverbal prayer is not responded to within a reasonable time, he may very well despair.

He may not yet be able to blame a given cause, but when he learns his first words, he will hang on to these early sounds that represent all his hope and despair; eventually he will learn to use them to summon help and to make it clear that he holds certain outside forces responsible for his continued existence.

Because of the way his brain stores information, the child will vaguely remember his state of helplessness, his inability to solve his own problems, and his total dependency on the sounds and gestures that once summoned help from his environment.

Later, this capacity to hold someone else responsible for our existence is still maintained, even though we are no longer helpless. In distress, which is a signal that our very being is threatened, we are likely to reexperience earlier helplessness and reach for the old magic formula to shift responsibility for our survival to an outside force.

In some societies more "primitive" than our own, the delegation of responsibility is ended by ritual at the age of physical maturity. At thirteen or fourteen, boys undergo initiation rites to become responsible men, and girls become responsible women. After initiation, the individual is expected to take responsibility for satisfying all his own everyday needs.

Because of greater longevity and the growing complexity of modern society, the legal age defining "maturity" has increased. Since our own society feels that seventeen-year-olds are not quite responsible, a good many teen-agers maintain the habit of delegating to others the responsibility for their own survival; they become blamers, or they remain blamers. They make the most of it when they run up against not being allowed to smoke, to buy liquor, to see the movies they want to see, or to hire themselves out for responsible work.

Consequently, a substantial number of young people learn to shift responsibility as part of their assumed birthright. When they are finally given responsibility legally, many of them are unable to accept it and have a hard time understanding that society will not continue to take responsibility for their well-being.

They will now gain great satisfaction from shifting responsibility to such targets as family, government, friends. In this way they can justify the fact that they are not as mature and successful as they believe they should be; other forces are in charge of their lives and they are the victims of these forces.

It's Got to Be *Somebody's* Fault

Blaming probably originated with the highly personal desire to avoid a feeling of frustration and helplessness. Yet it is quite possible that this human capacity is also responsible in part for man's massive effort to discover the causes, real or imagined, which move his universe.

The child's helplessness requires him to seek out means by which he can alleviate this feeling. As he matures, however, he will not only berate and blame the conditions he feels have made him helpless; he will also direct some efforts to reexamining the assumed causes of his pain and attempting to remove them. In this sense, the human need to find a blame target can lead to taking a second look. Instead of stopping his inquiry once he has expressed his frustration, he turns to study the apparent cause and thus broadens his inquiry.

People blame the stars for their fate, or the god of thunder for a disastrous crop, but a second glance leads them to a useful discovery about the relationship of the sun and the moon and the planets. First a person blames the scapegoat for disease and kills it, but then he looks at his sickness again and finds causes with a more predictable relationship to the sickness.

In this way, people become scientists, deriving pleasure from seeking for causes. They become problem-solvers, using their knowledge to *control* the cause they had previously only *blamed.*

In everyday life, unfortunately, few of us appear to have progressed beyond the first stage. We are interested neither in inquiry nor in evidence. We are content to have become the instant victim of a vicious, immutable world that mishandles its responsibilities.

Furthermore, we do not accept ourselves as "blamers"; we label our statements "descriptive" or "factual." We say to our son, "Somebody raided the refrigerator last night and ate up all the goodies," and we feel we have made an accurate descriptive statement. Our son, however, protests his innocence as if he had been accused.

If our intention is indeed to describe accurately, we will welcome further inquiry into the true cause of the event. If we choose to avoid further inquiry, we can be certain that we are blaming and not merely describing. In this case we are not only blaming but blaming indirectly, by implication, without taking responsibility for it.

Blame Targets: People, Forces, Self, Objects, Circumstances

People select varied blame targets. Most often they hold other *people* responsible for their ills. This seems to be the easiest way to express frustration. A second category of blaming has to do with *forces* perceived as being beyond one's own control, such as the government, a minority, money, or even fate.

A third mode is to blame *oneself,* or parts of oneself. Messages to oneself include blaming one's ugly nose for a lack of dates, one's size for being defeated in competition, one's health, or even facets of one's personality for any disastrous experience. This self-blaming has nothing to do with insight and there is no intention of seeking a change.

A fourth category includes all possible *objects,* such as a stupid automobile or a malicious hammer that has just struck a thumb. Almost anyone, any force, any object, can serve to turn us into instant victims.

A fifth category involves *psychological and social circumstances* as blame targets. People tend to blame their childhood, their parents, or the lack of a proper education for many of their ills.

1. *People.* Many blame targets are culturally endorsed and represent fashions. In the Middle Ages people apparently were blamed for giving in to the devil and losing their faith. Any disaster was largely interpreted as a loss of faith, and we can easily imagine a man claiming that a woman no longer loved him because the devil had possessed her.

During the first half of our century, the more commonly endorsed blame targets were maladjustment, lack of intelligence, and intolerance. Almost any personal disaster could be accounted for by one of these three concepts.

We blame our own unhappiness often enough on our observation that those around us are maladjusted. A young woman thinks of her friend (who does not pay enough attention to her) as a "neurotic" or a "sex deviant"; parents blame misbehavior on the fact that their child is "disturbed," and we all look for diseases that can be blamed for our misfortunes.

The American Psychiatric Association has been of great service in this matter by publishing a diagnostic list of mental disorders so inclusive that not one person can escape being classified as mentally disordered on several counts.

The "mental disorders" listed include *enuresis, feeding disturbance, adjustment reaction of childhood* (e.g., "jealousy associated with birth of a younger brother"), *adjustment reaction of adult life* (e.g., "fear associated with military combat and manifested by trembling, running, and hiding"), *hyperkinetic reaction of childhood* ("overactivity, restlessness, and short attention span"), *marital maladjustment* ("conflict in marriage"), and *social maladjustment* ("culture shock"). There is even a category *(nonspecific conditions)* for people diagnosed as mentally ill but with no particular identifiable symptoms.

This monstrosity secures for 230 million Americans the possibility of becoming instant victims of some undifferentiated sickness and a handy blame target for all of us. The violent delinquents in *West Side Story* can claim they could not help themselves because they were victims of an officially verified mental disorder, *dyssocial behavior* (not an antisocial personality, but "predatory, like racketeers, prostitutes, and dope peddlers").

Even immense, complex political disasters are blamed on the insanity of one leader, a Stalin or a Hitler. This blaming fashion has also affected those who have been officially labeled as mentally sick, such as patients in a mental hospital. They now can use the label as an excuse to live up to it; like anyone else, they are affected by the expectations others have of them.

Lack of intelligence is another handy target. "He is not very bright" and "He's terribly clumsy" are common excuses for dodging responsibility. This fashion is institutionalized by dividing school students into various grades of intellectual citizenship. The slow learners are in the lowest class. They have been given the official stamp for slow learners and they are likely to live up to that expectation.

All this is done in the name of efficiency and adjustment, citing the rationale that "slow learners" would only fail and be maladjusted in a "normal" class. By lowering the expectations for these particular students, the blanket classification serves as a self-fulfilling prophecy. This procedure is particularly insidious since class assignments are often made on the basis of very poor data and clearly inadequate definitions of intelligence.

Even schools for the mentally retarded contain children who are totally misdiagnosed. In a study of one such institution. we found that 27 per cent of the population was misdiagnosed. Such institutionalized "blaming" robs many a person of his birthright and his rights as a citizen.

The reproach of "intolerance" is another blame target. While discrimination by virtue of race or sex or age is all too common, there are many poorly qualified job-seekers who ignore their own questionable skills and blame their unemployment on the intolerance of a series of prospective employers.

2. *Forces.* Today another blame target has become highly fashionable: the government. The government does affect everyone's personal life, and constant attention by citizens is required to provide for changes; but blaming behavior does not give this service. Heavy blaming is often engaged in by people who don't even vote, and it serves to retard changes rather than foster them, because the expression of frustration is an end in itself and is not followed by further inquiry and action.

Other forces commonly blamed for our personal misfortunes include "communists." "the stars," "the establishment," and, more simply, "them." They all serve the same function of providing individuals with a ready-made vehicle to shift responsibility away from themselves.

3. *Self-blaming: I vs. I.* When the blamer blames himself, he splits his

own personality. One part carries responsibility and even wisdom, while the other part denies responsibility and says he cannot live up to the demands of the "good self."

A mother says, "I should not yell at my child." One of her selves realizes that yelling is bad; the other continues to yell. One self shifts the responsibility for the "bad" yelling to the other self, which conveniently shrugs its shoulders.

These interesting tête-à-têtes within one's own single head are a gambit we all engage in. Generally they result in a sense of well-being, since we are paying lip service to our faults. Additionally, we take the wind out of the sails of anyone else who may choose to blame *us*.

We say, "I'm so angry that I can't help myself." One self suggests that anger is bad and should be controlled, but shifts the responsibility onto the other self, which says we have a good reason not to cooperate with the reasonable self. We succeed in appearing to be "blameless" while nevertheless continuing to engage in the "bad" act we find so satisfying.

While such double-edged behavior is very common and bears no "sick" label, it is probably the basis of what some people call the "split personality." Self-blaming statements give us a sense of relief but also serve to keep us locked into the very situation we find intolerable. The student who blames his sleeplessness for his poor grades does not work on improving his grades; the man who blames his temper for his three divorces fails to put energy into improving his current marriage.

So the self-blaming statement, although it appears to be a sound alibi, deprives us of self-correction. Our correct "insight" that we should change is immediately counteracted by the "other self," which stops further inquiry. Our private, everyday "schizophrenia" leaves us impotent in regard to the cause of our trouble. It also blinds us to the fact that, after all, we are just *one* person acting in *one* way.

Somewhere, somehow, it is this one person who is in charge. The individual who explodes periodically and blames it all on his "temper" is really not merely a victim of his temper. He blames his temper as if it were an uncontrollable part of himself. Strangely enough, he does in fact control it; he must have control, since he indulges himself at some times but not at others.

He yells "uncontrollably" at his wife when they are alone, but never in the presence of his mother, who lives with them. He yells when she asks for household money, but when she asks for money in the store where they are shopping, he controls his temper. His temper is not a random occurrence that simply overwhelms him; it is a behavior he indulges in at certain times of his choosing.

When he says he cannot help himself, he uses his private schizophrenia to condemn, and at the same time to make inevitable, his own indulgences. He shifts responsibility for this to the part of himself which he arbitrarily (and wrongly) designates as immutable, beyond his control.

4. *Objects.* We claim we are dehumanized by the computer. We say we are late because our car isn't performing properly. We blame our poor skiing on faulty equipment.

There are many occurrences when we are in fact victimized—when the phone swallows our dimes without serving us or when the picture tube burns out—but these are not true blaming events. Blaming occurs when we use a complaint as an excuse for our own failure and do not even attempt to correct the problem ourselves. Because we are often victimized by machines in fact, anything mechanical has become fair game as a blame target.

As with any other act of blaming, accusing the object is a way of making ourselves feel better. We let off steam and take no further action in the matter.

5. *Psychological and social circumstances.* The most common culturally sanctioned blame target is our own childhood. We blame our sexual inadequacies on a punishing parent, our lack of sophistication on the poverty of our parental home, our current hang-ups on specific childhood traumas. Actually there is no hard evidence that childhood traumas can distort our lives; there has never been a thorough study showing that people who love life and appear to handle their affairs well have had an easy childhood or been free of traumas.

But it has become the fashion to blame our childhood because this helps us feel less responsible for what we are doing now; also, there is no point in trying to change things since the past is, by definition, unchangeable. Parents or siblings are forever blamed for having been too strict or too permissive, too unloving or too loving, too hostile or too overprotective.

Blaming psychological circumstances is also the *raison d'être* of profanity. When we cuss, we are looking for instant relief rather than for long-range solutions. Interestingly enough, the words we use do not seem to be arbitrary but are directly related to our cultural heritage. In Germany, toilet training used to be taken very seriously and people took pride in having their children toilet-trained within their first year of life. Consequently, in Germany the most distasteful cuss words are related to defecation. These words were especially shunned, and they provided people with considerable relief.

In the American culture, on the other hand, early toilet training was not so significant, and the pressures were placed instead on keeping the child from "playing with himself," something that used to cause a feeling of horror in many parents. The resulting restrictions appear to give sexual swear words extra power.

When an American seeks extra relief from frustration, he uses a prohibited sexual word. In an indirect way, he is blaming his childhood frustration for his present problems. Psychological circumstances make perfect blame targets since their origin is always ambiguous.

What Can We Do About It?

Self-blaming creates an artificial state of equilibrium; it maintains the behavior we are complaining about. A change can only occur when the equilibrium is disturbed.

Alcoholics Anonymous does this for the alcoholic—it disturbs the careful balance of the double message he has been giving himself. The organization does not permit the chronic drinker to indulge in the discordance, but encourages him to state at all times that he is an alcoholic who is now sober. In this manner A.A. philosophy does away with the drinking-behavior equilibrium created when the alcoholic blames himself for drinking.

In the same vein, the mother who yells at her children while "part of her" is saying she should not yell, has to learn that she is one person—a person who is now yelling at her children. By denying her the relief she obtains from saying she feels guilty about it, her "yelling" equilibrium is disturbed. Now she has to face the decision whether she wants to be a yeller or a nonyeller. She has to face the fact that she is only one person and that her private schizophrenia is no longer tenable.

Essentially, a mother who intimidates her child by yelling is not likely to change her behavior unless the child stops being intimidated by yelling. The technique (yelling) has to fail before the mother is motivated to abandon it and explore new options.

A therapist, or perhaps a rare friend, may be able to respond in an unexpected way (possibly by not reacting at all), thus giving the mother the experience again and again that the technique of yelling does nothing but put an end to communication.

If the yeller is repeatedly caught in the act of destroying communication by yelling, she is likely to be shocked out of it. She cannot be deliberately alerted to her blaming behavior by someone who is involved in the interaction, for this would simply set off a mutual blaming dance.

Blaming behavior is one of many options that we all are free to forgo or follow. We choose our targets with discrimination and we choose when and where to voice our accusations. Our choice may be unconscious, but we do choose again and again.

In a current study of blame targets in marriage (Beier's Communications Laboratory, University of Utah), it was found that these targets change after the first year. Newlyweds typically blame their marital unhappiness or discontent on money, on too-close ties to one spouse's family, on friends, and on "philosophical" values, in that order.

After one year of marriage, sexual problems usually rank first as a blame target, then choice of friends, and then philosophical values. In other words, as people get to know each other and find shortcomings in living together, they like first of all to blame their sex relations as the source of their problems—even though their sexual behavior appears to be a reflection of the quality of the marriage rather than the cause of it. Also, spouses become jealous of friends (they feel neglected) and show greater concern about the philosophical values of the other spouse (is he a Democrat, tight with money, religious?).

Blame targets change in marriage because people who get married are not knowledgeable about the qualities needed for a lasting marriage. Some young people today feel they can live together before marriage and thus experience more closely whether or not they are made for each other. They tend to get married when they have children, and in this circumstance new qualities are demanded of them. At this point, blame targets shift again.

Actually, blaming is a rich source of information about the blamer, conveyed to us with little censorship. By listening carefully, that is, by disengaging from the immediate emotional impact, we can learn what values the blamer holds dear, where he feels frustrated or incompetent, and to whom he typically shifts responsibility for his problems.

In order to learn more about another person and understand his blaming behavior properly, we must not take his blaming statements too literally, but we should listen for the real frustrations he expresses through them.

9

The Microcosm of Sex

It is easy to understand why Freud saw the sexual drive as the "life force," the singular motivation that underlies most other behaviors. It is the strongest reward system built into the organism and it surely appears to guide many human activities. Yet Freud gave this life force such continual emphasis that his view may very well distort a full understanding of human conduct.

We propose that sexual behavior is essentially a recapitulation of characteristics peculiar to—and central to—the individual's life-style. In other words, a person's sex life is a small universe of behavior that echoes his or her overall way of dealing with life.

This way of looking at sexuality leads to some intriguing conclusions. For one thing, we should be able to predict how a person will behave sexually if we are familiar with his or her nonsexual behavior, and we should also be able to guess how an individual deals with life's daily problems if we know how he or she behaves in bed. For another, it appears that sexual contact is not necessarily the main objective of either a short-term affair or a long-term sexual relationship. The couple's life-style, reflected in both their sexual and nonsexual behavior, contributes greatly to their experience of satisfaction, and it may become considerably more important to them than specific sexual contact per se.

Seeing sex as a microcosm of a person's behavior also has implications concerning the kinds of changes required for the resolution of sexual problems. A man who is habitually very self-concerned on the job, for example, is probably equally self-concerned in bed. His sexual performance is not likely to improve until he becomes more concerned for others in all areas of his life. His sexuality is intimately connected with, and subtly dependent upon, his general approach to life.

Explorations

Sexuality in human beings is above all a *means of communicating*. Each of us develops a sexual language, or style, which is influenced but not determined by sexual needs. It reflects the compromises and adjustments that a child is forced to make in all areas of his or her life in the face of an increasingly insistent reality.

First the child faces the demands of his or her own organism. Then there are external physical realities that limit the child severely, and psychological forces that bend, shape, and even break original genetic endowments to fit the expectations of those who inhabit the child's immediate world.

The psychological forces are in no sense limited to the educational efforts and intentions of the infant's parents. They are the sum total of the immediate environment—of the space in the child's crib, of the softness of the mother's gestures, of the ease with which the child can digest food, of the time he or she has to wait before arousing attention by crying.

As we grow up, we learn where we can touch ourselves without disapproval, how we have to control our bladder, how we can get results with a shrill cry, and to what degree we can count on maternal affection when we hold out our arms.

We have to coordinate an untold number of events with our own built-in demands to shape an environment in which we can survive with a minimum of discomfort and pain. The pressures we experience and to which we have to learn to adjust are very subtle and reflect only minimally our parents' conscious intentions. That is why parents often cannot understand how the child they raised so lovingly has such frightful problems. They are aware only of their best intentions.

By learning to master and find adequate compromises for all the subtle pressures made upon them, children develop their psychological styles very early, long before sexuality becomes a problem.

A girl of three may experience that her mother never hugs her, never kisses her, never plays with her. The only time her mother touches her in any significant way is when the child strays from her bed in the evening and refuses to go to sleep. Then her mother grabs her, throws her into her bed, and spanks her.

Assuming that this is the only "closeness" she is permitted to experience, she is likely to develop an emphatically anger-arousing style. Not that she consciously wants angry people around her. She has learned, however, that by arousing anger she can achieve a compromise between her need for affection and the only conditions she knows of under which the environment will respond to her.

The compromise does not fulfill her need for affection, but it is a half-happy solution that affords her some feeling of mastery, and she is likely to incorporate this assumption in her later behavior with potential sexual partners. A young woman may annoy a male friend by telling him of other affairs, and then turn his anger to arousal.

A milder trauma is experienced by the boy of ten whose father makes constant demands on him and yet severely criticizes his attempts to fulfill them. The boy is asked to help paint a fence. He feels the need to do the job. He is scared of his father; he also has a strong need to express his hatred of the constant criticism. He may therefore do the job with a frown on his face or he may do it with exaggerated slowness, or he may accidentally spill the paint.

He engages in these compromises without awareness, and he feels that he should not be held responsible for this silent rebellion. The compromise between the need to serve his father and the need to maintain his own integrity is likely to become a permanent stylistic feature in the boy's behavior. For example, he may, throughout his life and in all areas of his life, be willing to take responsibility—but always with a chip on his shoulder. When he matures sexually, he may act as if he is doing the woman a favor every time he makes love with her.

Before we are physically mature, we accumulate certain successful ways of dealing with pleasures and threats. (Freud called this, somewhat loosely, psychosexual development.) With maturity, we begin to apply our most successful compromises to every experience that comes along, including specifically sexual experiences. We learn that sexual contact is seen as an invaluable pleasure but is also subject to strong prohibitions, and we use all the cunning and skill we have accumulated over the years to secure it for ourselves.

People who have been subjected to more threats than they could handle during their early years learn to hold off involvement and to delay pleasures indefinitely; now, applying this well-learned technique to sex, they shy away from sexual relationships and may even give up all sexual pleasure. They also may have learned to hide their prohibited desires or even to suppress consciousness of these desires altogether.

Sexual Patterns

Heterosexuality is obviously expressed in many different behaviors. For years the term "heterosexual experience" was assumed to be a norm against which the quality and character of other sexual experiences (often called "deviant") could be measured.

Wilhelm Reich, in his work on the function of the orgasm, was the first to look carefully at the many variations in the quality of heterosexual experience. However, he went on to describe an ideal heterosexual pattern in detail and by implication classified other heterosexual behavior as inadequate, thereby failing to appreciate the promise of any person's remarkable diversity.

Still, Reich's attempt to open for discussion the variety of heterosexual experiences was long overdue. Together with the general trend toward exploring new avenues of behavior, it led to the investigation of techniques for enhancing sexual experience and the meaning of sexual styles.

. Technique and highly specific behavior must not be confused with style. When a male brings the experience of disdain for women into his sexual microcosm, it does not matter whether he has traditional intercourse or suggests oral or anal or manual stimulation. He will likely express his disdain by means of whatever technique happens to come to mind. His style may manifest itself by a failure to show any concern at all for the woman's satisfaction. Or he may refuse to take the sexual initiative as he knows he is expected to do. Or he may show his disdain by not bathing or by muttering obscenities when he is with a fastidious woman.

His style is evident in whatever he does—in a sexual encounter, in the way he carries it out, in the way he terminates it. He may change techniques and appear inconsistent to another person, but his style, his overall pattern, is constant since it is deeply anchored in his personal history.

Sexual patterns are specific to the individual, but some generalizations can be made. The most common variations occur in four related areas: commitment, concern for the other person, daring, and control. All four areas are involved in courting and sex relations, and our approach to a partner is largely governed by our specific attitudes toward them.

Commitment tells us about the duration, depth, and meaningfulness of a relationship. Concern has to do with understanding, giving oneself, and giving pleasure. Daring has to do with personal courage, as in the defiance of prohibitions. Control has to do with dominance, submission, and manipulation.

Whenever we read people, knowing about these attitudes brings us a lot of information about them. And since the attitudes are displayed very clearly in sex relations, we can learn about another person's general style from the microcosm of his or her sexual behavior.

Commitment

Perhaps the most frequently observed factor that determines an individual's sexual approach is his or her attitude toward commitment. Variations in commitment are best illustrated by the "Don Juan" approach. All Don Juans—whether women or men—are engaged in transitory commitment, but within this limitation they differ in style. While some promise commitment and even marriage to create the emotional atmosphere their style demands, others are frank about their desire to engage only in a strictly temporary commitment.

Both types apparently enjoy a great sense of dedication to sexual conquest, and apparently they have learned such mastery in pleasing their partners that they can expect the partner to express sorrow when they leave. To hit and run is part of their style, whatever their promises may have been.

While Don Juans are extreme in avoiding commitment, other people are more than willing to commit themselves firmly. Many people commit themselves to just *one* other person, often their spouse, with no serious consideration given to other, transitory affairs. In return for their commitment to one person, they often achieve a stable home and freedom (or relative freedom) from sexual competition.

Between these extremes, people have learned to enter into commitments in varying degrees. Even in homes where the spouses feel permanently and fully committed to each other, they may still want to keep a toehold on the outside.

Most commitment problems seem to arise from difficulties in separating from home during adolescence. It is in the home that children learn to trust or distrust others, and problems occur when parents demand either too much or too little dependency. When parents take over their children's lives, solving all their problems and making all their decisions for them, they make it hard for their children to commit themselves to another person without feeling controlled or possessed.

When parents go to the other extreme and insist that their children be independent in every way, those children are likely to expect an indifferent response whenever they express their own wish for commitment. In either case, the commitment dilemma experienced in the parental home is reflected in subsequent sexual patterns.

People who learn early in life to want both commitment to and freedom from another person are likely to seek a partner they can live with but nevertheless leave at will. They wisely look for a mate whose life-style reflects similar values, or one who is able to accept their style, regardless of differing values. If a person has learned as a child to cope with uncertainty by making incessant demands for reassurance, he or she will probably transfer this attitude to courting behavior and find a mate who will accept or even enjoy being constantly tested for loyalty. If he or she has learned that breaking commitments gives pleasure, this style may be reflected in a series of marriages and divorces. In this case such a person has to find a mate who will *not* accept his or her style.

Commitment is not communicated with words but with behavior. Total verbal commitment, such as vowing exclusive loyalty "till death do us part," may reflect little more than a style of making dramatic promises. Words do not really count. Behavior does, and people develop extremely complex behaviors with which to communicate their sense of commitment.

Some of these behaviors communicate mutually exclusive attitudes—for instance, a need for commitment along with a need for freedom from commitment. This combination was demonstrated by an acquaintance who thoroughly enjoyed the company of prostitutes and was always so loving and convincing in these starkly limited affairs that he literally caused an uproar with the prostitutes' pimps. He says he obtained a great deal of pleasure from building a very close (albeit transitory) relationship with each woman.

In line with his style in other areas, he had managed to achieve with prostitutes the transitory experience of mutual commitment in a setting where he nevertheless remained completely free. This man also happened to be married and apparently was willing and able to stay with his wife in his half-committed way.

Does such a "double life" contradict the thesis that the sexual microcosm reflects a person's life-style? We believe that it does not. This man needed a nest, a home, and he had used his considerable ability in obtaining a close relationship here as well. This commitment was durable because he was able to maintain a foothold somewhere else. He felt that he exercised control in his marriage in this manner. Not that he ever threatened to leave home, but he knew he could still count on his ability to draw women into a close relationship and yet remain free.

Multiple commitment was also a sexual microcosm for this man, a combination of durable and transitory commitments that proved to be characteristic of his general life-style as well. He had one job to which he was committed, but he also had a finger in other pies and was constantly exploring still further possibilities. He played an excellent game of tennis—his major recreational commitment—but he fleetingly sought out other sports that he readily gave up after a few trials. His social life, even his wardrobe, fell into the same pattern. His sexual pattern was indeed a microcosm of his style of dual commitment.

A rather different style is demonstrated by a Utah woman who selected males in terms of their importance in the corporation where she worked. During a single twelve-month period, she agreed to marry, in succession, eight different men. Each in turn was totally captivated by her, only to be discarded when a new and brighter (business) star appeared at the horizon. Her life-style, which included social climbing, was fully realized in her sexual behavior. Commitment was determined by rank.

Another woman, who was afraid of being trapped by commitments of any kind, sought out male prostitutes (through advertisements in an underground paper) and invited them to her home. In her bedroom she had hung a curtain behind which she was hiding when one of her "boys" arrived. She asked the man to embrace her from behind the curtain and in this manner she had sex relations without being recognized.

She never knew what her lover looked like; he never saw her; she even discouraged him from talking. She says she has always avoided commitment. Her behavior resembles that of some male homosexuals who have impersonal sex through holes in the partitions of public toilets. But the experience made her feel like a queen and she always enjoyed it. She was served at her own demand and did not care to put up with the "nonsense" of a relationship.

Some people think there is such a thing as "straight physical sex" without personal warmth or connection, and some people derive satisfaction from such a "cold" relationship. But the label is misleading. "Straight physical sex" is a style which involves the "nonsense of a relationship" as strongly as any other; in fact, to establish such a relationship often takes more careful planning than a more conventional one.

The effort to avoid warmth in a human contact is, in and of itself, a stylistic pattern, and the sexual pleasure involved is a minor component of the satisfaction the pattern brings. A sex act devoid of caring or concern is reflective of the person's life-style. It is not "physical only." It is a complex pattern, one among a great variety of sexual styles.

The variety of human sexual responsiveness is probably a result of the fact that humans can be sexually motivated at almost any time. With most animals, sexual attraction is controlled by cycles which make females sexually available only for limited periods, and most animals have developed mating styles that are uniquely specific for each species.

The human sexual response, on the other hand, is allowed a great variety of styles because there is no cyclic control and each individual is free to develop his or her own style. Commitment, therefore, is a matter of choice rather than of genetic prescription.

Concern

Another factor that determines the nature of human sexual behavior is the sense of *concern.* Commitment has to do with the seriousness with which a person enters a relationship and with its duration; concern determines its quality.

A sense of concern for others is a central ingredient in every individual's life-style, and it appears to be directly reflected in sexual patterns. Most people seem to yearn for someone who shows concern for them and for whom they can express concern. But each person has a different image of just what concern means, so he or she has to find someone who appreciates these personal feelings in the matter.

Courting behavior is the testing ground for responsiveness to sexual patterns. Much as a bat uses echo-sounding to find its way, we human beings, when courting, send out information and listen for the responses as the message bounces back. The "echoes" give us clues as to how deeply the other person may be concerned with us.

It would be reasonable to assume that most people seek out those others who show concern for them, but this does not seem to be the case. Many people become annoyed when they feel someone is showing them too much concern, and some are clearly frightened or even offended. The degree of concern we are willing to tolerate is sensitively reflected in our sexual behavior.

One person will be attracted to someone she perceives as unusually warm and understanding, while another will flee in fear. Still another person will be drawn by a "safe" expression of moderate concern. A few will be attracted by effusive overconcern or even by militant lack of concern.

An exaggerated case of concern is the boy whose loving mother wiped his behind regularly until he was twenty-six because she was "so concerned about cleanliness." (Yes, this is a true story.) The boy was left with a definition of "concern" that strongly influenced his sexual behavior as well as his everyday nonsexual style.

This young man lived alone, constantly engaging others to do things for him. Once he had elicited this concern, he would abruptly leave, escaping with apparent relief from the person he had just set up. He would seek out therapists and, after eliciting their deep concern for him, he would berate them and switch at once to someone else.

He had sexualized this pattern as well. He would invite a woman to his apartment, arouse her sexually, and when she appeared ready to make love, explode with anger and kick her out. In fact, he never had sex relations with any of these women. In his masturbatory activity he came to orgasm only when he daydreamed of a woman who remained totally unconcerned.

A psychoanalytic interpretation—that he wanted to eliminate the image of his all-too-responsive mother as a possible sexual object—is perhaps as good a theory as any to explain how he had learned his style. However, it does not explain why such a pattern should last into this man's early forties.

While Freud assumed that a sexual attraction to one's mother is repressed into the unconscious, our assumption is that this man, when he still was a child, developed a style that forced him into compromise. He had learned to act out discordantly both his wish for sex (he aroused the woman) and his need to protect himself from the consequences of this arousal.

He became extremely skillful at eliciting concern from others. He got his kicks from making the Grand Exit, and he was apparently willing to forfeit direct sexual pleasure in order to do so. This half-happy compromise permeated his life and was reflected in the microcosm of his sexual behavior.

There are many people who will not engage in sex relations unless they feel concern for their partner. Their behavior probably reflects a style that became fashionable only within the recent history of mankind. While it seems both normal and desirable to us to enhance sex with concern, the chances are that people engaged in sex long before romantic love and a sense of concern for the other individual became an ideal. In the animal kingdom we find concern for the young and competition for sexual objects, but it is doubtful whether pleasure-giving in the sexual act is of concern to any animal other than man and perhaps dolphins and whales.

Modern sex workshops attempt to train people to develop greater concern for each other and to be less performance-centered. The participants are trained to communicate with each other about their sexual pleasures and hang-ups, to discuss their intimate needs, and to guide each other for greater satisfaction. It is hoped that such therapeutic exploration will encourage people to change their sexual styles. In a sense, however, these workshops are putting the cart before the horse. They change the microcosm in the hope that the macrocosm will change also.

Changes in sexual behavior seem far more likely to follow changes in one's general style than the other way around. Changes in general style are necessary if "improved sexual functioning" is to be made a permanent feature in the individual's life. When we recognize that sexual behavior is essentially a reflection of one's general living style, we can see that changes in a "microcosmic" behavior alone are likely to be fleeting.

Daring

A third factor that determines an individual's sexual style is the *urge to take chances.*

In our society, a child grows up learning about rules, customs, expectations, and prohibitions, and about the nature of the punishment commonly inflicted when these are violated. Many of these rules appear arbitrary to the children who must obey them. They often feel they are giving in, forfeiting personal integrity.

It is hardly surprising to find that they are apt to rebel against some of the rules and that they enjoy the battle. Their rebellion is in part a communication to themselves ("I don't have to submit when I don't want to") and in part a communication to others ("So I may have to go to the principal's office—see who cares!")

In these communications, the "daring" component seems to be more significant than the direct gain. Sometimes we as violators are concerned exclusively with communicating to ourselves and others that we will take chances, and there is simply no other gain.

Daring is much encouraged in our society—in "standing up" to those who offend us, in competing with others in sports, and in risk-taking in business. Daring behavior does not always involve challenging the rules, and yet it is a way of reaching for prohibited fruit.

Most people have a pet behavior that is their preferred battleground. Some do their daring at income-tax time, others while driving on the freeway, still others by petty shoplifting (walking off with restaurant silverware or stealing stamps from the office). Some otherwise law-abiding citizens commit minor assaults, and many of us permit ourselves the luxury of a violent temper when offended.

Daring is also reflected in our sexual behavior and may be expressed violently (sex murder and rape) or mildly (the "crime" of assuming the "wrong" coital position with one's wife, which happens to be regulated by law in some states of the Union).

In order to understand how deeply sex and daring are associated, we only need think of even the most harmless contact between a boy and a girl. Society encourages a sense of shyness in the young, and it takes some daring to overcome it. Some children feel courageous when they finally get up enough nerve just to speak to a child of the opposite sex.

The cultivation of shyness, along with the cultivation of competitive feelings, apparently serves society by preparing the young to deal with the challenges they will meet as adults. By cultivating shyness in the young, society discourages early sexual contacts and promotes fantasy and the delay of gratification at the expense of immediate action. Shyness, fantasy, and the postponement of pleasure make for big dreams and a need to compete and win.

Control

Control by means of granting or withholding sexual "favors" comes in many forms. In any sexual approach, control is exerted both by the initiator and by the "object," who may accept or reject the other's advances. What is not always obvious is that in some relationships the manner in which the approach is made—that is, the style of conquest—becomes more significant to the participants than the sex act itself.

The style may even be "negative," as when the initiator sets up an experience of rejection. Or a person who is usually receptive to sexual invitations may reject an offer in order to experience or demonstrate control. With some couples, the initiator appears to be indifferent; rather than expressing a personal desire, he says something like, "We haven't had sex for a while. Isn't it about time?" This too is a "microcosmic" reflection of the life-style of the lovers. They have learned not to express personal needs or desires in any of their discussions, whether the subject be sexual intercourse or tomorrow's menu.

Satisfaction during sexual relations is communicated in many ways, by means of sounds, for example, or by high excitement or prolonged contact or a change in the quality of touching. Such expressions are commonly used to control the partner. They may serve to direct the partner's actions and to enhance sexual exploration, or they may be used in a "negative" manner.

By failing to emit the enthusiastic sounds which are customary in the relationship, one of the partners can communicate a threat of punishment or a loss of concern for the other's pleasure and well-being. The woman who resignedly makes herself "available" and constantly reminds her husband of the fact probably thinks of herself as a chattel, but what she is really communicating to her partner is that he is not good enough to bring her sexual satisfaction. She is in effect rejecting him and thereby exercising subtle but powerful control.

Particularly heavy control is possible in the wake of a sexual episode when one partner communicates to the other the significance he or she attaches to their being together. Some men (and perhaps a few women) go out of their way to make it clear who is in control.

A man may end the sexual contact the moment he is satisfied and get up to smoke a cigarette, thus reminding his partner that her main function is to serve his desires. With this gesture he controls the nature of their sexual exchange, and that exchange probably reflects their attitudes toward each other in other phases of their relationship—the willing female, pleased to do the bidding of the controlling male. It is reasonable to assume that this particular pair of roles will be played out in many of their other interactions, ranging from the preparation of meals to the education of the children.

The variety of sexual expression found in heterosexual behavior is, not surprisingly, also present in homosexual behavior. In both cases the individual engages in any of a number of specific sexual activities; both styles embrace a wide variation in terms of commitment, concern, control, and daring.

We do not really know why people choose to love some person of their own sex. There is no clear evidence of whether this is inborn, learned, or both. Some people may have had disappointments in their relationships with the opposite sex. Others clearly have not.

The recent official reclassification by both the American Psychological Association and the American Psychiatric Association of homosexuality as a variation of normally occurring behavior rather than as a "disease" is significant because it recognizes that homosexuality can be a chosen life-style.

While many people want to curtail the choices others make about their love relationships, our society and many European nations today have begun to liberalize their laws governing sexual conduct among consenting adults. Still, the homosexual person has to fight for many of the rights to sexual identity that are taken for granted by people who have made a different choice.

As with any label, the label "homosexual" communicates certain information to both the person who takes on the label and the people around that person, whether they react favorably or—as is more often the case—adversely, when they are made aware of the label.

If a person does choose to label himself or herself "homosexual," the option selected to play that label out is, as with all kinds of other behavior, an indication of the general style of that person's life, sexual or nonsexual. One homosexual man, for example, may choose to be a discreet private citizen and keep his sexual identity to himself, choosing in this way not to commit himself to others, or he may reveal himself only to his closest friends and thereby involve himself in greater commitment. Another homosexual man may choose to be daring and take the risk of being "found out." (It is interesting to note the significance of the communication conveyed by the use of this phrase.)

A lesbian may choose any of these options, too. Or she may act out her concern for others by making her sexual identity a very important characteristic of her life and openly fighting for it. She, like the homosexual man, can also use her sexual identity to control others—by claiming, for example, that an extraordinary amount of suffering is inflicted on her by society's prejudices and by using her sexual preference as a scapegoat.

In terms of the style characteristics we have discussed, then, the gay person can express the same variety of styles through his or her sexuality as the heterosexual person does. Labels are used in the same ways: Don Juan can be either straight or gay; having a child out of wedlock may provide some of the same rewards and satisfy some of the same needs for one woman as choosing a gay life-style may provide for another.

It is interesting to speculate on whether someone—anyone—chooses to love another *person,* or specifically another man or another woman, and, further, to ask why those particular choices are made. Whatever the choice, there are a multitude of needs and communications involved, some of which conflict with and contradict others. The resolution of this kind of speculation is not an easy, single answer.

Still, whether one chooses to love a man or a woman is not really the essential element in these communications patterns, though it may determine the channels used. After all, the sexual activity of any individual, gay or straight, is only the microcosm of a general life-style; naturally, many attitudes and feelings will be expressed in either.

Within the confines of this chapter, our discussion of the communication aspects of the homosexual's choice is necessarily very limited and incomplete. It is not our purpose to analyze the many questions raised, but only to suggest that any individual's sexual identity is a channel of communication that is of great significance to that person and to others.

That the word "homosexuality" is accepted by so many—both those who choose that label for themselves and those who label others with it—as an adequate designation for a whole person who does a thousand things other than sleeping with members of his or her own sex, testifies to the shallow listening habits many of us have carelessly come to adopt.

Sexual Discordance

Most of us have enormous difficulty dealing with discordance when it involves sexual behavior. Since we attach great symbolic significance to sexual performance, the man who does not function well in bed thinks of himself as a substandard male, and the woman who doesn't experience much sexual pleasure has some doubts about her womanhood. Such views are self-punishing and tend to maintain the discordance.

Sexual discordance makes itself known most emphatically in a number of well-known dysfunctions. Most frequently it manifests itself in both men and women in the indefinite delaying of pleasure (impotence and frigidity), in the failure to achieve orgasm, and, in males particularly, in the failure to delay pleasure (premature ejaculation). Only rarely are these dysfunctions due to organic causes.

There is enormous variety in human sexual experience. The kinds of pleasure—orgasmic and other—are limitless, and so are the kinds of displeasure that may accompany sexual dysfunction. We are going to look at sexual dysfunction as a discordant communication that serves as a powerful means by which the body can communicate messages that the mind may not wish to acknowledge. We will look first of all for what the discordant behavior has to tell us about the unhappy individual who appears to suffer from it.

Frigidity and impotence reflect psychosexual attitudes that may be as mild as a temporary loss of pleasurable sensation or as severe as total unresponsiveness or a feeling of repulsion when touched by another human being. Whatever the psychosexual attitude, they reflect a lifestyle the woman or man experiences not only while making love but in most other significant encounters as well. When a person claims that a lover's touch is repulsive, for example, this individual is probably also in the habit of keeping her or his distance in areas that are not in the least sexual.

Why should anyone prefer the experience of unrewarding sex to one of enjoyable sex? Apparently, unrewarding sex relations are not just "endured" but also desired. Neither frigidity nor impotence appears to be a deeply anchored pattern, and either may give way to pleasure as an individual's attitude toward life changes.

Impotence, and, in many instances, frigidity, appears to be mainly the result of performance anxiety. This anxiety is fostered by both partners' intense concern about sexual functioning—which of course is understandable, given past failures. Performance anxiety is the villain in almost all of the sexual dysfunctions, according to Masters and Johnson, but it is not clear why it should manifest itself in men as impotence in one case and as premature ejaculation in another.

A contributing cause of frigidity and impotence is the general sexual climate of a society that traditionally idealizes women as acquiescing sexual objects and requires "good" sexual performance of men. The woman, according to this image, is designed not to choose her own pleasure but to follow that of her man.

Part of her problem is that, in many instances, she has been systematically excluded from making her own choices in areas that go far

THUR. 16
     7:30
      18

JAN. 6

beyond the sexual, for example, in daily living, careers, and athletics. Consequently, she may not be familiar with the process of choosing or with the process of accepting responsibility for the consequences of personal choice. The woman in such a society is honored for assuming the culturally defined role of "wife" or "mother" (roles that are, interestingly, tied to sexual relationships), but she is seldom seen as an active, independent force in the world in her own right.

Men, on the other hand, are expected to be providers, leaders, and rulers, who must perform well and prove their strength if they are to be respected. Both these culturally sanctioned word cages lock women and men into roles where communication, sexual or otherwise, is difficult if not impossible.

Between the so-called sexual revolution and the emergence of the women's movement, more options for communicating seem to have been made available to both women and men. Though the discussion of sexual dysfunctions that follows focuses on sexual relationships between men and women, it should be noted that when women choose women or men choose men, some of the same problems in communication between partners arise.

Despite the heavy stereotypes, an unrewarding sex experience, even when it occurs regularly with a given partner, cannot be blamed entirely on society's expectations. It may be tolerated, or in some cases even sought after, because it can bring other rewards, many of which both partners fail to recognize.

Frigidity means that a woman does not experience sexual desire or that she does not experience pleasurable feelings when engaged in sexual activity. It also implies that she does not experience orgasm. We assume that the so-called frigid woman has sexual relationships not for the sake of sexual pleasure but as a gesture, perhaps as a way of maintaining a relationship she enjoys.

In a woman frigidity may deliver a meaningful unconscious communication from the woman to herself. For any number of reasons, she may want to prove to herself that she does not experience any pleasure and that she has no desire. Being innocent of desire, she cannot be held responsible for the act. In this manner, frigidity can serve as a discordant message; it allows her to have her cake and eat it, too.

The unaware message a woman's "frigidity" delivers will vary greatly according to her preferred style. One woman will suffer in silence and even pretend to have an orgasm, while another will respond with stoic indifference and still another will complain or even accuse her partner of clumsiness.

With a woman whose style is based on concern, the unconscious message may be, "You are the greatest lover of all." She pleases herself with her concern for her partner's pleasure, even at the expense of her own. A woman with a daring style may be saying, *"Are* you the greatest lover, after all?" She is willing to risk losing her partner in order to test the relationship.

Another woman's silent message—"You are surely not a very great lover"—allows her to feel justified in withdrawing her commitment to her partner. Finally, a woman concerned primarily with control may use her frigidity to determine the initiation, frequency, or duration of the relationship, and her lover literally has to jump not to disappoint her. In all these situations, the woman introduces her general life-style into the microcosm of sex, even though she is probably not aware of it.

When frigidity is accepted (and thus maintained) by both partners over a substantial length of time, we may conclude that both find it rewarding in some way. For example, it may allow the woman to express her feelings of deprivation and allow her partner to feel less than fully accepted sexually.

Both of these feelings confer some advantage on the person who experiences them; they are stylistic techniques for controlling a situation that suffers from conflicting pressures. They may provide an acceptable rationale for asserting independence or even for maintaining an outside affair. In this sense, frigidity can be a shared communication that has certain built-in rewards and is therefore quite acceptable to both parties, in spite of the cost.

In the extreme case, frigidity involves a feeling of repulsion for sexual intercourse. By means of such a feeling, the woman communicates to herself, and possibly to her partner, that she only indulges in sex as a sacrifice. In other words, she seeks the pleasure of becoming a martyr more avidly than she seeks sexual satisfaction. Her behavior demonstrates overtly that she only lives for others, but such self-sacrifice has strings attached. By giving up her own pleasure, she "earns" the "right" to make equal demands for sacrifice from her partner.

In most instances of impotence, the man is capable of having an erection but he does not have it at certain times when he claims to desire it. Actually, the word "impotence" is both harsh and inaccurate. The term "slow arousal" is probably closer to the truth. The man can be aroused, but he is in fact *not* aroused by certain situations and settings that he chooses to define as "arousing."

He feels that he has no say about whether or not he will respond sexually, and he sees himself as a helpless victim of circumstances outside his control—even though he may unconsciously want to anger his partner. Just as accident-proneness is anchored in a careless style of living, impotence is anchored in a style that involves extreme postponement of pleasure as well as resentment of the pressure of other people's expectations. Performance anxiety is an inevitable result.

Impotence typically has as much to do with the man's partner as it does with the man himself. Although they have experienced frequent bouts with slow arousal or no arousal, couples so "afflicted" rarely explore any other setting than the very setting which has so far produced repeated failure. As with frigidity, they both seem to cooperate in maintaining the status quo.

There are many conditions that obviously could be changed or experimented with. Diet, for example, the amount of alcohol consumed; the time of day or night reserved for lovemaking and the amount of time involved; the quality and duration of foreplay and the variety of sexual techniques employed; the physical setting—all of these elements affect performance anxiety and sexual functioning.

However, most couples seem to stay with the same old embrace at the same old time in the same old place. The only change they seriously consider is to try a little harder to achieve specific genital arousal.

Direct genital stimulation has its place in courting and lovemaking, but when it is the only stimulant (or the only one emphasized), it often serves to transmit a distinctly offensive message. One partner is saying that the other is failing yet again. It is as if one were telling the other, "Even when I go out of my way to help you, you won't respond. What in heaven's name is the *matter* with you?"

Not that the partner doesn't deserve this aggression. With his or her own discordant behavior (actions belie words), one has been telling the other that he is trying to make love to her because he feels obliged to. He usually denies feeling obligated and points to his own shame and suffering: "How can I *want* anything like that?" He would rather stay with the "sick" role than to take a hard look at his unacknowledged motivations.

Yet the chances are that slow arousal ("impotence") is an aggressive message. The man says he finds his partner attractive and seeks her out, but part of him says that she is really not quite his cup of tea, and it is this part that speaks in bed.

Failure to achieve orgasm may occur in women who are not frigid and in men who are not impotent. In most people, the absence of climax during sex relations does not mean climax is impossible; it simply means that it does not occur in this specific relationship.

Both women and men may very well achieve climax in other settings: masturbation, indulging in fantasies, or sexual contact with other people. The fact that such satisfactions often occur in total privacy implies that the individual is probably in the habit of refusing to commit this intense pleasure to another person.

A potent man, for example, who cannot obtain an orgasm does not seem to be depriving the woman of pleasure; rather, he seems to be overdoing it. He often thinks he is giving pleasure with a vengeance, though it should be noted that not all females perceive prolonged intercourse without orgasm as pleasurable.

The man in this case gives a special kind of message: he is willing to serve the female but not willing, in the end, to commit himself to the relationship. The woman may enjoy the man, but she also knows that he has not completed his sex act, he is not relaxed. It is almost as if he wants to keep himself in readiness for other, greener, pastures. Sometimes the woman will be much offended when her lover maintains his erection in this manner. She may verbalize this as a fear of not being attractive enough, or of not being his exclusive choice.

People have developed the notion that potency and orgasm ought to occur every single time they engage in sexual exchange. While this may be an ideal prescription, it just doesn't happen this way. Accordingly, people develop performance anxiety or "completion anxiety" and make each other's lives uncomfortable.

They need to learn to enjoy sexual contact whether orgasm occurs or not. And they need to listen for the messages their bodies transmit by way of sexual initiative and response.

In premature ejaculation, the male is aroused and ejaculates either prior to or soon after penetration. This may occur after extensive foreplay or it may occur without foreplay. There are usually two specific psychological consequences: the man, in spite of his orgasm, feels he has not performed well; his partner is likely to feel disappointed.

A great many couples suffer from this dysfunction, and the similarity of their individual experiences is striking. Premature ejaculation can be understood as a message in which the man is saying to his partner, "Your expectation that I am surely going to deliver is scaring me off. I'd better take my pleasure while I'm still able—even if you get left out in the process." But he not only punishes his partner; he punishes himself as well.

The self-punishment is a message that says, "Obviously I want to give you pleasure. Why else would I feel so bad about failing to do so?" He *has* to feel bad. If he were to have fully enjoyed his premature ejaculation, he would be forced to acknowledge that he was fundamentally a selfish lover and not just the victim of a disability.

The degree of punishment the man inflicts on his partner without consciously intending to do so can be reduced or changed by showing some demonstrable concern for the partner's satisfaction—something as simple and obvious as manual stimulation, for example. Again, there are many ways of showing concern and they vary according to the style of the participant.

We assume that the man has the ability to control the duration of his sexual arousal, but that he is presently caught in a habit pattern which serves unconsciously as the vehicle for an important communication. An understanding of this fact can lead to sensitive listening for the consequences of the unfortunate pattern and for the emotional anchors that hold it so firmly in position. Hopefully, the couple will discover how their joint sexual pattern reflects their more general attitudes toward each other. They then will have the option of making helpful changes in both their general behavior and their specific sexual behavior.

The man's sexual attitude is often a clear reflection of his everyday, nonsexual style. In one case, a man with a long history of premature ejaculation was known to be chronically distrustful. He spent his earnings the moment he was paid, and he grabbed every opportunity to make a quick profit, even though he knew his chances would improve if he were willing to wait. At length he became aware of this repeating pattern and learned to give up immediate gratification and postpone rewards in all areas of his life. This general change was almost immediately reflected in his sexual behavior, with results that pleased him greatly.

Most sexual dysfunctions, both female and male, seem designed to deliver a strong, specific message to oneself or to a specific partner. This is a powerful means by which an individual can express just how much concern, daring, and commitment he or she feels and to what extent he or she feels a need to control the course of the relationship.

When we understand that the sexual microcosm represents or reflects a life-style, we can see that new options in sexual function or behavior are achievable by changing one's general life-style.

Sexual Deviancy

Freud believed that all children go through a period of polymorphous sexuality during which they explore many possible forms of obtaining pleasure. Some of these forms become associated with more general motivations such as the wish to exhibit oneself or to watch others, the desire to steal, the desire to play with a prohibited object or person, the wish to punish or be punished, even the urge to play with selected objects such as shoes or clothing. Children thus provide themselves with meaningful experiences which are temporarily sexualized.

Most of these experiences are soon forgotten, but a few may become particularly meaningful to some children, probably because of certain traumatic experiences that occurred at the same time. If the child was beset by mutually contradictory pressures at the time, for example, the experience may have served as a compromise solution. Any behavior "fixated" in this way becomes part of the sexual repertoire of the growing child.

This can be illustrated by a case of exhibitionism. Exhibitionism occurs mostly in males, although female exhibitionism is currently on the increase. But it is really not sexual in nature, for it requires neither touch nor orgasm. It is, of all "sex" crimes, probably the most harmless since the "victim" is at worst left with some sense of shock and perhaps fear. Yet it is one in which the offender will engage time and time again. He may lose his home, his job, and his friends; he may even serve a prison sentence, and still return to his preferred pastime.

He does not do so for his sexual pleasure as we know it, though he is aroused and feels deeply excited. Many an exhibitionist has successful sex relations with women in which he functions "normally," but the real excitement is experienced when he opens his pants in front of a woman and shows her his aroused manhood.

What sort of compromise has he achieved that is so devastatingly alluring that he risks his freedom for it? A confirmed exhibitionist, asked to recall his greatest failure, gave us a surprising answer. He said he once showed his erection to an unsuspecting schoolgirl of sixteen who, in a blasé voice, told him, "What a shame, it's such a waste."

The man, in relating the event, was very much agitated. He could not forgive the girl for the injustice he had suffered through *her* action. He had wanted to surprise her, shock her, frighten her, perhaps to anger her. He had needed such a response from her in order to feel what he called "a sense of delicious well-being." The girl was either indifferent to his gross gesture or she was herself aroused. In either case, he felt he had been deeply misunderstood, and he left the scene in tears.

This man stated that he knew the whole game was stupid, dangerous, and undignified, but that he could not help himself. Apparently it represented an important compromise to him. It allowed him to prove his courage by risking his freedom and claiming his right to be recognized as a potent male. He only wanted to be recognized—not to act—but the recognition had to be accompanied by surprise, as if the woman had not really expected him to be such a potent male.

If she wanted him sexually, or if she failed to be surprised, then she was, he said, a "dirty whore." The woman's surprise and shock gave him the feeling of respect for her innocence. If the woman yelled and had him arrested, he would not resist; such a response was to be expected from women who were extraordinarily innocent.

Whatever else might happen, she had recognized him as a potent and strong adult. He had engaged her deep concern in a split second, and he enjoyed all the attention he got. His reward came from his style of shocking, not from sexual pleasure.

In other nonsexual areas of his existence, this man acted out a similar life-style. He was quite innovative at his job (he had been until recently a policeman) and was known for his silly but challenging suggestions. He once proposed that policemen on the beat should wear true-to-life toy machine guns on their backs to intimidate criminals. At another time he suggested that all policemen in his precinct wear high-heeled shoes in order to appear taller—a suggestion that was seriously considered. In both cases, his suggestions had to do with the appearance of power rather than with real power, and were very closely allied to his habits.

The exhibitionism was not so much a problem to him as it was a solution, a compromise among several conflicting pressures which he experienced. The source of one of the pressures was a childhood incident in which his mother showed surprise and interest in an unexpected erection. It was an innocent event and there were no sexual desires involved, but he was already possessed by an urge to impress people with the appearance of strength and power.

He found that he greatly enjoyed the startled surprise people expressed when he appeared to be a lot more grown up than they had imagined. They were surprised because they had expected nothing, and even a gesture would catch their attention. In his thinking, the gesture itself—the message alone, without any follow-up activity—became the most important communication.

The need to surprise people began to permeate his life-style. He had to think of ways of appearing more powerful than he was. He wore heavy wool sweaters, even in the summer, to hide how small he was. He was hoping to surprise people with his supposed strength and perhaps immobilize them.

Analysis of the offender's communications makes it easier to understand just how he maintains his behavior. Exhibitionism appears to be a bizarrely unfulfilling act, but when we look at it in terms of the message it delivers to us, we can understand that it is a rewarding experience for the exhibitionist. He feels strong, yet at the same time he is not called upon to prove himself.

In the past, the standard method of handling disorders such as exhibitionism was to prevent the offender from indulging himself any longer—typically, by putting him in jail. When we appreciate the breadth of his total pattern, we recognize that the sexual aspects of his behavior are rather insignificant. The general style—his need to arouse curiosity, perhaps to find some adventure and to provide the target of his exhibition with shock—probably accounts for a large share of the pleasure involved.

If the behavior can be accurately broken down into its components, our ability to help this person find better ways of communicating his needs will be greatly enhanced. We will begin to see why he might want to maintain such a strangely unfulfilling behavior.

10

The Jaws of Love

A fable.

Once upon a time there was a young man named Nubbin who was desperately in love with a beautiful woman named Sylvia. Nubbin approached her boldly. Sylvia shrugged. Nubbin tried flattery, pleading, and finally subterfuge. Sylvia tottered, but would not tumble.

As a last resort, Nubbin prayed. "Dear God, grant me the power to change how Sylvia behaves toward me, the ability—*some* men seem to have it—to make her be more like I wish her to be. I guess You know I want to make love to Sylvia more than anything in the world."

Nubbin's prayer was answered. Within a week he was able to control Sylvia's attitude and her actions toward him merely by *wanting* to. He wanted to make out, and they did. He wanted her to love him exclusively and forever, and that is just what she said she would do.

When he wished to be reassured of her love, she erupted with a flare of jealousy. Nubbin was forever grateful. (He had perhaps forgotten that, as a child, he could at will cause adults to react with instant consternation, love, anguish, embarrassment, or laughter.)

In the end, a certain sameness came to attend their goings and their comings. Nubbin, for all his power, could not keep Sylvia from acting in predictable—and therefore not very exciting—ways. He always knew ahead of time what it was he had willed her to do. At length he was reduced to praying once again: "Dear God, maybe that wasn't quite what I meant."

This fable, of course, lies close to everyday truth. We do indeed control others as if by magic. We get the results we wish for, often without asking overtly for them and sometimes even without taking responsibility for them. But there are three drawbacks.

First, the technique is like a trolley car: we get good mileage out of it but there is no way to steer it. Second, we often want things we don't permit ourselves to know about, and sometimes we even get those wishes fulfilled! Third, what if two people have mutually exclusive wishes?

This last drawback leads us to a sequel to our fable. What Nubbin did not know was that Sylvia had beseeched her own gods to grant her the power to control what *he* said and did. She needed to be loved for herself, not for her admittedly gorgeous body. She wished to imbue Nubbin with a fine taste for gourmet foods and a desire, on more homely evenings, to wash and dry dishes.

Her wish was granted, much as Nubbin's had been. Sylvia was overjoyed, and she made many wonderful plans for the future. Before long, however, a certain sameness became apparent and she began to realize that she was doing things that were not at all in line with her every unspoken desire. She finally confessed to a vague uneasiness about their idyllic life together.

What often happens in a "marriage," legal or otherwise, is that each partner unconsciously manipulates the other's behavior in some ways; they soon reach a stalemate, locked into an initially attractive maze of controls and responses. Each believes himself free but is unknowingly constrained by the other. Each is unexpectedly happy or annoyed and doesn't know just why. Each can move the other like a marionette, yet neither one is aware of the strings.

There are advantages, of course, or the situation wouldn't persist. For example, a husband can eat his cake and have it, too, by unconsciously wishing for his wife to start a fight so he can blame her for starting it. Sure enough, about an hour later she begins to complain. He continues to be friendly and cooperative, telling her interesting things about his day. "Remember Shirley?" he is saying. "You know, with the boobs? Now there's a gal who knows how to take care of herself. Saw her for lunch."

Then—as he told Shirley later—"right out of the blue, my wife comes over and whacks me with the flat of her hand. For no reason!" What else could the poor man do but stomp out of the house and, for consolation, telephone Shirley and invite himself over for a drink?

Another advantage of such subtle prompting is that one partner can control what appears to be the other's "spontaneous" behavior. A woman hopes that her man will fling his arms around her from pure joy—and he does. She never asks him to do this, since that would rob the act of its spontaneity, but in a dozen unconscious ways she lets him know that she is unhappy when he fails to.

Or she uses another common, ever so subtle arm-twisting device, "Have you ever been so in love before?" and he can't very well say anything but no. More and more, his motives stem from a sense of obligation, and so do hers. The two subtly adapt to each other.

Most couples do this in many areas of contact, and a certain loss of spontaneity is easily accepted and does not detract unduly from their happiness. But there are occasions when they adapt at the expense of their own integrity. They permit the other person's control, or sometimes seek it out, even though they bitterly resent it.

In a way here, too, each one gets what he wants from the other: a sense of abiding resentment which, for each of them, justifies keeping one foot outside of their relationship. The couple may even maintain a conscious aura of harmony while at the same time badgering each other ever so subtly, delicately rocking their static relationship.

Unmarried couples who are living together fall heir to the same problems, and under some circumstances the problems may be even more acute. A longtime, living-in relationship is similar to marriage today except for the lack of formal ties.

Insofar as it is freer than marriage, however, it is also a more difficult relationship to sustain. There are no fences, and either partner, when offended, can say to hell with it and take off. The joker here is that subtle constraints become more significant just because there are few formal controls. Lovers often make heavy use of their subtle, controlling skills to foster personal dependency. When one of them overuses such skills and treads on the integrity of his partner, he risks losing her.

A friendly affair is even freer than a "living-together" relationship and is therefore still more difficult to sustain, particularly if one or both partners are already married. There are no external bonds. In fact, if anything, there is some social pressure to split.

An exquisitely rich feeling of commitment is necessary if the affair is to survive its initial bloom. Here the sense of integrity of each individual is most important, for they have to live on the respect they have for each other. When respect for each other's integrity ceases, they stop listening to each other and the relationship begins to fall apart.

Divorcing Our Way Through Marriage

Divorce always happens day by day, in small increments. These "little divorcements" are too familiar to be noteworthy as they occur, but they solidify with each repetition, building up the load on the camel's back, straw by straw. The final straw, of course, could be any straw at all. The "key" disturbances are the little things that occur day after day; they erode the integrity of one or both partners.

A couple usually begins with a happy start and hopeful expectations. They initially enjoy common activities and tend to discover new areas of common interest. While courting, they test out each other's styles. They may discover similar styles of living and desire much sharing, or they may bring dissimilar styles and set up their marriage to draw enrichment from differences.

But they also control their styles in order to please each other, and this control eventually wears thin. A man who says pretty things to the woman he is courting because he is out for conquest may change his style once he has accomplished this goal. He may even come to express a lack of caring. He is then recognized as undemonstrative by the disappointed spouse.

Our styles are most easily seen in the activities that are truly important to us. Often, partners first see changes in each other when they begin to notice different attitudes concerning friends, money, and personal philosophy.

Style changes are typically perceived as dangerous, and they demand new solutions. "You go out with the boys Thursday nights and I'll see my friends during the day." "Here's *your* money, and I don't care what you do with it." "Vote like you want; just don't tell *me* what I ought to think!" In each case, one person reacts to style changes he senses in his partner, and these changes in turn demand that he commit himself with his own new demands.

Sex is the area in which differing styles are heavily tested. Husband and wife will most explicitly express their different life-styles in their sexual embrace, for better or for worse. Here they will make their silent agreements: "I am more concerned for your happiness than mine" or "I don't care what you do" or "You are only here to please me." The sexual act reveals our most personal attitudes about life in general and about the other sex in particular. Sexual talk may be deceptive; sexual actions tell the truth.

Another revealing area is child training. Here the new parents quickly learn about each other's social views. They reveal to each other their loving or hating styles, their harshness or ability to forgive, their sense of caring, responsibility, or self-concern, and their capacity to share love when immediate "rewards" are not forthcoming.

The elements of one's personal style are based on lasting attitudes, and they are so taken for granted by the person himself that he feels his integrity is constrained when he gets slapped down for them. The man who constantly teases his children and then finds good reason to punish them harshly for *their* flippancy will feel his own existence threatened when he is criticized for his belief in "honest discipline."

When a husband or wife attempts to change the other or censor his stylistic behavior, he meets instant resistance. The "victim" may be forced to confront the question of whether the relationship is as valuable as his own sense of integrity. Actually, this test of *relationship* vs. *integrity* is a necessary function and is repeated every day in one form or another.

Such daily testing can help the marriage to become a lasting experience (when people make a decision *for* the relationship), or it can lead to a highway with separate lanes. And of course it may also be instrumental in breaking a relationship apart. Testing is not a means of asking for a divorce. It is the way we discover where we are going. Eventually, it becomes a reliable compass, whether our course runs toward greater intimacy or in the direction of dissolution.

When a husband says, "Sorry, darling, but tonight I am going out with the boys," he does not mean to ask for a divorce; yet he may be quite aware that his wife will be dreadfully upset. He is testing her to see how much *she* values their marriage. Is she willing to recognize his freedom, his integrity, for the sake of maintaining the relationship? He may very well be less interested in going out with the boys than in testing how far his wife will go to express her commitment to him.

Little divorcements are "failed" tests; they involve testing episodes that end up with someone's integrity getting crushed. This simply means that one partner has failed a love test; he has given a lower priority to the relationship than to his own demands. The woman tells her husband she will not accept his going out with the boys; she *thinks* she is telling him she values their relationship.

Actually, she is telling him that the relationship is less important than living out her own style in her own way. She does not accept his freedom, and by denying it she taxes the relationship. His question will have to be whether the price is too high.

Little divorcements may be behaviors and messages based on thoughtful or frivolous demands, but they always question the relationship. In this sense, divorce is a richly cooperative process between the partners. They are not merely fighting each other; they are both fighting for their own freedom and at the same time are trying to preserve their relationship at a reasonable price.

Sometimes a couple agrees that one party alone is to blame, but the chances are that such agreement rests on false premises. A man named Stephen enjoys a very satisfying family life, he tells us, but his wife feels hopeless much of the time and regularly manipulates him into bitter arguments. She wants out of the marriage, but she cannot really say why.

"Sometimes I ask her what I can do for her," Stephen says, "but she always replies, 'Nothing. You're a very responsible husband and we have two wonderful children and a lovely house. It's just that I don't know what my life is all about and I am to blame, but I want to get out.' " Both apparently agree that she is the one who wants to break up the marriage.

A series of inquiries reveals that while Stephen has been struggling to keep alive the picture of a "good family life," he is more involved in the breakup than he lets on. His wife does consider him a "responsible provider," but when she lets her hair down she admits that she resents the fact that he is seldom home.

She does believe she has two wonderful children—girls aged fourteen and sixteen—but she is deeply concerned because they avoid her and clearly prefer the company of her husband. She loves her house, but it is large and cluttered and she needs help, which her husband does not provide. She never has experienced much sexual pleasure with her husband, and she feels that he closes his ears whenever she tries to tell him this.

So while she publicly accepts blame for breaking up her marriage, she is actually suffering from isolation. Through hundreds of little divorcements, she has found that her sense of integrity has been badly bruised and the relationship is no longer worth the price. Her style favors withdrawal, not protest.

Her husband is not an idle bystander in this split. Apparently he has won his battle for freedom, only to lose his home. His testing has backfired—with her full cooperation. She accepts the blame—saying, however, "Take your freedom, but I'm leaving since I wasn't included in the first place."

The story shows that divorcements and failed tests do not always involve hassles or angry exchanges. People can test each other subtly by means of withdrawal or passive resistance as well as by violence. In either case, they are saying the relationship does not permit them to experience a wholesome way of being.

Sometimes such testing is so subtle that it seems hardly noticeable to an outsider. A husband will repeatedly show his inattention in the middle of a conversation. A wife will be so busy talking that no conversation can take place. A husband will insist that he is needed at his workbench whenever the house begins to quiet down. One wife broke into tears every time her husband brought up a problem, and after a while he felt so bad about this that he stopped talking to her altogether.

Any two people who have been living together for more than a few months know very well how to please or antagonize each other. They also learn quickly the limits of each other's tolerance, which is to say they learn to test the other person for what sacrifices he is willing to make. For one couple, the critical test may include the man's "temper," which gives him an "alibi" for hitting his wife; for another, it may be the wife's sense of spontaneity, which permits her to throw a Chinese vase at him.

Instant testing also occurs when one partner manhandles the children or spends money erratically in the face of mounting debts. By such a critical test, a partner hopes to get reassurance that he is still loved in spite of it all, but he also risks discovering that the relationship is too shaky to salvage.

A woman enters therapy because, she says, "I really want to save my marriage." A repeating pattern in her marriage proves to be what she calls her husband's gambling behavior. Whenever he goes gambling, he loses a lot of money and cannot then provide for her. She says she threatened to leave him and once moved out of the house when he stayed away gambling for two nights. Now he has been away for three nights running.

She wants to save her marriage but she is no longer willing to tolerate the obstacles her husband sets up in his bid for "freedom." She says that if she were to accept these obstacles it would not be good for her or for her husband. In order to save her marriage, she resorts to a highly effective unexpected response—she files for divorce.

Actually, this action jolts her husband out of gambling and he is able to give it up. He now knows he must change his style if he is to save his marriage. The implications of this testing behavior are that the husband in this case has to *lose* the test for "freedom" in order to gain the relationship. He has to experience total rejection before he can feel he is really wanted.

No-fault Divorce

Divorce is becoming so common in the United States that it begins to rival marriage as the thing to do to attain, or perhaps to regain, happiness. The divorce rate continued to rise in 1974 while the marriage rate dropped for the first time in sixteen years, according to the National Center for Health Statistics.

There were forty-four divorces for every hundred marriages throughout the nation, sixty-six divorces for every hundred marriages in California, and 102 divorces for every hundred marriages in Marin County, at the north end of the Golden Gate Bridge. One sixth of all divorces involve marriages of at least twenty-five years' duration. And with increasing frequency, the subject of divorce is first brought up by the woman rather than the man.

Traditionally, our society has viewed divorce as something intrinsically negative and has assumed that the principals are most likely to be a victim and an aggressor or, in earlier times, an innocent and a cad. These two assumptions are not very often true, but their general acceptance has made the experience of splitting more destructive than necessary for hundreds of thousands of couples. They need to be reassessed in terms of what each partner communicates when he talks about divorce.

Divorce is almost always a cooperative venture. "Causes" such as boredom, alcoholism, and even physical aggression are themselves also cooperative ventures. Nobody can keep up aggression in a marriage without the cooperation of a mate who gets something out of being a victim.

Likewise, the daily testing for love and freedom (that sometimes becomes a divorcement warning leading to a permanent split) cannot continue if either of them listens carefully and chooses to confront the issue directly or to accept whatever the mate defines as his "freedom."

Splitting partners do not often realize they are cooperating, and one of them may bitterly contest the divorce action. This is often due to one of three common causes: the contesting party has misread the warning test and wants another chance to get his style accepted after all; or he is shocked out of his style and now wants to prove he can change; or he wants simply to antagonize his mate by making trouble.

When the responsibility for a breakup is laid on one partner alone, a complex problem is reduced to a simplistic question, circumventing the truth. The dissolution of a relationship usually stems from distorted communications; a test has been "failed" too often and at least one of the partners feels his integrity is endangered.

A sense of integrity is the basis for self-respect. If a husband associates integrity with the freedom to come and go as he pleases, he will lose his self-respect when he feels obligated to stay home.

This sense develops as a child grows from total dependence on others to relative independence. Most families expect the child to do more and more things for himself as he matures. He will have to learn to walk without a supporting hand, eat with his own spoon, tie his shoelaces, spend time alone entertaining himself, and get up in the morning by himself to go to school.

The child likes to remain dependent, but he also likes to become an independent person in his own right. Every child matures in his own way; some are held back by overprotecting parents while others may be thrust out on their own resources before they are able to handle independence. But once the child has learned a skill he is proud of, he will probably resent anyone who now takes it away from him. His integrity is threatened because he is forced into a dependency he no longer needs.

A boy may feel that his integrity is symbolized by his ability to withstand parental demands and keep his room in total disarray, but he can easily switch symbols and focus on smoking pot or going out with the "wrong" girl. A general rule is that the less ready an individual is to accept responsibility, the more exaggerated are the behaviors that signify integrity to him.

When a couple contemplates divorce, they usually declare a moratorium on further testing for integrity, and under certain circumstances this makes it possible to consider divorce as an act of constructive change. The problem, after all, is not the divorce. The problem is the long and increasingly painful history of a relationship that has backed itself into a corner.

Divorce is a solution that permits the partners to disengage from their habitual clashes and inspect their own styles. Now that separation is on the horizon, it is possible to consider changes just because the partners are no longer engaged. Some couples become better friends after a divorce, and some learn from their divorce just where they themselves have failed. Some couples learn enough from talking bluntly about the option of divorce that they don't even have to go through with it.

Talking about divorce, or even fighting about it, can serve as a powerful unexpected response. It can open uncomfortable questions that have long been in need of clarification and confrontation. Or it can reopen touchy issues that have been carefully put away in mothballs. When day-to-day adaptation has failed, talking about the option of divorce can be a step toward listening for what is really going on in the relationship.

A good fight can open new options if it serves to make each partner aware of his own contribution to the alienation. Both partners can become alerted to choices that they never considered before. They can say things they have wanted to say for a long while but never quite dared to.

Festering resentments are lanced. Blocked areas are opened up and fresh perspectives are inevitably stumbled upon. There is now a fair chance that they may learn to live together with a mature sense of freedom which is founded on mutual respect.

The End of an Affair

Separation is often painful, but the way in which it is approached can make the difference between a bitter experience and a constructive one. Two people who are about to break apart may feel they have very little choice as to the nature of their separation. They do have options, however, provided they want to listen.

We are talking about separations of all kinds—the breakup of a promising romance, the dissolution of an intimate living arrangement, a trial separation of partners, whether married or not, and the legal divorce of a married couple.

We shall describe the breakup of a relatively uncomplicated affair in order to illustrate several things: locating the hidden cause of discord, changing a partner's habitual controlling behavior, and making constructive use of separation.

A young divorcée, Marion, values strong friendships but values her freedom more. She has found what she considers to be, under the circumstances, an ideal lover—a passionate artist who is loving, thoughtful, forgiving, and only free to see her once or twice a week, plus an occasional weekend. His name is Jon.

A year later, Marion is feeling vaguely uncomfortable, and it worries her because she can see no reason for this. Finally, she says, "You're calling me more than you used to, Jon, and it makes me feel restricted." She is afraid he will be offended, but he says, "I'm sorry, because the last thing I want you to feel is any kind of obligation toward me."

This makes Marion feel better, but within a month she catches herself making impatient little sighs every time Jon telephones. She likes him very much. She thinks she still loves him. But it seems to her that he is *after* her all the time. She tells him carefully, "Jon, sometimes you make me feel as if you own me or something. On the other hand, when you don't call for three or four days, then it's a real delight to hear from you."

Jon takes this to mean she is delighted to hear from him, and he calls her even more often. She tells him again, but he hears only what he wishes to hear. She says, "Jon, damn it, leave me alone for a while."

Jon promises to wait until *she* calls *him,* but he telephones again that same evening, saying, "I was out for a while and I thought maybe you'd tried to reach me." Marion is furious, but when Jon asks why, she can find no really good reason. She then begins to listen, really listen—not only to the flavor of his invitations and suggestions and arguments, but to her own reaction to them.

She discovers that she feels particularly uncomfortable at precisely the times when he is most kind and thoughtful. One day it dawns on her that she herself has defined "generosity" and "kindness" as demands. She remembers her home and thinks of the iron fist of kindness that her mother often used to coerce her.

On the one hand, Marion consciously admires people who are considerate, loving, and forgiving. On the other hand, she realizes that she herself permits these behaviors to enslave her. When her friend is kind to her, she feels she should be grateful for his very presence; she cannot possibly be angry with him, even though she does not really want to do what he asks of her. She realizes she is like the woman who has to fall into bed with every man who says a kind word to her, and now she thinks a change is in order.

So Marion tries to disengage from Jon's "kindly," smothering control. Whenever he lavishes love or praise or consideration upon her, she refuses to respond in her usually grateful manner. When he tells her how much he respects her taste in men, she says she has just had an exciting dinner with an old friend.

"That's nice," he replies, "but you don't need to apologize. After all, you're a free agent." She adds, "His kisses haven't changed a bit." Jon says tersely, "And what else is like old times?" She says that is a personal matter, and he calls her a bitch.

Marion is delighted. She is breaking out of her automatic program and she can see a new pattern emerging. So now she delivers a new, unexpected response every time he brings the pressure of kindness to bear on her in the old way. She is no longer apologetic. She resorts to a great many noes and insists on making suggestions of her own rather than following his plans all the time.

She is in effect trying on a new style with him. The next time she feels annoyed, she says so directly. Jon replies sweetly, saying he understands exactly what she means. She says, "Jon, you're a shit!" He is very nice and he pretends he hasn't heard her remark. She repeats it, adding that she doesn't want to see him anymore until she is ready and calls him.

This barrage of unpredicted behavior hits Jon very hard. He appears grief-stricken. After five weeks without seeing each other, she calls him and he takes her out to lunch. As it so happens, their new relationship is a discovery for both of them. She has clearly changed, as she is now more in charge of the relationship than she had been before; she no longer responds helplessly to his kindly button-pushing.

But he has changed as well. Because of the split, he has looked not only at his own intent (being a "kind" and "considerate" person) but also at what his behavior is getting him. This in effect makes him a more genuine, less syrupy person.

The two finally break off, because they cannot quite overcome their painful history together, but they have both grown through their separation and are ready now for a more mature commitment.

Scene from a Marriage

The second major option immediately available to any couple contemplating divorce is to make some changes and continue in the relationship.

The repeated little divorcements that build toward a major break are not just passing errors or character flaws. They are freedom and love tests anchored in the general style of both parties and reflected in many different facets of the relationship. These tests change for the better as the security of the partners increases, but this requires skill, patience, and a reasonable capacity for disengagement.

All of these considerations are visible in the following case history—a marriage that has survived so far because of a number of sturdy compromises. But now that the last of four children is off to college, the compromises are no longer effective and the relationship is beginning to deteriorate.

The wife, Ann, has tried many little "stabs in the dark," as she calls them, hoping to improve the relationship, but to no avail. Her husband, Robert, she says, is very uncommunicative, never talks to her, and only pretends to listen. At dinner he lets her talk about her daily problems, but his typical response is an occasional nod. She feels totally isolated and she suspects she is being manipulated into separation. She is desperate.

Encouraged to think about how she might be contributing to the situation, Ann admits that she talks too much and that she usually rejects her husband's occasional sexual advances because of her anger. When asked if she wants to make the effort involved in trying to save the marriage, she thinks for a long while and then says, "Yes, for I guess I really haven't much to lose."

A discussion of her resources for changing her style in their relationship makes it obvious that she will have to work hard and face much adversity. She anticipates that her husband will resist any change, and when she faces the question of their sexual life she is extremely reluctant to approach him. "Why should I give myself to a man for whom I only exist as a sexual object? And why do I have to do all the dirty work?"

The answer is that she doesn't *have* to; she has already chosen of her own free will to make this effort. She then asks herself, "Do I really want him to talk more than he does? Now that I have to be very honest with myself, isn't there some advantage to shutting him up?"

When she asks the question in this way, a number of events from her distant past suddenly come to mind. At one time, for example, her husband had talked a lot; in fact they had been close to what she termed "an ugly divorce," and almost every statement made by either of them had led to a painful clash. She now admits that the two of them might have made a silent agreement at that time to avoid discussions that would end up in wild accusations. The marriage was thus enabled to survive for eighteen years.

Ann makes a list of all the things she thinks she will have to do and is overwhelmed by the fear that she can't handle them. She begs her therapist for answers that she can only unearth for herself. She is certain that the whole effort will fail. But in the end she sticks with her decision to demonstrate that she cares, sexually and otherwise, however formidable the task might be.

Her moment of truth comes one evening when her husband arrives home at the usual time. After his customary half-hour rest he comes to the dinner table prepared for his wife's usual complaints. However, he is met with an unexpected response: no complaints are forthcoming. Ann speaks little, and then only about things such as the butterflies she has seen in the garden.

Robert becomes restless, and after ten minutes he places his fork on his plate and says, "Aren't you feeling well?" She replies that she feels fine. He endures her good nature for a short while, but then he puts his fork carefully on the table, places both hands on the arms of his chair and announces, "This sort of supper makes me sick. Don't we get anything in this house but chicken and pot roast? There must be fourteen hundred different dishes you can invent, but always you cook the same thing."

Ann knows he is pleading with her to return to the routine that has served them for so long. She smiles and says, "Robert, I do want to please you with a fine dinner. Perhaps I should give it more loving attention." Her attempt is not quite genuine, and it nearly backfires. Robert is infuriated. "Loving attention!" he yells. "I do my job and give it loving attention. Why shouldn't you give your job loving attention? This whole conversation is disgusting."

Ann suddenly sees her husband as a small, angry child responding predictably as she pushes the button that triggers his tantrums. She says, "What I meant was, I'll try to make better meals, and I would enjoy varying the menu also."

On the following evening Robert acts as if nothing has happened, and he is annoyed when she is again friendly and quiet. Only on the third night does she feel confident enough to take a gentle initiative in bed. She tells herself she is not comfortable in the to her "unnatural" role of a desirous, available female, but once she has committed herself she feels as if a great weight has been lifted from her shoulders.

She has dared to experiment, and it excites her. Her timing must have been excellent as well, for she later reports that she now knows her husband needs her and that she herself has experienced pleasure.

The two of them talk together regularly after this, fight occasionally, and soon agree that they are actually beginning to like each other. The style change has paid off, although it is only a beginning. The eternal test of motivation is time. In this case, the couple is able, in time, to establish new ways of living together although it apparently is not as easy as the record may imply.

There are always times of crisis when we fall back into our old molds, but if there has been a strong new foundation of good will, such crises tend to strengthen the relationship.

The kind of change required to make a disturbed marriage rewarding again is of course neither simple nor unilateral. There is not one big issue to be repaired, but a large number of little divorcements, some of which appear trivial to anyone outside of the family. Here is an instance of how one such "trivial" freedom test was worked out. It is one of a number of divorcements that characterize this particular marriage.

The wife has a problem that disturbs her greatly, she says, and she describes it in these few words: "My husband is always late for dinner. That's all there is to it."

After being encouraged to identify specific actions in which the objectionable pattern might be anchored, she describes the problem somewhat differently. "At 5:10 P.M., I am in the kitchen working on a quick dinner. At five fifteen, my husband brings me a mint julep and a scotch for himself and we take ten minutes out for drinking. There is a good feeling between us, even though I typically refuse a second drink. Then, just about every day, I say to my husband, 'Rather than having that second drink alone, why don't you stay here with me and give me a hand.' However, he leaves and I have some angry thoughts about woman's lot and all that stuff.

"Then comes six o'clock. Everything is hot and ready and I call, 'Come and get it!' Five minutes later I yell, 'Come and get it. The hell with your drinking!' Five minutes after that I go into the living room in a fury and tell him to come to the table or *I'm leaving!*

"He comes. For the first five minutes we don't talk, but then he is sweet and acts as if nothing has happened. We eat, and he actually helps me with the dishes. Every day. That is our *daily* routine."

The woman has described the entire series of tests that holds the "daily routine" in place. She realizes immediately that she has to focus on more than the "simple" target (curing a case of tardiness); she has to consider the entire pattern if she is to make adequate changes.

Her most difficult task is admitting the ways in which she herself might be contributing to the problem. Do any of her husband's objectionable responses follow directly from something she herself does? Is she manipulating him in some manner?

She notices that neither her first nor her second request to "come and get it" ever works. Her own behavior is the same every time and it is always followed by a ten-minute delay in getting her husband to the table.

It becomes obvious to her that the parts of this exchange that are satisfactory to her include not only the good feeling she establishes with her husband before dinner but also the opportunity his tardiness affords her to complain about woman's lot. She realizes this complexity when she is asked how she would feel if her husband in fact came in and helped her cook. She is firm in her answer: "Dishwashing yes, but cooking is not for my husband." In other words, she does not really want him to come and help her, even though she has asked him to do just that. She wants to complain to him (and to herself) about her lack of freedom.

She now has to decide whether a change will really make things better. She knows she does not want him to help her cook; but is she really willing for him to give up being consistently late for dinner? Her first reaction is, "My God, yes!" On second thought, she wonders if he will continue to bring her a drink and sit with her in the kitchen every evening if their fight pattern is broken up.

She also realizes that her threatening to leave him is somewhat rewarding. It gives her the feeling that she is a free agent and not overdependent. Also, his coming to dinner despite this magic threat reassures her that he doesn't want to leave her.

She now has several choices. She can make a small change in their pattern, minimizing the risk but accepting some compromise. Or she can risk real uncertainty in the relationship by giving him an ultimatum and following through with it. Or, of course, she can decide to leave things as they are for fear the risks involved are not warranted.

What she in fact does is so simple that her friends wonder why she hadn't tried it years earlier. She starts calling him to dinner ten minutes before it is ready. She still yells at him and she still threatens to leave, but the meal doesn't get cold. Her husband is aware of the ruse, and it amuses him. He comes to the table in good spirits, and dinners no longer begin with a fuming five minutes of silence.

This is a new compromise and a distinct improvement in terms of how both of them feel about that unique hour of the day. On the face of it, the problem appears trivial and so does the solution. In actuality, the overt exchange every evening between this husband and wife serves as a ritual that provides important satisfactions and dissatisfactions for each of them. The change keeps the satisfactions alive but reduces the dissatisfactions by making a game out of it.

A New Lease

Obviously, confronting our own contribution to a serious misunderstanding can clear the emotional landscape. This disengagement in turn enables us to make changes—either changes that can improve a frustrating relationship or, if the road seems to be too long and our integrity is too deeply involved, changes that will establish clearly the need for separation.

In either case, the all too familiar pattern of a long-term relationship is opened for reassessment. Even if we should choose to separate, the *process* of investigating our own behavior will give us guidelines for the future.

There is no ideal style of living, for we have to deal with many different internal and external pressures. The discordant compromises and unvoiced pressures that disturbed Nubbin and Sylvia will always be with us, and our unaware communications will often prove to be incompatible with our declared intentions. So we cannot hope for a "perfect" style. But we can understand the process of changing and we can appreciate how dependent this process is upon the delivery of accurate information to ourselves—especially in those areas where we experience failure in our relationships with others.

Changing our style is like an operation. There is a time of searching for the source of the pain; there is a time of risk and danger, and then there is a time for healing. Listening for the consequences of our behavior is the key to discovering the source of the pain. Delivering unexpected responses and committing ourselves to an unfamiliar option inevitably involves risk. Allowing time and space to consolidate new options is the time of healing.

The risky part of changing our style comes when we first try out some new behavior. No one is comfortable with uncertainty, and a new way of acting always seems unnatural. So we need the space and time to recuperate, to heal. The new behavior now has to become "natural." Once this occurs, the relationship is on a new footing.

Is it possible to have a dynamic, growing relationship that is free of problems? Of course not. Problems of dependency, of freedom, and of style are part of the substance of emotional relationships. Furthermore, there are no clear solutions for any but the most trivial of problems. The problems that attend a marriage or other committed relationship are not only highly complex, they are constantly changing. They cannot be finally resolved. They have to be kept open. They have to be solved and resolved, confronted again and again.

If we are involved in an intimate relationship that is growing, we can expect to be repeatedly surprised—our predictions thwarted, our complacency jolted, our assumptions sometimes turned upside down. That's the nature of learning, changing, and exploring new ways.

11

The Trans Parent Child

Whenever two people attempt to direct each other's behavior, problems burst into bloom. When the two people are husband and wife, and children are added, interpersonal problems continue but take on a new dimension.

When we listen to an individual's behavior within the family, we may be learning a great deal about the role—the black sheep of the family, for example—and almost nothing about the person. To listen for what a child is "silently" saying about his own personal needs, therefore, we have to be familiar with the specific emotional setting in which the family operates.

This setting is partly determined by the culture—and, in heterogeneous societies such as our own, by the subculture as well. And it is partly determined by the peculiarities of the specific family. The setting includes family expectations, role assignments, and coalitions. It transmits a vast amount of information to the child and it greatly influences the form of his personal communications.

In the human species, the child at birth is about one twentieth the bulk of the adult and cannot survive on its own. This biological fact requires that the child be taken care of and that he be trained in behaviors that will help him survive physically and psychologically. Because of this initial helplessness, he makes a great many demands on his parents.

As the child grows up, he needs less and less care and becomes increasingly more independent of those who are raising him. In order to realize his own potential, he must progressively "divorce" himself from his original family. The most frequent problems that confront parents have to do with the difficulty of accepting this simple course of events.

Within any given society, the role of "child" is well defined. In one culture a child is first of all a burden—one more mouth to feed. In another, the male child is appreciated as a prospective worker while the female child is a handicap and sometimes, in an early form of population control, she is killed. In other societies, it is the girl child who is adored.

In our own culture, the role of "child" varies in a general way according to heritage, social status, and geography (Southern or Midwestern, rural or urban). In the middle and upper middle classes, the birth of a child is commonly a joyful occasion. Friends are notified, and the parents even brag about such incidentals as the baby's weight. Birth adds to the family's prestige and the parents do not count on any financial return for the large investment they are making in their child.

Furthermore, the child is expected to remain a dependent far beyond the age of sexual maturity. He is in effect trained to accept that even when he is sexually mature and at his prime in body strength and intellectual capacity, he will not yet be judged ready to take care of himself.

Before the dawn of what we choose to call civilization, a seventeen-year-old human being would never have been able to comprehend such a state of affairs. He or she would have been already far beyond the age of initiation into manhood or womanhood. But in our society today a seventeen-year-old is given so much protection and so many guidelines and restrictions that he has great difficulty developing his own identity and establishing his independence.

The obvious ground on which to assert his integrity and work out his own compromises is his own home. Here he sharpens his teeth, and he may put great effort into resisting the "overcare" lavished upon him. Strong adolescents rebel, forsaking the comforts of being a "dependent" and claiming the right to make their own mistakes. Others stay with the discordance by remaining dependent while still doing their "own thing" on the side. Some suffer for a lifetime because they cannot find a sound compromise, a role to fit their varied and conflicting needs.

Prolonged childhood, traditionally accompanied by lengthy training, seems to be of some advantage in a growing society that believes dissatisfaction to be the seed of ambition and upward mobility to be its goal. But when there is rapid change in such a society, the children may be *mis*trained; they may be carefully prepared for a society that no longer exists, even though it was once familiar to their parents.

Family patterns, marriage customs, professional ambitions, the uses of leisure, the place of children and the elderly—all can change drastically in one short generation. Belatedly, we reevaluate and change our ideas about the number of children we want, the kind of success we're looking for, how we want to run our lives emotionally and sexually.

A child finally completes his training, only to find the goals he has been training for are being seriously questioned by everyone and may prove to be already obsolete. The role a child is trained for in a rapidly changing culture may leave him badly confused and even psychologically crippled. The more his dependent training period has been prolonged, the more out of step he is likely to be.

Trans Parent: Listening to Our Children

We have discussed the art of listening to another adult. There are some essential differences in the art of listening to a child. The child uses body language more freely. When he feels warm about another person, he comes close; when he feels on edge, he backs off. His posture, facial expressions, and gestures are generally less inhibited than those of an adult, and they give us more accurate information concerning his moods and how comfortable he feels. He has not yet learned to hide his emotions or control his expression of them.

Children also "read" the feelings of others with greater sensitivity than do adults. They are keenly aware of subtle bodily cues and they retain many of the infant's remarkable preverbal skills. They are still tuned in to the messages conveyed through the tone of voice, posture, involuntary gestures, and unaware facial expressions of adults who are important to them. They can see through their parents with unsettling directness and they—unlike adults—are very hard to fool for any length of time.

The adult's problem is simply that he knows too much. He knows how people usually act in familiar situations and he thinks he no longer has to listen very carefully. He understands that people can express one thing yet feel quite differently, so he has learned to discount much of the information that does come his way. The child, on the other hand, experiences directly the consequences of his own misreading and therefore gets constant training in reading the subtle expressions of others correctly.

An adult usually assumes that a child, like himself, maintains one consistent style throughout a wide variety of circumstances. He misinterprets the child's sudden switches of style, since he does not realize that the child is still in the process of developing a style and is still experimenting.

The child has not yet worked out his own techniques for coping with his world. Any change in his home or in the people he is with regularly constitutes a direct threat to his security. And to him, security means survival.

Another problem we adults face when listening to children is that we have preconceived notions of what a *child* is. Many parents have a weakness for children of a particular age and tend to treat their own children as if they belonged to this age group even when they are younger or older. They may use baby talk with a four-year-old, or they may expect a two-year-old to remember all his promises.

A child will feel accepted if his real age and real capabilities are respected; otherwise, his development may be retarded or, conversely, he may feel constantly driven by demands he cannot possibly meet. What we hear when we listen is grossly affected by what we expect to hear, particularly if we imagine that we know precisely how children should behave.

When it comes to controlling or guiding or otherwise changing a child's behavior (as opposed to merely listening well), the adult has an obvious advantage. But much of our educational impact on our children comes about by unintended and very subtle influences: the values implicit in our actions, the quality of our daily life, the nature of our relationships with those we love, and our unspoken attitude toward children.

When we try consciously to guide a child, we are far less subtle about it. We typically think of two modes of control: approval and disapproval. There are many other modes—understanding, kindness, concern, simple acknowledgment, encouragement, or sarcasm, anger, hate, destructiveness, for example—but straight, unadorned approval and disapproval are what we usually resort to.

Approval and Disapproval

Some families make overt use of the fact that approval can motivate a change in behavior, by setting up "point" programs whereby they schedule approval for the accomplishment of certain tasks. There is serious doubt, however, that approval alone does the trick.

Within the formal setting of behavior modification, for example, parents are instructed not to use any other mode of control. Their total interaction with the child changes; they are encouraged to look at his accomplishment rather than at his failures. On the other hand, the parents are forced to express nothing but approval, thereby denying themselves the accustomed privilege of saying whatever they feel when they feel it.

Approval communicates to most of us a feeling of friendly support, but the moment we sense that the approval is scheduled, we become suspicious. If we suspect that the other person wants something from us in return, we feel manipulated. We recognize that approval is being used, without our knowledge, as a means for controlling our behavior. If a child picks up this kind of message, the parents' entire program is likely to backfire.

When approval is spontaneous, however, the child is usually affected in two ways. First, he feels good, he probably gains confidence in what he is doing, and he may even become enthusiastic and want to excel in the area that draws approval. Second, he learns another reliable way of pleasing adults. Both experiences are very much to his advantage.

Disapproval, or punishment, as a means of educating the child is a popular tool because it seems to work well. When a child is punished, however, two things occur: the child temporarily lets go of the undesirable behavior, and the child learns what sort of behavior can be counted on to draw adults into an emotional relationship with him. In this sense, punishment is a double message.

The way punishment is perceived is directly connected to the general relationship between parent and child. If the parent often gives approval and maintains a warm relationship but shows his disapproval occasionally, the child won't have to make a bid for punishment in order to establish a relationship.

If, on the other hand, punishment is the only major relationship the parent offers, the child may come to rely on the knowledge that a certain undesirable behavior triggers an intense emotional relationship with his father or mother. He is likely to use this information whenever he feels a need to relate with the parent, even though he knows this involves pain.

If the punishment is too severe, the emotional cost of this particular engagement becomes too great. The child then will, without being aware of it, try some other, equally upsetting behavior, but he will choose this behavior in such a manner that he cannot be directly held responsible for it. He may have accidents; he may become ill. He may become incompetent in talking, in schoolwork, in sports, in mechanical skills—or in any endeavor his parents believe to be of value.

One of the most common mistakes a punishing adult makes is to administer the punishment but continue to carry a grudge afterward. The message the child gets is that he is being punished more than once for a single misdeed.

Generally speaking, punishment is either physical or psychological. Physical punishment (if not excessive) is usually immediate, and the adult, having acted out his anger, can forget the grudge. Psychological punishment always involves a delay. It is often expressed by persistent anger, by indifference, by threat of future hurt, or by an unemotional administration of discipline.

Each of these expressions communicates a different message. Anger is a mood unconsciously designed to intimidate the child, and unless it is followed immediately by physical punishment, it implants the threat of delayed punishment of some unpredictable kind.

When a child is punished with indifference, the adult overlooks the offense and avoids a confrontation. Parents and policemen play a similar role in that both have to judge whether an offense warrants attention. Policemen observe many minor offenses which they choose to ignore. Parents have an additional burden in that, once an offense is judged punishable, they have to choose a "fitting" punishment and execute it.

A parent plays a triple role—legislator, policeman, and jailer. When he overlooks too many offenses, the child gets the message that he, the child, is in charge; the parent will then have a very unruly child on his hands. If the parent plays the role of legislator and policeman but fails to administer the punishment after threatening it, he is telling the child that he disapproves of the behavior but that his bark is worse than his bite.

On the other hand, if the parent punishes every offense he notices, he helps create a climate wherein the child is likely to learn to either submit totally or rebel. This is particularly true in families where the offense is judged and the punishment executed without any further participation of the child, that is, where the parent makes no attempt to understand what really happened. When a child comes home late and misses his dinner he may have committed an "offense," but he may also have been a victim of circumstances beyond his control.

When the parent uses a threat of future punishment ("You cannot go to the birthday party unless . . ."), he delays *immediate* punishment and tells the child that both of them must now live with the burden of *impending* punishment. The parent should consider ahead of time whether he really wants to execute the punishment. If his threat is not really serious, he leaves himself open to the bark-is-worse-than-bite dilemma.

If he regularly does carry out threats of withdrawing a social privilege, then he communicates to the child that social activities are not a right but have to be earned by good behavior. While there is nothing wrong with such a message when it is used occasionally, the repeated use of such real threats may train the child to give up social activities altogether. This often happens and the child becomes a loner.

Threats—whether executed or not—are essentially devices for maintaining anxiety. The threatened child is forced to expect an impending disaster, and he comes to associate the offense with the anxiety that follows it. The parents hope he will worry about dire consequences *before* he commits the offense, but it doesn't seem to happen this way very often. And anxiety *after* the offense, if it represents the dominant parental punishment, is likely to make the child extremely sensitive to fears of impending disaster.

The unemotional administration of punishment tells the child that his parents have decided to hurt him but don't want to feel personally responsible for it. They blame their sad duty ("This hurts me more than it hurts you") on rules and regulations that presumably give them little choice in the matter.

The good intention is to teach the child about fair, impersonal laws, but the parent forgets he is three people in one—the legislator who makes the laws, the judge who determines whether the accused is guilty, and the person who executes the sentence. This does not sound like a good setting in which to teach the majesty of the law. In fact, since the parent often acts as if he himself had no say, the administration of "uninvolved" punishment is likely to teach more about hypocrisy than about justice.

Punishment does of course have a place in the raising of children, despite the dangers inherent in its misuse. In most homes there is a single dominant style of punishment and there is enough positive support so that punishment does not represent the only or the major relationship with the parents. Also, most parents are reasonably forgiving and a child can discount occasional injustices.

All parents should make certain that their children are clearly aware of what constitutes an offense and what punishment is likely to follow. It is meaningless to caution a child to be, in some general way, "good." He needs to know, before he acts, what kinds of behavior are going to be prosecuted and what the penalty is likely to be.

Rules, Requests, and Suggestions

Among families we have worked with, those who seem to have the least trouble make use of a simple system for applying rules, requests, and suggestions.

A young child needs more *rules* than the child of ten, and a young adult has no need at all for such rules as "don't steal" since he knows by now the "rules" of society. Home rules such as "dinner at 6 P.M." are necessarily spelled out.

When rules are broken, there should be clear consequences which the child is aware of ahead of time. Punishment is best administered only after inquiry and proper participation of the child. The adult listens, but then goes by the best evidence available to him. Rules can be renegotiated as the child grows older (bedtime, for example).

Rules are not much good unless they can be enforced. Unenforceable rules like "don't smoke on the way home from school" can only lead to confusion and entice the child to test how far he can go without getting caught. When events occur that are not covered by the "home" rules but that other members of the family find highly objectionable (Johnny brings home friends who clean out the refrigerator), parents might do well to discover what responsibility the child carried for the event and whether it is likely to occur again. If there is willful damage, corrective measures should include restitution rather than punishment.

Requests differ from rules in that they are specifically negotiated. In a given home, a rule may state that the child has to be in bed by nine o'clock on school nights. A request would be that the child get good marks in school or that he keep his shoes polished. A request, by this definition, is always a give-and-take proposition.

The parent makes a request and in this manner communicates that he himself will offer a child some reward for fulfilling the desired request. Inherent in this negotiation is acceptance of the possibility that the child may not want to comply.

Rules must be clearly distinguished from requests. Much havoc arises in families where a parent makes a request but refuses to honor the child's decision if it is negative. Such a parent typically proclaims that the "request" was really a rule all along, and this ex post facto shift of definitions violates the child's rights.

The mildest form of influencing another person's conduct is *suggestion*. Suggestions are communications of simple statements, opinions, or wishes that have no power. They do not "have" to be followed, as rules do, and there is no give-and-take element involved. A parent suggests to a child that he stop scratching himself; he will not offer a bribe to the child, nor will he be upset when the child does not follow the suggestion. A suggestion by definition leaves the decision totally up to the other person.

When there is great confusion as to the nature of a parent's wish, or when the nature of a "suggestion" or "request" changes so that dire consequences are suddenly attached to it, the child is literally trained to become a disciplinary problem.

He can no longer predict the consequences of his behavior, so punishment, from his point of view, comes randomly; it no longer makes any difference to him whether or not he follows parental rules or requests.

Power Politics

One characteristic of family life that profoundly affects each individual member is the formation of *coalitions*. A coalition may involve everyone in the family except one person—the "black sheep." It may consist of just one parent and one child against the rest of the family. It may be a children's coalition against the parents. In all cases, coalitions bring chronic discomfort and pain if they are fixed and unchangeable.

A coalition means that the partners never fight against one another, particularly concerning issues on which they have disagreements with outsiders. They agree with each other whenever they sense opposition and consequently they exercise heavy political power within the family system.

Coalitions always threaten the health of the system. The members of each faction predictably vote together and thus create a communication strategy that inevitably polarizes the group. In such a situation, reason seldom prevails; the group is not concerned with reason but with political power.

In the case of a coalition of all family members but one, the lone "black sheep" may be a child or it may be one of the parents. Typically, he is deprived of many of his rights, blamed for any and all troubles, and repeatedly characterized as negative, stubborn, and inferior. He becomes the coalition's victim.

At the same time, however, he usually accepts this role (it does provide him with certain satisfactions), and the coalition's prophecies thus have a strong tendency to become self-fulfilling. The black sheep, alienated from his family and unable to find support for his views, may even adopt with a vengeance the negative expectations that have been laid on him.

A family recently sought help in dealing with their "problem child." He was a fourteen-year-old boy who had just run away from home and, after thirty hours, still had not returned. Asked why he had run away, the mother replied, "I don't know, but it figures. He's the one who's always getting into trouble. Furthermore, he's lazy and dishonest. Even his younger brother and sister have been remarking about *that.*"

We met with the whole family and asked them to *listen* to what they were telling us and each other about the missing boy. What messages had they been giving him and what messages had he been giving them? It soon became obvious that the boy's parents and three siblings all expected him to be dishonest, disloyal, and lazy. They had lectured him constantly about his "faulty" character and reprimanded him regularly for "bad" behavior—some of it apparently true and some of it only imagined.

The boy seemed to have gained a certain strength and pride from successfully defying this powerful coalition, but he had at the same time been backed into a cage of labels from which he could find no escape short of running away.

The family was able to appreciate the fact that they had been ganging up on the boy for as long as they could clearly remember, and they decided to make a real effort to break up their coalition.

The boy returned home after three days and all members of the family participated in the difficult task of changing his behavior by changing their own. To his predictable challenges, they now responded in a very unexpected manner: they offered him—without strings—an equal place in the family, even when this required rewarding him for his offenses.

The boy was upset by this inexplicable change in the familiar family pattern, and he tried to recover the pattern by escalating his "bad" behavior. Two days after his return home he was caught shoplifting ski equipment. The family, prepared for possible outrages, all went to court, made restitution to the store, and bought for the boy a good set of skis, boots, and poles, plus a lift ticket for the season at a nearby ski resort. They told him they wanted him as a full-fledged member of the family if that was something he cared to accept.

The boy was puzzled. He accepted the gifts but did not ski with his brothers. Two weeks later he refused to go to school. His parents wrote excuses for him and his older brother offered to help him keep up with his schoolwork at home. The boy refused to work with his brother, but after three days at home he voluntarily returned to school. Apparently he was still suspicious of the motives of what used to be an antagonistic coalition.

The boy's next move was to steal an automobile. This heavy test shook up the family, but they nevertheless showed up in court—all six of them—and all participated in a long session with the juvenile judge. The judge agreed not to press for more extensive punishment when he was told about the family's efforts.

The family decided they would all contribute to the purchase of an off-road motor bike, which they gave the boy, with the comment that he could let his brothers use it or not, as he wished. After one week the boy let his brothers and sister use the bike. The intensity of the many unexpected responses was so great that he could not believe that his family really meant it when they stopped fighting him, even in the face of his impossible demands.

He now asked to be permitted to borrow the family car to drag Main Street. The family held a council to which the boy was invited, but he did not appear. They decided that they could not go along with this request (the boy did not have a license), since complying would not, in this case, communicate a truly caring attitude.

The boy was told of the decision, and to everybody's surprise, he seemed relieved rather than angry. In fact, he then called for a family council and told everyone that he had had enough. He began to resent special treatment; he just wanted to be another member of the family. All concurred that the time had come to stop treating him as if he were—as his seven-year-old sister put it—"sick."

The episode was almost like a textbook description of a system change, and the results were gratifying to the whole family. There were no further problems. The major political power, the coalition, had listened to the boy and looked at itself.

By changing its own behavior, it provided for changes in the one family member who was thought to be unredeemable. None of their expected fears came true, and none of the other children started acting out in order to get special treatment.

The Parts We Play

If coalitions are power plays that always polarize family behavior, *role assignments* are simply a means of dividing psychological territory. For example, an older son may assume responsibility and represent the view of his parents, particularly in relation to younger siblings, while his younger brother acts out aggressive feelings as a regular thing.

The family does not consciously desire an aggressive younger son, but the two roles seem to be maintained by subtle communications from everyone in the family. It is common for one of them to say, "We'd better ask David," or "Someone's going to scream about this and I'll bet I know who!" In competitive families, the assumption that older brothers are by definition good boys implies that they are better than somebody else, and there is usually a "somebody else" available.

Such role assignments arise from the dynamics of family interactions and are not based on fundamental personality components. They are determined by the silent expectations of the family members. The father may want his sons to be football players, while the mother wants them to be scholars. The two sons may divide these roles, each carrying the acceptance of one parent and the disappointment of the other. Or one of the sons may choose the role of player *and* scholar while the other chooses the role of bum.

The point is that such role assignments are just that: a role is assigned and then played out. Each brother *acts* a part in the family drama, and whichever role he accepts, he will accumulate appropriate skills. It appears that he is acting out his own unique personality. In fact, he is capable of many other roles, and he can change roles if he is able to break through the word cages that the entire family has constructed for itself.

Sometimes one of the "actors" in a family will be removed from the scene, leaving his role vacant. A pair of twins carries the "good" and "bad" label, but the "good" twin leaves home for a year; immediately the "bad" twin becomes unexpectedly civil. In another case of good and bad twins, the pair exchanges the roles every few months. They apparently have a silent agreement that one of them will deal with family disapproval so the other can take advantage of various "good twin" benefits, such as driving the family car, which he secretly shares with his brother.

But good-bad is only one of many dimensions in silent agreements. Siblings often make silent contracts among themselves, with trade-offs of an entirely different nature. Two brothers may divide the spoils of competition, one of them focusing on scholastic success and the other on sports. The bargain is never verbalized but it is nevertheless communicated by other means and it may last a lifetime.

Breaking into the other brother's territory is punished as severely as similar breaches are punished in the animal kingdom. Once the contract is in operation, each brother accumulates skills in his "assigned" area, and a change becomes increasingly difficult.

Yet the situation can shift under the pressure of major outside changes. Upon the death of an older brother who was a somewhat pedantic A student, his younger brother, who had been indifferent to intellectual challenge but excelled in art, became the top student in his class within a single semester. His parents (and even his intelligence test!) would have predicted otherwise. The capacity was obviously there all the time, but as long as his brother was alive, the younger boy would not permit himself to challenge him.

A similarly perplexing situation occurred with seventeen-year-old twin girls. One was an average student, charming and very popular, who dated heavily, while the other was a bright student and dedicated musician who was somewhat neglectful of her dress and appearance. When the "charming" twin got married and moved away from home, her sister cultivated the role of charmer and became very popular. The change in her appearance was sudden and astounding; she now affected the bearing of her sister and even let her grades slip.

Removal of one sibling is not the only motivation for reassigning a role. Sometimes this occurs through important changes in the parents' expectations or as a result of a friendship, a prolonged illness, or therapeutic intervention. Switching roles is always surprising since the original role had been accepted as "real"; that is, the individual's behavior was assumed to be his consistent expression of his "true" personality. The individual himself believed that he *was* the role he filled.

Our observations make it clear, however, that the roles we play make use of only a limited, tightly selected segment of our actual capabilities. They are maintained because they fulfill certain functions in our lives, both within ourselves and in relation to others. Role reassignments can occur throughout our lives and are always related to the choosing of new priorities and the development of latent abilities.

Coalitions and role assignments are two of the most significant "settings" that influence not only a child's conduct but also our own efforts to listen for the child's needs and discordant compromises. Preconceived notions are a form of chronic, selective deafness. The parents of the boy who excelled academically only after his brother's death had always "known" he wasn't very bright. They were astonished at his newly revealed capabilities. The parents of the musician had believed she was simply by nature not a charming young lady.

Such events should alert parents to the fact that the children they know so well have many capacities other than those that happen to have been selected by the child and by his place within the family. The particular capabilities that are developed and displayed are a function of motivations, compromises, and style rather than of basic endowment.

Acting as a Sounding Board

Listening to a young person can easily be an act of love. Listening with concern but without judging is an art, and it helps the child explore his motivations, his style, and the compromises he has so far achieved. This kind of listening does not mean letting the child know what is expected of him. It means giving him a safe place where he can speak at his own speed and explore new options, however unrealistic they may appear to us.

When a child says he does not know what he wants to do, he may be asking us to make his decisions for him, or he may be sounding us out to see how we will react to some of his wilder fantasies. Or he may feel that he has no idea at all what it is he really wants. On the other hand, particularly when it comes to choosing a profession, he may be simply unwilling to commit himself, since any commitment means giving up other possibilities.

During the past century, in the middle and lower classes, young people seldom had to make such a choice since their trade was often already prescribed. Today, young men and women are faced with the difficult task of voluntarily making a choice of one among hundreds of possible options about which they have been given very little solid, practical information.

The listening adult should know that the "I-don't-know-what-to-do" phenomenon is part of our current culture and that, for the young today, a choice also means a loss. Many young people want to take time out to let some of the confusion settle in their own minds, and they travel if they can or experiment with alternative life-styles.

This modern delay tactic is contrary to the values of many adults who feel that an early professional direction makes a person competent and successful. If we are to listen without misleading preconceptions, we have to understand that our definition of success is not always shared by the young.

Listening to a son or daughter can be a most rewarding enterprise. As a child grows into and through adolescence, one of his great needs is for a listener—a resource person, not a controller or critic or promoter of old, established ideas. He has a lot to say and a lot to question. He needs a sounding board. He has no use for a critic or a preacher.

Most parents do not "naturally" listen in this way, and they have to train themselves to do so. They should expect to be challenged and tested when they first attempt to listen with unengaged concern. A daughter may casually refer to her sex experiences or talk about a marijuana high; a son may speak lovingly of his "undesirable" friends or of his skill at cheating on examinations. Or they may both make up shocking exploits. A parent who really wants to listen must understand that he is being tested to see how trustworthy he is as a listener.

The problem facing many well-intentioned parents is that they cannot find an opportunity to talk with their children. Many a mother is quite ready to listen but her daughter is not ready to talk. At the same time, many young people complain that they are quite ready to talk but their parents don't want to hear.

One young man of eighteen had responded several times to his mother's heartfelt request to know what he thought about life and love, but every session had ended with her sobbing, "What have I done wrong?" Either way—whether we are the parent or the child—reestablishing contact requires patience and the acceptance of the fact that our efforts will probably be rejected a good many times.

A father who had lost contact with his son tried for several months to show interest in what the boy had been doing, but he was met with blunt answers at best. Suppertime remained a time for sulking silence. The boy was an avid race-car fan, however, and one day the father invited him on a trip to watch a big race in a neighboring state. The father became interested in what his son was thinking about (cars), and the son responded. That was two years ago, and they still sit together and talk, and not only about race cars.

Sometimes, as in this case, the crucial step is a message of considerable consequence. To this son it meant that his father was not hopelessly lost in the business world, but was willing to give more than dinnertime lip service to understand and share in what excited him.

The most frequent error a listening parent can make is to adopt a "parental" stance. A good listener will not push his own opinions (as the stereotype of the good parent would do), and he will not pressure his child for solutions to the problems that are brought up. What is valuable is not a neatly worded solution but a clear statement of the problem; premature solutions are often destructive.

The good listener must know what he himself represents to the child; many successful professional people fail to understand that their very existence represents a heavy pressure because they are such hard models to follow. The good listener must also know how to tolerate uncertainty and how to leave personal questions open-ended. (Son: "What should I do about Ruth?" Father: "That's a tough one. It may take a while to figure out.") Answers are necessary at times, but not while acting as listener. A definitive answer is always a good way of shutting off a conversation.

The rewards of good listening are immeasurable. Listening communicates a strong sense of caring and permits the other person to sort out his thoughts and consider new options. To become a resource for our own children, as opposed to being a director, is a new role for most parents and can last a lifetime.

Listening is the foundation of respect; it gives our children the subtle and convincing message that we are interested in them as they are, not as we might wish them to be.

12

Withdrawal

A cockroach has essentially two known ways of escaping danger. He can run away or he can stand still and play dead. Both are apparently passive defense, or withdrawal, maneuvers.

Man behaves essentially like the cockroach when he resorts to physical withdrawal to escape a threat. But his peculiarly human way of "playing dead" is far more complex than the simple "freezing" of the cockroach. The human being plays dead by remaining physically present but withdrawing inside—mentally and emotionally. He backs off psychologically. He hides within himself.

Withdrawal behavior can be most directly observed in the young child. Under unpleasant circumstances he will simply increase the physical distance between himself and the object he is afraid of. We find that this is also true for some adults. We measured physical distance between newlywed couples who did not seem to be too fond of each other: they would place their chairs farther apart when given the choice and also lean farther away from each other than loving couples would. They engaged in this very primitive withdrawal response and perhaps used it to communicate to each other about their unfriendly feelings.

Singin' the Blues

Withdrawal does not necessarily take place by an increase in physical distance. Sulking behavior is a form of withdrawal and occurs very early in childhood. The child of three or four has learned that he can "run away" from an unpleasant situation by crying or looking very sad and that he can punish the doting parent at the same time with such behavior.

The parents' efforts—"Show me a smile," "Be happy," "Now, don't cry"—may sometimes be successful, but these comments certainly give the child the information that his withdrawal has been noted and causes pain. The child also learns that the adult is tuned in to reading his mood and that his moods are important. As a result, the child himself will experience his moods as important events and as events he can use to communicate to the parent.

The most dramatic lesson the child learns, however, is that he can often use his moods without being held personally responsible for them. Many parents treat a child's mood as a state that he has to be coaxed out of, that cannot be ordered away; he has to be *motivated* to leave it behind. This gives him the right to claim throughout his life that the mood is not under his control, that he "cannot help himself" and that he himself is a victim of his moods.

In other words, when sulking, he can withdraw and feel he has been victimized, even though he indulges in his tantrum quite willingly and enjoys the effect on those around him. He finds gratification in the "message" that he is suffering.

Withdrawal allows one individual to tell another that he is helpless, that he is not overtly aggressive. By saying he "feels blue," the child also communicates covertly to the adult that he, the adult, has failed the child. The adult often correctly understands the message; he hears the child say: "I am suffering, and *you* cannot make me happy. I am *your* failure." The child is probably not aware of his covert aggression, but having the power to drive his parent to desperation is in any case a pleasure.

The unconscious use of moods to control others is very often a skill maintained for a lifetime, and hidden aggression through withdrawal may become a major stylistic feature of the child's behavior. It expresses a highly sophisticated compromise solution for two heavy needs: the wish to punish and the fear of being punished.

The result is punishment a person can administer without being recognized as the willful punisher. The suffering the child endures is apparently a small price to pay for such an accomplishment.

Actually, withdrawal behavior is one of the most covertly aggressive acts known to man. It is "expensive," however, since the child who adopts sulking behavior because he does not get the ice cream also accepts that, at least momentarily, he will not have the ice cream. He is willing to trade ice cream for the covert satisfaction of punishing the person who failed him.

If offered ice cream as a bribe at this point, he may refuse it because of his delicious decision to punish by withdrawal. The trade-off is that the subject denies himself all satisfaction at the moment and in return enjoys the covert power, which he uses to work on a future victory.

This technique is used effectively in all kinds of negotiations, from intimate personal interaction to politics. In hospitals in India, patients like to kiss the doctors' feet since the doctors then feel obliged to work harder for them. In Bombay, if you let a beggar kiss your shoe, he "owns" you, and you then have to give him some blessing (in the form of money) because he has humiliated himself. The same values are reflected in the religious rites of self-humiliation and in vows of poverty, forms of withdrawal that command respect.

Withdrawal on a large scale was also practiced by the flower children in the United States in the late sixties. For example, an upper-middle-class boy withdrew into the life-style of the very poor—or what he imagined that style to be. He wore his hair long and uncombed, dressed in thirdhand clothing, and ate out of garbage cans. He used drugs, was sexually promiscuous, and dropped out of school.

His withdrawal was successful because he was willing to say to his family, "The worst you can do to me is throw me out! I have nothing to lose, I am leaving anyway. I want nothing from you, so I can do as I please." This boy was not beyond accepting the bribe money his parents provided to save him from disaster. He did not interpret the check as a sign of love, but only as a sign that his parents, too, had to do their own thing.

When we told this fifteen-year-old that his behavior (disappearing for six months from his parental home without notification) was an aggressive act, he was astonished. He had never thought of it that way. He said he would be extra sweet and considerate to his parents for the short time he planned to spend at home.

Interestingly, the boy's hidden aggression against the values of his parents was not without remarkable consequences for them. They began to loosen up, smoke pot, give a higher priority to leisure, and cut down on their work. Even their clothing became more informal, and the father's hairstyle changed.

Withdrawal behavior, when seen as a communication, has much in common with passive resistance. By withdrawing, an individual gives a message that he no longer wants to accept responsibility; he refuses to cope with these problems. He passes the initiative to the outside, to another person, to the environment.

He refuses to participate, often in settings where his participation and his decisions are needed. With his active withdrawal, he not only shifts responsibility to others; he also gains the advantage of not being recognized as the author of the aggression he perpetrates.

The essential ingredients of withdrawal behavior are also present in alcoholism, sexual dysfunction, depression, and some types of crimes. Such behaviors are often means of "withdrawing" from an unbearable home situation. By pulling away from his home, a person makes a desperate attempt to consolidate his own territory so he can live his life with some sense of integrity.

He drinks and accepts the consequences because he also punishes his spouse, for example, by withdrawing from her, at least partially. He does not actually run away from home or get a divorce, but he does the next best thing. He stays around and becomes a symbol of reproach. He makes his wife suffer by implying, through his very existence: "See what you made of me."

This confrontation expresses his covert aggression and yet permits him to maintain certain rewards the relationship has for him, such as maintaining his home. With this compromise he does not see himself as responsible for his aggression.

In a similar manner, sexual dysfunction, as well as certain "compulsive" acts, serve to express reproach to the partner or relative. For example, a young man who is not in need of money frequently passes bad checks. He cannot help himself, he says. He claims he suffers from his condition (a great sense of failure), but he knows his parents will either bail him out or feel guilty about not doing so.

Both these responses cause in his parents a sense of impotence and give him, incidentally, a sense of control. The partial withdrawal permits him, at least temporarily, a sense of integrity and equality with his parents.

Busy, Busy, Busy

Let us concentrate on some of the less obvious partial withdrawal behaviors in everyday living. We are particularly concerned here with partial withdrawal from a specific relationship with another person.

Most marriages in Western cultures permit a maximum togetherness of husband and wife of about six waking hours on weekdays and thirty-two on Saturday and Sunday. This much togetherness allows for very little privacy. It is not likely that many marriages would last with so much unleavened exposure.

Fortunately, there are a number of conventions that make some partial withdrawal permissible. These conventions range from sports and hobbies to a night out with the boys, a bridge evening, and business engagements. Some marriages, of course, permit greater latitude and accept semiprofessional trips or even pleasure trips by one spouse alone. Males have been favored in these conventions, and one of the great efforts of women recently has been to gain equal status so they will not be automatically bound to the house while the man has his freedom.

The standard agreed upon differs with circumstances and with the characteristics of the partners. A truck driver's wife probably would agree to being left alone for "legitimate reasons" for weeks at a time when her husband is on the road. A professional person is likely to be away from home much of the time because of his professional meetings and obligations, and there is some convention that governs this absence.

From a communication point of view, these realities are not often chance factors. The truck driver often chooses his job because he feels that he needs to be alone and because he likes the experience of the comradeship of the road. The professional man also can be said to have chosen his profession because it permits him to withdraw from an exclusive commitment to his partner. Even so, he probably could often limit his professional enterprises without ill effect on his profession.

The businessman who brings work home, the employee who moonlights, the housewife who keeps so busy cleaning house that she cannot spend time with her husband, all show a partial withdrawal. Not that keeping busy is an undesirable behavior or that marriage ideally should be a sixty-two-hour-a-week proposition. Keeping busy is simply an acceptable way of withdrawing.

By exercising such options, a family communicates to each member just how much mutual commitment is desirable. Problems exist when the priorities for outside activities differ among family members.

Why should people withdraw from a "too-close" human commitment? There are many reasons, not the least of which is that learning about the dangers of commitment occurs during our most impressionable years. With a mother who defines love as possessiveness and a father who defines caring as control, the child learns to keep one foot out of a loving or caring commitment because he wants to maintain his own integrity.

Withdrawal is thus an expression of our concept of what a human relationship should look like. The restless Don Juan who goes from bed to bed till ripe old age may be thought to be a sexual adventurer; he may also be characterized as a person who is totally unwilling to commit himself.

A change in partial withdrawal behavior can cause a crisis in a relationship, particularly when the change is dear to only one of the partners. Retirement often poses similar problems. A thirty-six-hour-per-week marriage is converted into a hundred-hour-per-week marriage, and the strain of such a change can result in grave alienation or even early death. Why? Because the "job" is a legitimate withdrawal behavior whereas an unexcused absence is ordinarily not acceptable.

A Salt Lake City man retired several years ago and immediately became involved in frequent heavy fights with his wife. He tried to develop an interest in adult-education classes, but found this was not an acceptable withdrawal behavior to his strong-willed wife. He had been able to deal with his wife on a several-hours-a-day level, but he did not have the will or strength to resist her demands on a hundred-hours-a-week basis. In short order he became an invalid, withdrawn into senility before his time.

Withdrawing Just a Little All the Time

Some people do not choose to keep busy as a legitimate means of being physically or psychologically absent. Married couples may spend many hours together under the same roof without exchanging more than a few words. They absent themselves by silence.

They like their common home, and perhaps even their sexual relationship and some of the social advantages that stem from their life together, but they simply have withdrawn from the type of commitment which involves vocal expression. They have very little to say to each other, even though they would never abandon each other at times of emergency.

In the extreme case, such people are strangers living under the same roof. There are the TV hours and the newspaper hours and the workshop hours and the talking-to-children hours, and there is no excuse needed for the silence they encounter with each other.

These couples have only a minimum of interest in each other as people. One might say they are technically but not personally committed to each other.

Partial withdrawal may also be accomplished by "helplessly" falling in love. An individual feels he cannot help himself. Meeting the woman of his dreams was a matter of fate, and he is not really responsible for the fact that he now has to separate from his wife. He "really" has no choice. The new commitment is so urgent, his new potency so overwhelming, his feeling of their having been made for each other so absolute, that he is simply a helpless victim.

In fact, people can be so convincing in their enthusiasm that they almost legitimize their reasoning. The communication of this kind of withdrawal is very clear. It simply means that the person concerned wants to find a way out of an established relationship but needs some "higher authority" to make it all right.

"Falling in love" (with someone else) serves as a message to the wife or husband. It means "I have to leave you, even though I cannot tell you so directly." Many of these "helpless" victims of love have in fact helped things along enormously.

Before the Fall, it turns out, they have engaged in search missions, made obvious demonstrations of availability, or at least shown enthusiastic responsiveness to new prospects. Such statements as "But I love my wife and my children" are not convincing. They are merely communications that precede the reordering of important priorities.

In some cases a man may actually fall in love with his *wife* after twenty years of marriage. Here the communication is a demand for a change in partial withdrawal, this time toward more togetherness. This, too, can cause trouble, as in cases where the wife fails to respond.

Another form of withdrawal has to do with providing. An increasing number of people leave their jobs or, in some milder cases, switch to jobs that demand less and less. This depresses their standard of living. They feel they have to upgrade the quality of their lives by working less and "living" more.

Often such changes contain a subtle message to the family. One partner says to the other, "Will you stay with me even if we become a lot poorer? Are you concerned for our happiness?" This type of test may result in withdrawal, because the spouse who does not accept this choice implies that his living standard is more important to him than his "happier" relationship with his spouse. It is a communication that tests the commitment of the partner.

There are many cases where husband or wife withdraws from commitment because of illness, imagined illness, or mysterious pain. Typically, a reduction in sex relations serves as a reasonable, clear warning that the commitment is in danger. This is, of course, particularly true with young people. Older people can sometimes get away with total sex withdrawal because of the mistaken assumption that the sex drive decreases or that sex is less desirable in later years.

Anyone who has a lot of accidents is probably indulging in partial withdrawal. Like the chronic sulker, he seems to be saying, "I don't care whether I participate in life or not." Being accident-prone is the result of increased risk-taking.

While a person may not actually desire an accident, he may be tempted by the kind of daring displayed in Russian roulette. When he takes large risks, particularly in ways that endanger his home and property (as in heavy gambling) or his own life or even the lives of his family (as in careless driving), his act can be seen as a communication: The status quo is not worth preserving.

In some cases the message is even closer to Russian roulette: "Love me or let me die." This strange alternative is apparently an exaggeration of what some of us have learned as children. The young child is often overindulged when he experiences some accidental harm. When parental concern occurs at such occasions and not at others, the child may seek out (and exaggerate) such harm. When accidents occur too often, parents should recognize that the child has to go to desperate and painful means to experience being an object of concern.

We also are aware that certain illnesses, often termed psychosomatic, have physical symptoms but are related to emotional stress. It is not clear whether a person can become ill specifically in order to communicate, but there is some evidence that this happens. There are fashions in fainting spells, headaches, and stomach upsets. But beyond the physiological symptoms, sickness can be used as communication in a secondary way. The headache that means "no sex tonight" is proverbial in some marriages.

Even such clearly organic facts as the loss of a limb can become a communication. There are also people who lose a limb and act as if nothing had happened. Some amputees who learn to ski on one leg have a desire to communicate to themselves and others a sense of mastery in adversity.

There are others who refuse to learn to make use of the remaining leg; they use their loss to depend on others, whether they need to or not.

Still others use such adversity to withdraw into loneliness with the rationale that they do not want to experience false sympathy.

A person's ingenuity is the only limit to the number of choices open to him when he wishes to communicate distance. He displays infinite skill in achieving compromises between his desire to be gregarious and his wish to remain independent. He uses his skills to hide his demands for independence from those he is committed to, as if it would take courage or even recklessness to admit to such needs.

He takes advantage of conventions that permit him to shift responsibility for this wish away from himself. He goes to bars because "he cannot help himself"; he falls in love and "he cannot help himself"; he gets overworked in his profession because "it's the way things have to be."

Someday we might want to ask just why our civilization makes all these excuses necessary.

13

Depression and Suicide as Communication

A convincing way to communicate unhappiness is to display the symptoms of depression. These symptoms—clear, conventional signs closely related to sulking behavior—involve real suffering. At the same time, they are far more than passive responses. They serve to relay important messages to ourselves and to others. We may unconsciously want to make sure the person who rejected us knows what a terrible blow we have been dealt. We may need to use the aftermath of a bitter failure to kill forever the high expectations people have always had of us.

A mental state of depression is most commonly observed when a person experiences grief. We may be enduring unavoidable grief and at the same time need to assure ourselves that we do indeed feel as bad as we think we should. We may simply wish to affect others with our feelings because grief is easier to bear when shared.

Or we may broadcast our unconscious sentiments by refusing to grieve at all. Some people won't let on that they have been touched by a loss; sometimes they go to extremes to assert such denial, as in the case of a woman who went out dancing when her mother died.

The use of grief as a communication becomes clear when we think of a Middle Eastern funeral procession that includes women who are hired to weep aloud and utter convincing signs of bereavement. This demonstration is designed not only to publicly express the sense of loss, but also for the public sharing of the grief.

Our funerals are characteristically more sedate, but the sharing aspect is still represented by neighbors visiting, newspaper announcements, calling the whole family together, and sending flowers. Public concern elicited in this way seems to serve as an emotional support to the bereaved. While in some societies funerals are festive occasions, in most Western cultures, the tears, the sad face, the slow walk, and the thoughtful, hesitant speech are the norm. Once these behaviors are displayed, we have a convincing sign that a person feels deeply about the loss.

While we ordinarily think of grief as a very private feeling, the conventions of public sharing in any society are deeply established. People do not often "put on" or fake their grief, but they do normally fall into the conventional role.

Other life crises besides loss of a loved one may serve as triggers for depression—loss of a job, destruction of one's property, an automobile accident, loss of a part of one's body, even the loss of a skill. A depressed individual is sharply conscious of this triggering crisis. He blames his depression on the crisis instead of looking into the underlying causes, for neither the depressed person nor those close to him know the true cause of the depression.

Depression, like schizophrenia, comes more easily to some people than to others, and there may be a genetic or an organic basis. At the same time, a predisposition is not sufficient cause. We also need experiences to activate this unfortunate facility.

What are these other ingredients? One of them appears to be the experience of having observed depression in an adult who played a significant part in our upbringing. A great many of our behaviors are imitative, and we adopt them when we are exposed to them at an impressionable age.

Another probable source of depression is that, at an early age, we were deeply impressed by the intensity of concern our sulking brought us. If parents pay attention to us when we sulk, and fail to pay attention when we are happy, we are likely to adopt such depressive features as a sad face, a sad posture, inactivity, and speaking in a low, depressed voice.

We learn, probably without awareness, to make this trade-off: to accept suffering as a way of eliciting attention and love. The sense of suffering must be real, for if we were to complain without really suffering, we would feel that we were manipulating and would feel guilty.

As with all compromises, we take the bad with the good, and along with our suffering we also experience extra caring. We become "manipulators" without knowing it.

Paying the Price for Control

A family has one depressed member, the wife. The rest of the family agrees that the wife is the "patient" and that the husband, son, daughter, and the patient's mother-in-law (all living together) are simply observers. The wife is "sick," so it is really *her* problem.

She can no longer do the housework, she neglects her church duties, she does not permit sex relations, she goes around with a sad face, cries a lot, drinks occasionally, speaks in a low voice, and complains of hopelessness. She has taken tranquilizers, to no effect. She also sleeps a lot, does not seem to be able to get up in the morning, and has lost all interest in social life.

No one can find a good reason why the wife should be in such a depressed state. The children are doing well in school, the husband is a good provider and loving, the house is in good shape. No reasonable person could be, or should be, depressed under such benign circumstances.

But the diagnosis made by the rest of the family looks at the wife's behavior in isolation, as if she were all alone. It does not account for the fact that everyone in the family influences the wife's behavior.

The story unfolds slowly. The wife is most depressed on Tuesdays and Fridays. She is depressed all week, but she goes to bed only on those days. Why do Tuesdays and Fridays always bring heavy bursts of suffering? The answer comes when we look at what happens with the rest of the family on Tuesdays and Fridays.

The husband comes home early from work to sit with his wife, talk to her, and hold her hand. With her husband at her bedside, she takes a few drinks, even though they depress her further. The husband always discourages her from drinking, mentioning that her father was an alcoholic. The father, it turns out, has taken her husband into his business, and the husband has built it into a very prosperous enterprise.

The husband's mother, who lives with them, is a very strong-willed woman. Her latest complaint is that her son, while he owns only half the business, is working himself to death, without the help of the father. The father was the founder and draws a much larger salary than his son-in-law, even though he seldom shows up at the office.

This theme is the subject of a heated discussion between the wife and the mother-in-law on one particular Tuesday afternoon. The mother-in-law wants the wife to talk to her father, to straighten out these injustices. At this point the wife's depression lifts a little, and she says she has always felt that adjusting the salaries was her husband's affair. She feels that the pressures laid on her to talk to her father are unfair.

The wife reveals that about six months earlier, shortly before the onset of her depression, she had given in to these pressures and tried to talk to her father. At first, her father had been friendly (and drunk) and had boasted about his many efforts to keep the business going. She did not have the heart to speak as urgently as she knew her mother-in-law wanted her to.

In the many discussions that followed, her father became more and more abusive. She got sick, and during the first month of her illness her father visited with her every Tuesday. He let it be known that he was very concerned about her drinking, as one alcoholic in the family was enough. He came on Tuesday because he knew he would encounter his son-in-law at her bedside. Whenever he saw his son-in-law, he always told him that he should leave and get back to work because the business was going downhill.

On this particular Tuesday the two men and the children join the women. The mother-in-law complains that her son was deprived of his rights in this business, and she says it is her duty to ask her daughter-in-law to fight for her own and her husband's rights. This time there is no response, for the family is tired of fighting. Several of them say they want to clear up the problem.

At this moment, the old man's face starts twitching, and his daughter flies into a rage—apparently for the first time in her life. She tells her father off. She says that if he did his share the business would not go downhill, and that if he wants to go on and neglect the business and do his drinking, he should at least let her husband have the reins and divide the profits properly.

Then she directs her anger at her husband and her mother-in-law. She wonders why they have been sitting by, pressuring *her* into doing all the talking. She has always resented this unfairness. And while she's at it, she also reminds her husband that they had agreed to help his mother to find a home of her own. That time has now come!

The family is stunned. The father's face stops twitching. It is as if a cool breeze has cleared the air. After a few more get-togethers, the old man retires at a smaller salary. He does not like it, but under the circumstances he accepts it. The husband takes the reins and the mother-in-law moves out. The wife becomes her former effective and contented self.

A fairy tale? No; a true story. The wife broke out of her depression, the verbal cage that defined her as *the* sick member of the family. She came out of it and was once again in charge of herself. The change was so abrupt that for a time the husband took to sulking. He could not quite accept that he was now in charge of his business. He felt undeserving because it was his wife who had accomplished it.

The case is unique in that the verbal cage ("I cannot fight for my rights") was broken so suddenly. It was as if the wife, by exploding, had found the courage to make her wishes known.

Actually, such sudden "conversions" are not as rare as we might think. They are based on a stylistic feature that acts like the straw that broke the camel's back. A critical mass of frustration accumulates and now the emotional climate is just right for clearing the air at one stroke.

The togetherness of the family, their fatigue with fighting, their readiness to pay attention, were all properly sensed by the ailing wife. She had carefully laid the groundwork.

She communicated to her father—by way of her own drinking—that he should pay attention to her before she destroyed herself. She punished her husband for not speaking up by neglecting her responsibilities in her home. She punished her mother-in-law for pressuring her by turning the housework over to her and by becoming too depressed to take responsibility for talking to her father. Finally, when she exploded, she had the proper audience—one which at that moment was ready to share responsibility for the family problem. She no longer needed her depression.

This story supports the contention that depression is an efficient way of communicating a compromise solution. The wife had punished her husband, her father, and her mother-in-law without having to take responsibility for it. When she finally did take responsibility, she got well.

Power Through "Weakness"

But does depression always carry a communication? Sometimes depression hits a person who appears very much alone, where no other significant participants are visible.

A young man who has few friends and no clear commitment to anyone is brought in by a concerned neighbor. One morning this neighbor had noticed that the young man failed to leave for his job. The neighbor first thought the young man was ill, but after a few days' observation, he decided he had better find out what was going on. The door was open, and inside he found the young man cowering in the corner, undernourished, dirty, and obviously incontinent.

The young man is taken to the hospital and is discharged after a few days. He is still depressed but seems in somewhat better shape. At least he knows he needs help. He tells us there is nothing he wants to do and that all desire has left him. He claims this has never happened to him before. He knows he cannot make friends, particularly girl friends. He feels utterly lonely.

He returns to his job but still lives without joy. Eventually he discusses his problem concerning women. He feels most strongly attracted to those involved with his best friends. This is a disastrous kind of attraction, and it often enough results in his being beaten up and even shot at by his "best friends."

He reports that shortly before his depression he had obtained a promise to marry him from a former lover of his present closest friend. Three days after her promise to marry him, she ran away and married the friend he had "deceived." He cannot understand why the woman agreed to marry him and then went back on her promise. He sees himself as a victim. His woman broke her promise to him and his best friend deceived him.

It becomes apparent that this man's stylistic behavior is getting him into deep trouble. He sees his friends as pawns. He makes friends easily but just as easily loses them by being "on the make" for the women they are involved with. He comes on as a deep and lonely person, arousing the sympathy of these women, and he often succeeds with them.

This kind of conquest, deceiving his friends, represents to him "an important experience in caring." To him, this means that a woman chooses him in preference to a friend—a friend who is in fact aware of his victory and who will therefore fight him.

The "unfair" fight of his latest victim is what brought him into his depression; this victim was not playing "fair" since he irrevocably reconquered the woman. Irrevocably? The young man actually tried to "win back" the newlywed ex-fiancée. Only after he failed in this attempt did he explore new options for ordering his life.

In everyday life many forms of depression serve useful purposes. A boy of sixteen, from a family that holds schooling in high esteem, refuses to attend school or take a job or even seek company. All he does, apparently, is to sleep, run around with a sad face, look at TV, and smoke pot alone. His parents argue with him, threaten to turn him over to a detention home, but are impotent to deal with him. His depressed style is a constant worry and annoyance to them.

The father wants to kick him out of the house, but the mother vetoes the idea. She says that now is the very time her son needs help, even though she does not know what sort of help she can give. He is a bright and sensitive boy, but he has learned to obtain a sense of power by an aggressive display of aimlessness, irresponsibility, depression, and a habit of being accident-prone.

He seems to have a need to punish his parents for torments he feels they inflicted on him, and perhaps he has a deep wish to get his father out of the house. His parents are not innocent bystanders; when he was small, they had used him as a pawn when fighting their own battles.

One day the boy achieves a complete victory over his father by sparking a bitter argument between his father and mother, both of whom feel guilty for having somehow failed him. The father explodes with anger and says he is leaving home. The boy is elated. But his victory doesn't last long, for he overplays his hand. He appears too happy when his father announces his decision.

At that point both parents sense that the son is playing a game with them, and the father changes his mind about leaving. The father and mother, together then—for the first time in their lives—tell the boy to move out of the house; they don't even care whether or not he goes to college.

The boy does not move out, but he takes responsibility for himself at once and is soon working hard in college. Until the big confrontation, he had focused his energies on punishing his parents and getting his father out of the house. He used his "lack of motivation" to do so, but he was not a faker. He accepted a trade-off in suffering in order to make his communication more powerful, but his game was neither flippant nor a matter of gross manipulation. It was an unaware style he had learned some years earlier.

Aren't we ignoring genuine suffering, where no games and no styles are involved, and where no communication is contemplated? "Real" feelings are always involved in depression—as they are in joy and jealousy and other states we can express with conviction—but this fact is not incompatible with the fact that these feelings may also serve as communications.

We can of course play a role, con, fake, pretend, or wish to deceive, and we can communicate with these behaviors; but we also can feel genuine warmth, real love, real grief, or real jealousy, and communicate with these behaviors as well.

The word "real," in this context, simply means we have no conscious motivation to deceive. When we send discordant messages without knowing it, we may say one thing and do quite another, but the *intent* of our message is not deceptive.

When we use our suffering to make someone else feel bad, we still feel genuinely miserable ourselves. The discordant message is a device that gives us many advantages, but it also victimizes us, since we use it to create in other people emotional climates different from the ones we consciously desire.

You'll Be Sorry Once I'm Dead

Suicide is responsible for some 30,000 deaths a year in the United States. Many more probably go unreported because of the stigma attached to the act and because of life-insurance clauses that exclude payment when death occurs "by one's own hand."

Chronologically, the suicide rate is almost directly proportional to age, although it has gone up 92 per cent in the fifteen-to-twenty-four age group since 1970. Geographically, San Francisco leads the nation with a rate of 37 per 100,000 (260 a year), compared with 17 for its nearest competitor, and a national average of 12. Everywhere, the rate is much higher than average among alcoholics and among divorced and widowed adults.

The problem is statistically greater than the figures indicate; it is estimated that there are eight to ten attempts for every "successful" suicide. Furthermore, a good many accidents appear to be suicides. Of 52,000 fatal car accidents per year in the U.S., somewhat fewer than half are single-driver accidents, and research indicates that at least one half of these may be suicides. Many of the drivers, in fact, leave suicide notes.

Whatever the mode, the place, the age, or the "reason," suicide and attempted suicide serve as powerful messages to one's friends, to oneself, and to the world.

The phenomenon of suicide has been carefully investigated by two

Los Angeles psychologists, Edwin S. Schneidman and Norman L. Farberow, who started the movement toward suicide-prevention centers. Their theoretical position was based on the observation that the characteristics of suicide victims can be divided into three categories: those who commit suicide even though they want to survive, those who commit suicide without really knowing whether they want to survive or not, and those who clearly want to die. They labeled the categories in terms of Hamlet's dilemma, "To be or not to be."

First, there are the "to-be" suicides, those who really wanted to survive but misjudged an important variable. They may have slashed their wrists more deeply than they had planned to, or they may have jumped to the street from a second-story window without realizing there was a truck coming. The researchers estimated that some 50 per cent of all suicides fall into this category.

Another 44 per cent fall into the "to-be-or-not" category. These "maybe" suicides take heavier chances. For example, someone pulls the trigger in a solitary game of Russian roulette and loses the gamble. Or a woman sits in her car in the garage with the motor running at 5:55 P.M., when her husband is due home, but this time he is half an hour late. Or a boy takes an overdose of sleeping pills at a time when he expects his mother to show up, but she doesn't.

Only about 6 per cent of all suicides, according to Schneidman and Farberow's estimates, fall into the "not-to-be" category. These people make certain that there is no chance of being saved. They are those who cradle a hand grenade and pull the pin.

Some 80 per cent of all suicide victims leave notes, and these are most often covertly aggressive in that the subject denies any wish to hurt the addressee but nevertheless singles him out for guilt arousal. Some suicides are extremely cruel—for example, a mother who hangs herself in the kitchen shortly before the children are expected home from school.

Attempted suicide ought to be taken seriously; 95 per cent of the "to-be-or-not" suicides try several times before actually carrying it off. The suicidal person usually gives warning—he is willing to risk his life, but does not really want to die. This is the reason suicide is now commonly called a cry for help. This cry is not just a slogan; it is the reality that underlies the existence of hundreds of suicide-prevention centers throughout the country.

The warning signal given by potential suicides is not always solely a cry for help but a composite of a need for help and a discordant message expressing hidden aggression. This view seems to be supported by the fact that when people call in to a suicide-prevention center they feel cornered. They ask for help that they cannot obtain in their own families, and they harbor a feeling of anger or hate for someone close to them. They often name the target of their aggression: "I'm no good and my wife deserves much better." Such a statement sounds humble but is really soft-sell anger.

Suicides often state that they cannot communicate directly with this significant person. When helped to sort out the problems, the feeling of aggression toward the target person becomes overt. They claim that they have been "done wrong" by this target person, and some even add that they have contemplated killing this person before killing themselves.

The "to-be-or-not" group uses suicide as a communication to self and to others. They are most likely to do so when several distinct conditions prevail simultaneously:

1. Often, but not always, there have been previous, unsuccessful suicide attempts designed to pressure a target person to straighten out a significant relationship.
2. There has been a life-crisis situation such as loss or separation from a loved one, which may precede the suicide attempt by as long as a year.
3. The person has shown a predisposition to using guilt arousal to involve and punish others, preferably by means of physical disability or pain ("You caused my headache!").
4. The person has a tendency to have sudden mood changes (as opposed to being constantly in a depressive state).
5. A "preferred" method of taking one's life is readily available.

This last condition might sound puzzling, because we might think opportunities for suicide are ever-present. That is not so. Suicide preferences are very strong; women by and large prefer taking pills, wrist-slashing, jumping from high places, and carbon-monoxide poisoning (car), while men prefer guns, hanging, and car accidents.

Everyone knows exactly how he would *not* commit suicide; certain people feel incapable of jumping from a bridge, others think pill-taking as far too passive a way to go. Therefore, the very presence of a gun, when all other conditions are ripe, seems to stimulate some to go through with their plan; the presence of a bridge or a high building is stimulating to others. The availability of the preferred method, at the right moment, seems essential.

There are also fashions in suicides. Sometimes a bridge (like the Golden Gate Bridge) or a high campus building achieves a certain status, and there are people who would not think of killing themselves in a less fashionable way. There are also varying suicide fashions among subpopulations. Suicides, for example, often occur in sudden waves; the suicide rate among blacks in the age group eighteen to twenty-four has doubled during the past few years, and the rate for women is also increasing, soon to be equal with men.

Many people apparently think of suicide not only as a way out of a problem, but also as a covertly aggressive act. It becomes extremely important to them to express this aggression in the most forceful manner, possibly even at the risk of their own survival.

Food abuse, alcohol abuse, smoking abuse, and drug abuse (which might be called "slow suicides") may serve as messages of punitive aggression. The aggression implicit in suicides, slow or fast, is best illustrated in suicidal self-immolations of individuals who become "living torches" to call attention to a cause sacred to them. Such causes apparently are enhanced by the self-destructive act, which has reverberations throughout the land.

Most suicides act out their aggression for more personal causes, which are just as sacred to them. There was a rash of suicides at the beginning of the Depression in 1929, when many businessmen took their failure personally and killed themselves. This was probably not done because these men wanted an easy way out of the "shameful" situation they found themselves in. Surely it would have been easier to run away or declare bankruptcy.

Perhaps these men had a deep and sacred cause, namely the demonstration to their clients that they were honorable men. They used their self-sacrifice to show the world that they had the courage of their convictions, that they deservedly earned the trust of those dependent on them and had done so honorably. In other words, these men felt betrayed, and their "voluntary death" expressed dramatically their anger and disgust at having been betrayed by the system.

Suicide in Everyday Life

When we suspect that for a given person the conditions for suicide are ripe and he is likely to take his life, we really have very few options. We can encourage him to talk to us, or to some professional person. If feasible we might want to discover whether there are instruments such as guns or pills available to the person and remove them. We might additionally alert people who live in close contact with this person, but we should never do so behind his back.

We cannot use force and we cannot easily commit this person, since we live in a society which at least pretends to rule out "preventive detention." Detention is a possibility only after an act has been committed, which of course is an ironic possibility in this area. However, some courts seem to accept the substantiated threat of suicide as such an act.

Many people, laymen and professionals alike, commit the error of denying the seriousness of a suicide threat or even of challenging the suicidal person by telling him that he is just fooling. Others do harm with overconcern, whereby they suddenly give in to every whim of the potential suicide, often with great fear.

Both responses may have effects precisely opposite of what is hoped for and can drive the subject to a suicide attempt. The challenge as well as the overconcern may communicate to the potential suicide that he has found the specific target person he has been looking for. The person threatening suicide sometimes needs to find such a target, one who is likely to feel specifically guilty when the act is committed.

Both challenge and overconcern can be perceived by the suicidal person as a living proof that he has been wronged. When challenged in his statement that he wants to kill himself he may despair because he is not being taken seriously; when overconcern is expressed, he may feel resentful that he gets caring only now, when he is resorting to emotional blackmail. In both cases the suicidal person is given the opportunity to direct his covert aggression at a target, or at least a pseudotarget.

It has been observed that suicidal persons ordinarily do not have a "weak ego," but are often strong and successful in their lives, and to give them specific advice at the time of a suicide threat may very well communicate to them that the adviser thinks of them as weak and hopeless. Solutions to their problems have to come from their own resources, and the helping person should only show listening care.

One of the authors was recently called in by the police to talk to a young man who was poised on the ledge of a building, ready to jump to the street eight stories below. His transcript of the events follows.

As I approached the window through which Jack had crawled. Jack yelled, "Stay away or I'll jump!"

I replied, "Don't worry, I will not use trickery to save your life. May I sit on the windowsill?" The purpose of this approach was to demonstrate quietly to Jack that he, Jack, was in charge.

"Okay, but I will make my own decisions. And don't you bring my mother here."

"Your mother is in the room already. Would you like me to suggest to her that she should leave?"

"No," Jack called back. A moment later, "Well, let her stay, I just don't want to talk to her."

In an attempt to simply reflect Jack's feelings, I said, "It would be painful to face her in this awkward position."

The attempt misfired, and Jack made gestures as if to jump. "*She* is the pain!" he yelled. "She kicked Ruth out of the house."

The mother's voice rang out. "That was a month ago and I did not kick her out."

I said, "Your mother wants to tell you something even though you just told her you don't want to talk to her."

"Shut her up if you can."

This remark sounded almost humorous, and therefore encouraging. I said loudly to the mother, "Your son asked me to keep you quiet. If you want to help him, perhaps you can convince him that you can keep quiet even though you are scared about what is happening." The mother began to cry audibly and I said to Jack, "I don't know if I can keep her quiet. I guess you feel that the situation with Ruth and your mother was desperate, to go to such extremes."

"Ruth left me after Mother threw her out."

"She left you, and your mother is to blame." I must not have tuned in on this stranger very well.

"She is *not* to blame," he said. After a long pause he said, more quietly, "Mother thought Ruth was no good."

"I did not," said the mother.

"It *is* hard to keep your mother quiet."

"That's the story of my life." After a long silence, Jack began inching back along the ledge. His only remark was, "Anybody tries to grab me, I jump!"

Jack eased himself back in through the window and took a long, deep breath as he looked us over. I said, "I'd like to help you, if you'd care for that."

Jack slumped into a chair, exhausted, and said, "Okay, you win this time." I set up several sessions with him and invited him to bring his mother.

The story illustrates the hidden aggression in a suicide attempt and reveals the nature of listening responses. Jack was never advised to come in or not to jump, although he obviously knew this was what everyone wanted. He knew he had a listener who was really listening, and he proceeded to talk himself out of jumping, or out of the feeling he had to live up to his threat of jumping.

Jack felt himself to be in a crunch between his girl friend and his possessive mother. But even after losing the woman, he couldn't sustain anger at his mother because she meant so well. It was as if he couldn't imagine any way to express his anger except by threatening to kill himself.

Well-meaning parents can be severe tyrants, for they do not often permit aggression to be directed against themselves. A wicked mother can be attacked; a well-meaning mother can escape direct attack and thus control for a lifetime. The only escape from such control is by some covertly aggressive means. When things get desperate enough, the ledge is about as effective a means as you can invent.

On such occasions, as well as on the help line in a suicide-prevention center, people will call and say they need to solve a particular problem immediately. The man on the ledge said that much when he brought up the problem of mother and girl friend, which gave him the feeling of being cornered. But it would be most unwise to help a threatening suicide by presenting him with specific solutions to his problem. Not only do we not know for sure what these problems really are, but he may find our suggestions uninformed or wanting.

We must provide such a person instead with the climate of concern and caring and convince him that we trust him to find a solution himself. It is apparently the caring experience that brings new hope by breaking the word cage ("I have no choice!") motivating his suicidal behavior. With hope, people can escape that moment where all conditions are "ripe" for suicide.

Withdrawal, depression, and suicide are very much alike in their communicative aspects. They most often seem to be designed to punish others by means of self-hurting. They are discordant messages that represent compromises between two conflicting motivations, to care and to aggress. Typically (but not always) the person himself is only aware of the unhappiness he feels. The aggressive component is expressed covertly and is unavailable to awareness.

14

The Rewards of Addiction

It is no news that modern society is drug-oriented. The average American swallows over a pound of aspirins a year. The prescription drug industry is a multibillion-dollar enterprise and is, according to many physicians, starkly overrated in regard to the value it delivers. Alcohol consumption is enormous, and the cost to society of this drug alone probably outranks all others. Cigarette smoke has been found to be a poison that injures and often kills.

Television sponsors incessantly promise that one drug or another will cure physical illness, make us more attractive, make us fall asleep, keep us more alert, make us happy. When we are depressed, drugs will pick us up; when we are excited, they will slow us down.

Sometimes we use drugs for flagrant communicative purposes. The young often smoke in order to look grown up or to let us know they are rebelling. They may go on hard drugs just to appear daring or to impress their friends. Many people use alcohol to improve their ability to communicate—to overcome shyness, fear, anxiety, or weakness.

While all kinds of drugs may serve the ends of communication, we are concerned mainly with those that are addictive—such as hard drugs—or psychologically habituating—such as tobacco, alcohol, and hallucinogens. Common to all these abuses is the exploitation of the fact that the abuse is *known* to be habit-forming. The "abuser" can claim he is not responsible for indulging in his pleasures because he can't help it; he is coerced by the drug itself.

Smoking abuse is similar to food abuse in that dependency on these substances is thought to be habit-forming rather than addictive. A person who smokes regularly or overeats can still choose whether or not to indulge himself, although the choice may be difficult to carry out. Either may say, "I really should be able to give up this bad habit, and I've tried a number of times, but I just find it too hard."

This communication has a different ring to it than the message of the hard-drug addict, who feels he is caught and has no choice whatever. The "hooked" smoker as well as the compulsive eater, on the other hand, can use his habit all day long to tell himself that he is engaging in prohibited pleasures. Whenever he says he shouldn't do it—while doing it nevertheless—he is delivering a clearly discordant message.

In principle, this message is not different from the husband's statement, "I know my jealousy drives my wife insane, but I love her so much I can't help it." Such messages provide the sender with the excuse that he is "well-intentioned" even while indulging himself.

His statement that he ought to control his smoking or eating implies that he knows it can be done and that others have done it. By delivering his discordant message, the smoker and the overeater apparently gain pleasure not only from smoking or overeating but from the message itself—the constant reminder that they are daring to partake of sinful pleasures.

The Dangerous Pleasure: Smoking

The nature of the pleasure is tied up with an individual's particular history, though it clearly fulfills needs of the moment.

A young man who desperately wants to give up smoking asks for professional help. He says he began to smoke as a boy of fourteen, under very rebellious circumstances. Smoking was prohibited in his home, under threat of religious condemnation.

Each day when the boy came home from school, his father smelled his breath and, if there seemed to be any evidence of tobacco, damned him and punished him. The boy used all sorts of devices to fool his father. Sometimes he had friends blow smoke at him but he did not smoke himself, just to trick the old man into giving him punishments he did not deserve. At other times he did smoke but disguised the odor by chewing gum or wild onions, just to prove he could get away with it.

As there were very few other things that caused such strong emotional exchanges between father and son, the exploration of just and unjust punishment by way of cigarettes became very important to the boy. In his concern for justice, he later studied to become a lawyer, quite against the advice of his parents, who badly wanted him to become a physician in the family tradition.

He developed an appetite for masochistic experience during his sexual relations with women, who had to smell him and then had to spank him for his bad smells. Obtaining prohibited pleasure became the theme of his life, and his smoking behavior was deeply anchored in his life-style. Smoking gave him a feeling of integrity, but he also berated himself as a way of bidding for his father's "approval."

We succeed only in breaking one part of the discordant message, namely his habit of constantly telling himself, "I shouldn't be doing this." He now smokes because he likes to smoke, and the coercive component of "pleasure" that comes from self-criticism is no longer active.

A few weeks after this he gives up smoking rather suddenly as a result of an external incident. He notices an acquaintance wearing an *I Quit* (smoking) button, and he quits, simply and neatly. Quitting is not always this easy, but when a discordant message dissipates, the habit loses much of its compulsive character. The smoker can then deal more rationally with his problem.

Every individual develops his own compromises, his own discordances, which strongly fortify his habits. But we really know very little about the general conditions that enhance smoking. Typically, smoking behavior starts early in life and sometimes is patterned by the smoking behavior of the parents. Parents who smoke may shape smoking rituals in their young; by being extremely restrictive, on the other hand, they may foster smoking as an effective means of rebelling. For some youngsters, smoking simply becomes established as a gesture of sophistication, as a way of living up to peer expectations, or as a source of physiological pleasure.

It is not surprising that so many young people take up smoking, but it is surprising that they later become concerned with their health and still fail to change their smoking habits. Why doesn't smoking follow the pattern of other exciting activities, like the driving behavior of young American males? After an early teen exuberance, concern for physical survival greatly modifies driving practices. Why do people continue to abuse smoking in spite of the widely publicized dangers?

The smoke abuser clings to a pleasure he knows to be dangerous, and perhaps it is this discordant message, this psychological compromise, which coerces him to stay with it. In that sense, the statement on the package is not a warning to him but an extra satisfaction. He lives dangerously for his pleasure's sake. In a culture that threatens to dehumanize people, we need to remind ourselves day in and day out that we have the power to overcome the controls and to experience our share of pleasures in spite of them.

A case in point is a woman who cannot give up smoking three packs a day, even though she has emphysema and her doctor tells her she has to quit or die. She asks for help. She has tried hypnosis without success and she has even tried shocking herself every time she feels like smoking. She says she discarded such devices after a short trial, since she usually forgot to use them anyway.

We can appreciate the constant self-berating that allows her to call smoking a health hazard while still indulging in it. The woman tells us she is in the middle of a difficult struggle in her job, which she hates with a passion. She describes smoking as her one pleasure, her one badly needed relief—even though she hates cigarettes!

She is upset that she now faces having to give up her "slavery" and take a step to eliminate this grave threat to her health. She claims that any time she forces herself to forgo a cigarette she becomes extremely anxious and is sure she cannot continue her professional battle.

The woman is divorced and has no local family ties. Because her smoking behavior has been discordant all along—she insists these hateful cigarettes are essential to her job—she now feels a loss of integrity when her doctor tells her to stop. She does what all of us do, she tries to prolong her present compromise. Smoking is now defined as necessary; she "just can't give it up." "Not giving it up," however, clearly means that her very survival is threatened.

We inquire why she might want to die and get a surprising answer. She has made a number of suicide attempts before divorcing her husband and she thinks about suicide whenever she is depressed about her job. She cannot stand her job without smoking; if she has to quit smoking, she will also have to quit her job. She defines "smoking" and "job" as absolutely interdependent. Why?

We discover that her ex-husband and his new wife work for the same company as she does and that it is this woman with whom she has all the trouble. She knows that she cannot stay on the job without the comfort of smoking, but neither can she leave her job. That would mean another defeat; it would be like permitting the other woman to win again. Smoking behavior is directly related to her standing up to this woman. She would rather kill herself than stop competing.

Once she finally breaks out of this word cage ("smoking" equals "integrity"), she is able to find another compromise. She obtains a transfer within the company. She then gives up smoking, though with much pain. The coercive, discordant message that helped her maintain the smoking behavior (and which she experienced with every cigarette) almost led to her demise.

The specific nature of the discordance can give us a deep understanding of the conflicting motivations governing an individual's conduct. Here, smoking means to compete and to risk death; not to smoke means to live without integrity and lose out a second time. Once the sensitive balance of these two motivational forces is disturbed by a shockingly unexpected response (her doctor's warning), she has to redefine her alternatives and find new options.

How do we get at the motivation expressed in the discordant message? If we are asked by an inveterate smoker to help him stop smoking, we have to listen—to discover just what the smoker is expressing to himself by smoking while simultaneously berating himself for it.

For most people who want to quit smoking but "can't," smoking has been given a very meaningful place in their lives. Generally speaking, it helps them feel that they are maintaining their integrity, that they are courageous in risking danger, and that they must fight for their pleasures. (These, of course, are favorite themes for the admen. "If I'm going to smoke, I'm going to do it right!"; "Come to Marlboro Country"; "I'd rather fight than switch!").

We can gain further understanding of such word-cage definitions by listening to the stresses keeping the discordance alive. The act of lighting up a cigarette while knowing one ought not to is not only a habit but the anchor of a coercive life-style. It is a noble gesture that tells him, "Despite everything, I remain master of my fate." For those willing to listen, it is a warning, a message that urgently calls for a reorganization of activities, a search for better options, and a redefinition of critical words and concepts.

Freedom from Choice: Alcoholism

When someone drinks too much, what he is communicating to himself overlaps, in the broadest sense, with the messages transmitted through the abuse of tobacco, food, and drugs: the abuser feels he is caught in a vise, he has no free choice.

The difference between smoke, food, and alcohol abuse are easily detected when we observe what people believe smoking, eating, and drinking will do for them. Alcohol is defined by many as a drug that brings about mood changes, primarily in the direction of happy and relaxed moods.

Actually, it is a depressant; even though it does not cause "depression," it depresses the inhibitory centers of the brain, permitting a person to act uninhibitedly. Even the lonely drinker can benefit from lack of inhibition, because he can at least permit himself the imagery of strength, beauty, and integrity.

Food and smoking abuse, on the other hand, do not encourage uninhibited behavior. A cigarette does not permit us to tell off a rival. Alcohol does. A cigarette does not permit us to think of ourselves as strong and creative—if only we could break the habit. Alcohol does.

Alcohol is often used as an excuse when someone asserts himself too heavily. ("You should see him in his cups. He's a little Hitler.") Also, alcohol permits a shift of responsibility away from oneself, even in criminal behavior. ("I was drunk. I did not know what I was doing.")

The propensity for developing alcoholism may very well have a genetic base; that is, some people may have a greater than average physiological "bias" toward using alcohol to work out their problems. But greater propensity only implies that genetic predisposition may be a contributing cause; it is not likely to be sufficient.

Alcoholics ordinarily do not call themselves alcoholics but often state, particularly when drunk, that they could stop drinking anytime. They commonly boast of a sense of control they probably do not possess.

Alcoholics Anonymous, still the most effective way of helping an alcoholic stop drinking, reaches only those who voluntarily join the organization. Many who need help just as much are not getting it. A.A. teaches the alcoholic first to accept that he is an alcoholic.

From a communications point of view, this is a sound procedure because it forces the alcoholic out of discordant behavior. The discordance in alcoholism comes from the alcoholic's conflicting motivations; he says he is motivated to stop drinking because of his social and personal crises: losing his job, his home, his friends, his property. But he is also deeply motivated to continue drinking. A.A.'s demand that the alcoholic first accept that he is an alcoholic means he has to commit himself to giving up the rewards he obtains from fighting himself with every drink.

Apparently there is no one personality pattern that fits the alcoholic. He is not typically weak, dependent, or unassertive. While individual alcoholics will use alcohol for all sorts of reasons, the one common feature is the specific means of shifting responsibility away from oneself.

Apparently alcohol permits a person to improve his self-image without the necessity of providing proof. The alcoholic may feel sexually strong, desirable, and desirous, but he often cannot prove his potency —and does not need to in order to maintain that glow. He feels very witty and clever but does not need the smiles and admiration of others for support. He feels physically very powerful, but even if he is pushed over he can celebrate his victory. In other words, alcohol temporarily dissolves discordance as far as the drinker himself is concerned.

Let's look more closely at one of these imaginary victories. Think of a male alcoholic who has a self-image of a sexually strong and desirable stud, even though he cannot perform. He is quite different from the person who experiences sexual dysfunction. The alcoholic may undergo sexual defeat but he does not berate himself for it. A man with a sexual dysfunction, on the other hand, expresses a discordant message; he wants sex relations, but he does not provide an erection; then he punishes himself and the woman by feeling bad. His desire is to perform more adequately, but he is also motivated to fail.

The alcoholic expresses his discordance through the conflicting motivations inherent in his drinking behavior. He does not experience discordance in his sexual failure. The specific reward of alcohol is experienced in neutralizing his performance anxiety, in relieving himself of the pressure of social expectations. If he runs into a telephone pole with his car, he is likely to be amused by the odd shape of the hood.

This wondrous and beautiful relief from performance anxiety (he can fail and still feel on top of the situation) appears to us to be the psychological basis for the habit-forming characteristic of alcohol. The alcoholic seems to have found a miracle drug to reduce or even temporarily eliminate aversive pressures and, in spite of all its negative consequences, provides him with a feeling of integrity. He no longer has to fight himself.

Many alcoholics in hospitals claim with great sincerity that they are through with drinking, only to get drunk at the next opportunity. They set up false expectations in others, which they apparently do not want to honor; it is as if they found special pleasure in deceiving others with these expectations.

Yet alcoholics in many hospitals are also known for their great capacity to function well when sober. In many wards they are leaders. Many successful businessmen are alcoholics; apparently they can function as well as they do because they have also found a way of alleviating the strain. In fact, some industries maintain a pool of alcoholics working together on a limited number of jobs—for example, ten alcoholics for four jobs. So alcoholism does not have to be totally debilitating; it sometimes can be lived with and represents only a partial shift of responsibility.

When an alcoholic is under the influence of alcohol, however, the discordance between what he is and what he feels he ought to be dissolves, and this results in low performance anxiety. He actually sees sober, successful performance as dangerous, since it threatens to raise performance anxiety. He defines success as selling out. But he cannot accept personal responsibility for not succeeding, so he shifts this responsibility to alcohol. And with discordance temporarily reduced, he gains the ability to laugh, to thumb his nose at those who demand performance, and even at himself for demanding integrity.

For example, a composer fears his powers are dwindling, and he is afraid to complete a half-finished symphony because he is sure he will be pilloried by the critics. So he writes bawdy little songs that he sings regularly to his friends at the local tavern—to his own piano accompaniment. When asked how the symphony is coming along, he almost boasts, "I'm tired of being a longhair. I'd much rather enjoy myself. And besides, I'm too drunk to carry it off."

The difficulty of treating the alcoholic is well known. In many treatment models there is a demand for immediate cessation, which is like taking away the only peace the "patient" knows. With hospitalization, rules of this kind can be enforced because temporarily the alcoholic can find comfort in attaching a "sick" label to himself. In nonhospital settings such rules are not very effective. The demand for total abstinence is made in the belief that one drink leads to another.

Some contemporary procedures attempt to train the alcoholic to drink socially rather than to abstain. He is trained to drink in small sips with long pauses between sips, and in pleasant social surroundings. So far there is no evidence that these technical approaches have been very successful.

Neither is Antabuse, a drug that makes the experience of a drink dangerously unpleasant. Under such circumstances, people gulp for air and swear they will never drink again; and they usually don't as long as they take their Antabuse. As soon as they are on their own, however, they are likely not to take the Antabuse. Unless forced, very few people will give up the miracle of instant peace.

By and large, talking treatments in private sessions are also unsuccessful. As soon as a patient begins to deal with the problem, he performs better and then becomes anxious about having sold out to society. On the other hand, when the whole family can be persuaded to participate in the treatment and share responsibility for the expected performance, success is more frequent. In a family setting, the degree of performance expected of the alcoholic is reduced accordingly. He apparently no longer needs to feel he is selling out when he is successful, and his need for "instant peace" wanes.

The effect of family involvement is illustrated in the case of an alcoholic who went on a binge every two weeks, directly after receiving his paycheck. (He was working in his father's business.) His pattern was invariable; he drank heavily at a neighborhood bar, invited all present to share his two-week income, and following this was given to writing checks he could not cover. At closing time, his father would appear to carry him home and put him to bed. The father supported him for another two weeks and covered the bad checks.

In the family therapy session, the father had to learn that his good intentions carried a different message than he imagined. He wanted to help his son when the son was in trouble—a noble intention indeed. We suggested that his help was misplaced, that by taking the initiative and softening the consequences of his son's drinking bouts he robbed his son of self-respect.

It then became apparent that the son was under heavy family pressure to take over the family business. His drinking behavior was probably triggered by a dilemma. He wanted to do well, but he felt he was not his own man while working for his father. Facing a loss of integrity when successful, he resolved this discordance by getting drunk and writing bad checks. He was thus able to laugh at his own performance anxiety and to show his covert aggression toward his father. The father's coming to the rescue contributed significantly to the son's continued indulgence.

The pattern of their collaboration was discussed in one of the family sessions, and the father decided to withdraw his helping hand. He told his son that he would not drag him home from the bar and would no longer cover the bad checks. The son, he added, could live at home for a limited time only, and he would have to pay for room and board.

In short, he let the son know that he (the son) was now accepted as a person: he could be responsible or irresponsible, drunk or sober, but he now was on his own. The father had to accept the risk that his wish to have the son take over the family business might come to naught.

This sudden shift, worked out in the family session, was not without pain. The father and mother were afraid the son would "go to the dogs."

The son resisted, saying, "I guess I do need you to help me. I am sick." But in the end, the father's message did lower the son's performance anxiety.

At first the son tried very hard to reestablish the old pattern by getting into fights; he even landed in jail one night. Then one day he moved out of the parental home, used his paycheck to cover some checks he had signed while drunk, and started to straighten out his life. His first act was to quit the family business and start one of his own. He eventually went to A.A., and has remained sober ever since.

Unfortunately, such talking treatments are not usually so successful. One reason is that the alcoholic's discordance between performance demands and personal integrity poses a dilemma that extends into the therapeutic hour. Whenever a talking treatment "works," the alcoholic soon feels the need to undermine his newly successful performance and reestablish his integrity. Hence, another binge. Through skillful use of covert communications, he creates a self-perpetuating system.

In the above case the father had become engaged in the system; he served as a biweekly trigger that perpetuated the familiar cycle. The son had successfully shifted responsibility for his own conduct to the father.

During therapy, the son introduced this same style. He invited the therapist to "help," but as soon as the therapist felt he was getting somewhere, there would be another binge. The son had to upend the therapist's expectations in order to enhance his own sense of integrity. The therapist's ego involvement in his own therapeutic success becomes his undoing. But just as the father could accept the son's own choices, the therapist can remain disengaged. He must learn that he is facing a discordance of two significant values: performing as expected and maintaining personal integrity.

To control drinking behavior, the alcoholic needs to restructure his life-style. He has to experience that high performance does not have to be threatening and that standing on one's own two feet can be very satisfying.

The image of alcohol as a devil's brew that destroys people in small doses is potent, but we must recognize that alcohol specifically serves the alcoholic as a friendly scapegoat; it explains his poor performance, reduces his performance anxiety, and allows him to believe in his own essential integrity without having to prove it.

How to Be Carefully Stoned: Drug Abuse

The smoke abuser, the food abuser, and the alcoholic have in common that they have an alibi—a habit that permits them to claim they obtain their pleasure under some sort of duress. It is believable when they say, "I tried to give it up, but I just couldn't help myself."

The hard-drug user also has an alibi habit that allows him to shift responsibility for his indulgence to the drug itself. By "hard" drugs we mean addictive drugs, not marijuana or hallucinogens such as LSD and psilocybin. We also distinguish between "nonviolent" use and "violent" or "criminal" use. In either case we are concerned with an understanding of the hard-drug user's motivations broader than is implied by the "dope-addict" stereotype. The physiological effects of hard drugs are still highly significant, of course, and the "cause" of addiction remains an unsolved problem.

One of the major communicative features of hard-drug use is that it is illegal. We shall first look at individuals for whom the "criminality" of using such drugs is minimal, that is, where there is no great problem in securing the drugs.

Long before the present preoccupation with hard-drug abuse, hard drugs were most often consumed by doctors, nurses, and jazz musicians. The criminality here involved securing the drug illegally, but without violence. These groups of users are similar to the drug abusers in the armed forces who could secure drugs in Vietnam and other countries at a price they could afford; they could indulge without violence. (Prior to the present drug problem, there were also "lower-class" drug abusers who used violence to secure the drug, but they were relatively small in number.)

The nonviolent abusers used these drugs with some care. Ordinarily, they did not fall victim to illnesses and death, which occur from unexpected dose strength or from infected needles. Because they rarely came to the attention of the courts, we know very little about this group.

Many physicians and nurses who had these drugs available seem to have functioned adequately enough in their positions that they were ordinarily not recognized as abusers. They apparently could experience pleasure, even a sense of euphoria and total relaxation from the pressures of everyday life, and yet they could feel (privately, as it were) that they, too, were partaking of the forbidden fruit.

Unlike alcohol, hard drugs permitted the nonviolent user to withdraw from the environment without having to act anything out. He walked in a land without barriers, without responsibility; performance anxiety was a foreign word. He experienced an altered state of consciousness, almost a religious state. But even when active—a stoned jazz musician, for example—he could explore new worlds of thought and feeling. In a very private sense, he was living in a universe of his own creation.

These drugs, even more than alcohol, rendered the abuser uninterested in and often incapable of sexual performance. That, too, may have been an added attraction for some, particularly for those who suffered from sexual performance anxiety. Such self-denial is not as unusual as it sounds, for there have always been people—priests, nuns, and many others—who adopt a whole life-style that rejects sex relations altogether.

The main characteristics that set the nonviolent hard-drug user apart from the alcoholic, the overeater, and the habitual smoker are the need for secrecy (because of his illegal status) and the need for reducing or even eliminating interaction with the immediate environment. Often it is not only the drug but society which serves as an object onto which responsibility is shifted.

A physician we interviewed said, "To fake the prescription is really part of the fun; it's always exciting to have to do so. With that, I'm telling society off, a society which puts too much pressure on me and doesn't want me, or allow me, to relax." This physician's style included his feeling of integrity for taking a stand, his overly strong need to perform, and the compromise that allowed him to goof off and still feel good about himself.

Interestingly, returned veterans who had been on hard drugs without violence felt the same way. They were also more likely to accept methadone maintenance programs, that is, the free noncriminal use of a drug probably as addictive as heroin. They could accept the free drug because their style did not require excuses for violence, whereas those who had taken the criminal route to drug addiction had a much harder time accepting free drugs.

Returned veterans as a group appeared more willing to reorganize their lives after returning to the United States, where they were faced with the necessity of criminal activity to obtain the drug. On the other hand, users who developed the expensive-drug habit while fully aware that they had to commit crimes to support it are in a very different class. We might think that they especially, living constantly with the possibility of death, sickness, and jail, would prefer a free, legal drug. Apparently that is not so.

Paradise Is No Good if It's Legal

Why does a free-drug program not work as readily with people who got into drug abuse by way of the criminal route? The communication afforded by using a decriminalized drug like methadone does not usually answer the needs of users who became addicted to an extremely expensive drug obtained by criminal means.

These people apparently are attracted not only by the drug but also by the life-style that goes with it—a style characterized by the use of force. Some have learned to appreciate their indulgences only when they are associated with violence. In the sexual area, this includes men who like to commit rape or, in the extreme case, to kill their "love" object. Perhaps they want to communicate to themselves and others that they have a desperate right to their pleasures.

Hard-drug users are often exposed to the drug at an early age, but not all children exposed actually take the drug or become addicted. Very young users come from strict homes, from amoral homes, from loving homes, and from unloving homes, and initial use is probably prompted by the fads and fashions of the times.

Not everyone who starts with the drug stays with it. Some take it for several weeks and find it doesn't do anything for them. They may have started because they were shamed into it by their peers, or because they wanted to appear daring, or because they wanted to make a loud statement to their parents about their own freedom.

Those who stick with it and continue until they are addicted, however, need more than a sense of alienation or a feeling of comradeship with their friends. They are very soon aware that this is a hard drug to get hold of—financially, at least—and that it is thought to be dangerous and given to ruining lives.

Our hypothesis is that the youngsters who continue with the drug do so for a number of reasons: because they like to play with danger, because they have learned they have to fight for their pleasure, because they feel good about avoiding the "rat race" of school or regular employment. Also because their life-style discourages the delay of pleasure and because drugs are a prohibited fruit, which can only be obtained by standing up against the establishment.

The drug is a miracle worker. It gives immediate kicks. It slowly draws the child into an ever-increasing show of force against the establishment so he can act out his anger and feel powerful without feeling guilty. It lifts him out of the pressures and expectations of his life; he can maintain his sense of integrity without having to succeed and he can act out his aggression and anger without feeling bad about it.

He can shrug when confronted with warnings, for he has already discounted the danger. The discordance of conflicting motivations finds an almost perfect—though momentary—compromise. He has left home but found a violent family that offers him a new home.

The new family of drug abusers has its own loyalties, its own language, its own despair. It may not provide rich human relationships or love or even kindness, but there is a common direction and a deep understanding for other members of this family. All are pleasure-gatherers bound together by a "religious" commitment. All are living in fear of hell—of not being able to obtain the miracle drug—and it is not surprising that so many former drug users have become Jesus freaks. They share the comradeship of scoring, of violence, and of ever-present danger.

This meaningful, exciting life, which represents to the addict his strength, is now combined with an immense sense of well-being and relaxation when the drug has its full effect. The combination, the compromise of needs, makes it very difficult for a young user to come home to his old family. Home is a different country, with other habits and another language.

Since the compromise includes violence, the young addict cannot accept a nonviolent solution, and he becomes suspicious of a decriminalized drug such as methadone. It is inconceivable to him to accept pleasure from society without a fight; it threatens his entire life-style. He needs that part of the excitement that fighting provides. It is not unlike the more sedate feeling of the physician: "Part of the fun is faking the prescriptions." For the "violent" drug abuser, part of the fun lies in the direct confrontation with society, often in the form of innocent bystanders.

The communications of the addict go something like this: "There is too large a distance between myself and those who are successful. I cannot and do not want to learn all the skills you tell me to learn. I am gathering my pleasures now. All I need is a fix, and my feelings of having to do your thing are gone. And I *do* need it—by force if necessary. I can't help myself. That is what all my new family is about."

When offered treatment, he is not willing to talk about himself, as required in psychotherapy. His very existence is a rebellion against requirements. The last thing he wants is to reorganize his life, for he has put all his resources into, and gets all his satisfactions from, his present, violent way.

To learn to live in society again rather than in the street, he would have to learn how to derive a feeling of integrity from sources other than the aggression for which he disclaims responsibility. In order to change, he would have to listen and care and open himself up to experiences that involve warmth and concern. Living styles can be changed, but change requires a great deal of patience and an understanding of the meanings that change has for the person involved.

Methadone maintenance programs were introduced because it was finally recognized that arresting drug addicts did not reduce their number. The decriminalization program was designed to do away with the addict's need to support his $50- to $100-a-day habit through violence. It started with the laudable intention of reducing violence in crime-infested cities and helping the abuser to reorganize his life.

As with many other programs, early problems threw the whole thing out of gear. The first step was to decriminalize the fix. The new free "high" attracted a large number of people, but while it was helpful to the "nonviolent" users, it largely failed with those whose life-style revolved around street crime.

Something could have been learned from the early visits of street people who came because they were curious and wanted to find out what strings would be attached to the gifts. But the program was not designed for *listening* to the people it was set up to help. There was very little listening, even less caring, and almost no research.

The philosophy was to use abusers who had overcome the habit to carry out the day-to-day contacts with the active addicts. This seemed to be a good idea, as there were many helpers available and the cost was moderate. The program was styled along the lines of Alcoholics Anonymous, where the alcoholic who has stopped drinking becomes the guide for one who hopes to stop, but some important conceptual differences were neglected.

A.A. workers are recruited as volunteers, and they do not decide how much alcohol a new convert may drink; they assume that even one drink is too much. The convert has to make the decision not to drink on his own; he is not sentenced to A.A., and A.A. is not a place where alcohol or an alcohol substitute is legally dispensed. There is, therefore, no structural coercion to attend.

In the methadone maintenance programs, however, a drug reasonably similar to an illegal drug is legally available, and this of course is a form of coercion. The paraprofessionals in this program have to decide (or recommend to their superiors) how much methadone the "client" is to be given. Within a very short time, this dispensing function was the only major contact with the abuser.

There were some efforts at psychotherapy, but the group sessions were often devoted to discussion of dispensing problems. The workload of the paraprofessional became very heavy, and he received only a minimal amount of training in listening and other modes of caring. He was merely instructed to help the abuser to taper off, to take smaller amounts of the drug.

The intentions were good, and some people were doubtlessly reached with the message that "this is your opportunity to get out of the drug rat race." But many, particularly the street people, could not have cared less. They saw in the program just another hassle or just another opportunity to rip off the establishment; certainly their way of life was not understood. They saw only the prospect of losing their pleasures, their social life, even their language; and no one gives up his way of life without some hope for a new and better one. So they had a free ride as long as it lasted, manipulated the paraprofessionals as well as they could, and returned to their old ways when it all got to be a bore.

If the managers had listened for the consequences of their acts, they would have realized they were missing the best chance of reaching the people they were committed to help. As for the paraprofessionals, being a former drug abuser does not necessarily prepare a person to make wise decisions or to care or to convey the message that a better life is possible. Had the managers given a high priority to training these people, the underlying philosophy would not have been one of taking away a familiar life-style, but rather one of providing hope and skills for a new life.

What the hard-drug user needed was exposure to models for closer human relationships and encouragement to seek affectional ties. He needed help with his immediate problems, with legal difficulties, and with the task of finding living quarters away from the street. Such efforts were actually made by one chain of drug treatment centers, which did not believe in methadone maintenance, the nationwide Odyssey House program. However, this program appealed to only a few addicts, those who found comfort in the heavy discipline of a new family.

While the methadone maintenance programs have been heavily criticized, they are a long step forward as far as society at large is concerned. The very existence of the program tells us that society is beginning to recognize that making drug abuse a criminal offense has devastating consequences. It also implies that adults whose life-style encourages drug use are no longer quite as frightening to us as the old stereotype would have it.

Alcohol abuse always has been a bigger problem for society than drug abuse, yet it has been accepted as a tolerable life-style. Drug abuse, were it decriminalized, would probably be less violent than alcohol abuse. Furthermore, those who are presently attracted to the drug because they can indulge in violence without feeling responsible would probably stay away from it altogether, or would shift over to alcohol as an alternative alibi-habit.

Hard drugs have always been "unacceptable" in our society. Anyone who wants to turn inward in his own way and does not care to participate in society is embracing a life-style that threatens the *Weltanschauung* of Western culture. "Progressive" Westerners today are concerned with problem-solving, with living standards, with intelligence, education, and science, and with amassing material goods and services; anyone who claims he can be happy without such goals is not only suspect but threatening. He must hit a sensitive nerve of society, because somewhere, sometime, everyone dreams of getting out of the rat race.

Decriminalization of currently illegal drugs would at the very least communicate, to users and nonusers alike, that this "foreign" style is no longer quite so foreign in its nonviolent, decriminalized form. It would leave room for the alternative of seeking happiness by turning inward.

Is it not appropriate for a democratic society to facilitate a variety of life-styles rather than to decree what our individual paths to happiness shall be?

15

Violence

Society, when it confronts crime, thinks largely in terms of property loss, the invasion of privacy, and the injury and distress suffered by the victim. The "cure" is typically assumed to be providing punishment and the threat of punishment.

If we are interested in reducing criminal behavior and not just in punishing criminals, we shall have to start looking at aggression as an interactive event involving a number of significant communications on the part of the criminal. He has needs that go far beyond the obvious rewards of an isolated criminal act, and there may be many other ways of fulfilling these needs.

At present, our typical attitude toward crime prevention is that of the parent who lays on his child all the "don'ts" without offering him any of the alternative satisfactions that could help him accept the "loss" of his undesirable but rewarding acts.

We are in the habit of perceiving crime in terms of the "target behavior" alone, imagining that a robbery is fully explained by "the need for money" or a murder by "vengeance." We could come a lot closer to understanding (and thus influencing) criminal behavior if we would look at "undesirable" behavior as part of a fixed action pattern stemming from a number of related motives and bringing many rewards beyond the one obvious goal.

An undesirable act may be first of all the communication of a desperate need. An upstanding family man who commits his first burglary may be communicating to his wife that he is taking a desperate risk "in order to save our future," and that he is forced to do so because he never really had a chance to live up to her expectations.

Vaguely aware of his motives, he apparently wants to communicate both his despair and his unadmitted feeling that she is to blame for it. Once we understand this communication, we can see that in order to rehabilitate him, we shall have to enhance his communication with his wife. Punishment alone will reinforce, not inhibit, his criminal means of communicating.

The Individual: A Violent Plea

We are interested in aggression and violence as *communications* here and now: what does a society or a person hope to communicate to others (or to himself) by engaging in aggressive behavior?

Every individual has his own unique style for expressing aggression and his own very personal reasons for doing so in his own peculiar way. Aggressive styles and motives are often hidden and diffuse, but they are sometimes revealed with remarkable clarity in psychotherapy. Here is a case in point:

A patient who had been in a mental hospital told me during a critical hour that he had one evening tried to destroy his infant son with a fly swatter. He said he saw imaginary flies sitting all over his son's face and body. He said he knew the flies were imaginary but he nevertheless swatted at them harder and harder until his son's face and body turned blue all over from the bruises.

As I listened to the story, I felt more and more disgusted. I was thinking, how can a person *do* such a thing? But then I remembered my role, here, as a therapist who is not supposed to judge but to heal and help.

I began to realize that this man was trying to induce in me, with his description of his violent act, feelings of disgust and rejection, perhaps to test whether or not I would then reject him. Perhaps he would derive satisfaction from making me respond with disgust, proving that I was no better than any of his other so-called friends.

Either way, achieving success in my case would allow him to go his way, confident that he could at any time involve other people by getting them to hate him. He watched me carefully, but I did not permit him to "succeed" this time. His voice droned on, describing his indifferent feelings while he was doing violence to his own child.

At one point I looked at the patient and I knew I was right—he was a desperate man, struggling, a man grasping for something solid to which he could cling. I felt warm toward him for a moment, and I said to him, "You have beautiful eyes. You do have beautiful eyes."

The patient, having worked so hard to generate in me a response of disgust and rejection, suddenly sensed my reaching out and became totally uncertain of himself. His familiar strategy was no longer working. He apparently realized that here was someone who did not feel disgust but saw through his designs.

He must have experienced that perhaps there was after all something worthwhile about him. He started to cry, and through his tears, in his oddly unemotional voice, he said, "Thank you."

I thought about this young man for a long time and thought how easy it would have been to condemn him and feel frightened by him and do the very things he wanted me to do. I thought how very often we do exactly what violent people want us to do.

I am reminded of a psychiatrist who came into a staff conference and said,

"Today I saw the most depraved human being I've ever seen. He had hit a woman. He was walking down the street and with tremendous force struck a woman in her face. Fortunately, she agreed to report the incident, and the man was brought before the court because of unprovoked violence. He was sentenced, but he claimed a psychiatric history. He is not in the hospital, but I swear he will not escape his sentence."

I am reminded of this statement because here was a psychiatrist dedicated to helping people, but the act of violence triggered a predictable response: this man had hit a woman and tried to escape punishment; what an evil man he must be! Possessed by this information, the psychiatrist forgot his mission.

In both cases, the aggressor seems to have chosen unprovoked assault as the means for generating strong condemning responses from the righteous people of the world. In the latter case, the man involved an innocent bystander, a judge, and even his doctor, and he knew they each hated him with a passion.

He must have felt a great sense of power, being able to make a doctor forget his professional commitment by delivering no more than a fifteen-second flow of information. It must have been gratifying to realize one's ability to change the immediate environment that much in so short a time. With remarkably little effort, he had not only caused the world to pay attention to him; he had manipulated several important strangers to feel strongly involved with him.

Criminal Acts

A professional burglar often communicates through the very specificity of his crime; in large cities, police investigators may be able to identify a major burglary suspect from his characteristic "signature."

There are a great many of these "signatures." Some burglars specialize only in fifth-floor hotel rooms; some never take anything but money, while others take only pearls. Still others work with unique tools that leave a distinctive mark. Some burglars have developed specific routines which they repeat every time—checking the premises by telephone, singing on the job, returning to the scene the next day at noon. There are also those who leave behind a literal signature such as a scrap of paper bearing a name like "Zorro" or "Zodiac."

In other words, the burglar, like the rest of us, has developed a particular style, and we get the impression that living out this style is as important to him as the loot he comes home with. Many burglars could have increased their haul considerably if they had been free to break their established stylistic patterns.

In what way is this "uneconomical" behavior a communication? What is the man trying to tell the world—or tell himself? We talked with a burglar who had committed ninety acts of burglary, each of them bringing him approximately $4000. He burglarized only food stores, and only those that kept their receipts in a certain kind of safe—"the only model I have any fun cracking." Whenever he found a safe that was too easy, that would not call upon all his skills, he would leave without taking anything.

Typically, he cased the store ahead of time and never failed to buy a chicken and garlic salt "for good luck." His style required also that he break into the drug counter and steal an enema syringe. He never took amphetamines, which he used occasionally but preferred to purchase; he reasoned that "it isn't good to have too many of them around." The syringe he broke and left in front of the store.

With each job, the burglar apparently wanted to communicate to himself a number of very personal things: that he preferred to "earn" his way by risk-taking rather than by working, that he wanted to demonstrate that the world owed him a living, that each job was undertaken, at least symbolically, for his mother (who loved chicken cooked in garlic sauce), and that he was skillful enough to leave clues and still avoid punishment (breaking the syringe).

Communication to oneself, of course, has to operate within the symbolism of a private language, which is highly idiosyncratic and determined by one's personal history. This burglar, however, was also communicating to the police and to society at large. He was called the Syringe Burglar, and it was widely known that he favored chain food stores exclusively and that he was highly skilled in the art of safecracking.

The trademark he always left behind—the syringe—was seen by the police as a symbolic curse ("Fuck you!"). His police "profile" described him as a person of regular habits, intelligent, highly skillful, angry at society, and possibly subject to a few serious hang-ups. It was interesting to note that, while these characteristics are common to a great many people, they were the very characteristics he stressed in himself.

Stylistic expressions are probably intended to serve as communications and are certainly received by others as such. The way a person commits his crime tells something about him, and it appears that he in fact *wants* to communicate, through his act, some important aspects of his self-image.

In certain tribes in eastern Africa, the chief once a year randomly selects from his most esteemed advisers a number of individuals who are then put to death. Clearly this act is not to the chief's immediate advantage, but it is a communication to his people that he alone governs, that he is totally in control.

In a similar gesture, Henri Christophe, king of Haiti from 1811 to 1820, was known to march his own elite soldiers off a precipice to impress visiting dignitaries. Christophe, incidentally, had been born a slave. His life ended in suicide when he shot himself with a silver bullet.

Violence to Grow By

Such "acting-out" behavior is not really all that foreign to us in everyday life, even though the extreme cases sound cruel. We often do use violence to communicate to others that we are in control.

A tantrum is the simplest and most infantile example; it is a way of testing control. The child throws a tantrum to establish the nature of his power relationship with his parents. He generally cannot attack his parents directly because he is too weak. He cannot gain control by threatening overt aggression, because they are not afraid of him. But he can confront them by means of a tantrum and thereby test their willingness to act, communicate to them a deep sense of dissatisfaction, and make a bid for a greater share of control.

The adult may be frustrated and may react with anger or even with ridicule, but he cannot ignore the message that the child has reached his limits of endurance and is no longer to be trifled with. Clearly, the tantrum is a demonstration, a communicative act of alerting the adult to the fact that adult control has its limits.

A child in school is brought to our attention because he throws glass into other children's faces or beats them up or uses abusive language. The child might be described as simply "acting out his aggressive impulses," but this is not very revealing. We need to know a lot more. Why does he indulge himself by acting out his aggression? Why here and why now? What is the information he wants to get across to the teacher, to the other children, to himself at this time?

A nine-year-old child, unless he is mentally retarded, knows very well that when he throws glass into another boy's face he will hurt the child and will arouse the attention of teachers, the principal, other children, and probably his parents. His aggression is a manipulation of his environment and a very effective one: he gets results.

But his communication is directed toward himself as well. He may want to assure himself that he is desperate—desperate enough to challenge the world, if necessary. He may want to test how far adults will go to control him, and perhaps he wants to earn, with his communication, the fear and respect of his peers.

In the adolescent, aggression is typically employed as a means of locating the psychological and physical limits of his own being.

Adolescent rebellion has been clearly noted for many centuries; the adolescent wants to tell something to others as well as to himself, and a delinquent act is a most effective communication. Often he just wants to locate (or perhaps to create) the "enemy" he needs in order to discover and test his own strength.

For example, a boy tells us, when we inadvertently move an ashtray an inch or so in his direction, to stop criticizing him about smoking. He is not a smoker and we have no particular view about smoking, but it is important to him to have us as an enemy at this moment.

The adolescent develops his style during these years, or at least he reaffirms it. His style becomes more firmly channeled, and the channel he selects has everything to do with what he wants to communicate. He needs to express his new-found strengths, which he can do on any or many levels, from overt physical violence to the display of very subtle forms of "strength" expressed in tone of voice, gesture, posture, dress. He may even resort to messages we generally call self-destructive, such as having accidents or sinking into depressions.

The adolescent wants to realize his growing sense of control over his world, and he sends out information to test its effectiveness. In a recent study of male adolescents imprisoned for having murdered one of their parents, there were no regrets to be found. In fact, the young men felt good about it. In every case they said the victim deserved it. They had been so desperate that now they saw their jail sentences as a reasonable price to pay. Apparently, the communicative meaning of murder is at least as important as its consequences. The son says to himself and to the world: "I could not survive any longer without my self-respect."

Communication also plays a role with the adolescent who does not wash, wears torn clothes, and won't look for a job. He sets up, for all to see, his daily experience of rejection—and he knows precisely how to get rejected. This proves that adults in authority are incompetent and do not appreciate the real human values just beneath the surface. The urgent need to establish a personal value system is repeatedly the source of an adolescent's desperate communications to himself and others.

Since human culture is dependent upon the rechanneling of primitive aggressive (and sexual) instincts, and since all of us have been taught to inhibit violent impulses, we usually prefer not to appear as the author of our aggressive acts. But we still like to engage in these acts. The dilemma is resolved by our capacity to shift blame and elict aggression in others.

We communicate subtle cues that prompt violent acts on the part of other people; then we can respond or join in without being held responsible. This shifting of blame and subtle prompting of aggression can be directed toward ourselves as well as others. We can literally talk ourselves into a state of explosive anger and then say, "I had to do it because I have such a temper."

An adolescent, for example, may talk himself into a white-hot fury concerning the ways in which the establishment discriminates against youth, and then use this "freaked-out state" as an excuse for robbing or mugging an elderly victim. He actually feels courageous and righteous. He may even convince himself that he is on God's side because he is robbing the rich and thus encouraging equality.

This kind of self-deceit looks "evil" when used to justify a criminal act, but the mechanism is common to all of us; it enhances our ability to live with our own behavior and it represents a compromise among various expectations we feel we have to live up to.

Peace, Officer

Looking at crime as an interactive pattern requires that we look at the victim as well as the criminal. The victim's response is often the principal reward the criminal is seeking.

Many crimes directed against policemen, for example, probably have more to do with a predictable "police response" than with the victim's individual actions. When one policeman is killed, all policemen feel the blow, and the results are breathtaking. Kill an ordinary pedestrian and you are just another murderer; kill a cop and you are overnight hated by policemen the world over—which can be a rewarding response if you relish giant enemies.

The killer has murdered not just a man but a symbol. Policemanship itself has been threatened, the manhunt is pursued with a vengeance not accorded the ordinary murderer, and this communicates to the criminal the information that the police are more concerned with their own image and vulnerability than with justice.

On the other hand, the police are also guilty of crimes motivated by their response to a class (hippies, longhairs, students, and drivers of gaily painted VW buses, for example), regardless of the actions of the individual. Again, all members of this class feel the blow.

Shortly after the Kent State murders, a University of California drama student walking along Telegraph Avenue in Berkeley, passed two policemen who were raining blows on an unarmed boy lying on the sidewalk. The student turned and in a calm voice said, "Officer, this kid has had enough."

Without a word, the policemen knocked the student down, handcuffed him, and led him to their patrol car. As they returned to the injured boy on the sidewalk, the student noticed that the door of the patrol car was not locked. He kicked it open, ran across the street into a bank, and begged for help.

Immediately, several students surrounded him in order to disguise the fact that he was handcuffed. They walked him to the street and flagged down a couple who readily agreed to drive the student to safety. While the police were searching lunch counters and bookstores, the student was driven to Oakland, where his benefactors found someone to saw off the cuffs.

When one student is hit, all feel the blow. Neither the "student image" (in the eyes of the police) nor the "police image" (in the eyes of the students) was greatly enhanced by the incident.

The police also project a power image to the general public, largely because of their style and their costumes. Many law-abiding citizens feel uncomfortable in the presence of policemen, except on rare occasions when they suddenly need help. Most of us encounter police only in negative confrontations such as being ticketed for speeding. Despite the fact that our "peace officers" are literally hired by us to keep the peace and make life less threatening for us, they have in some sense failed to communicate that they are here to help us.

The black boots, the helmet, and (in the U.S.) the ever-present gun suggest brutality rather than the more noble aspects of law enforcement. Few softer communications or directly helpful activities counteract this impression.

The curious fact is that the criminal himself is probably less intimidated by these appearances than is the ordinary citizen. In turn, we as citizens consistently fail to give the police the support they need. In other words, the cops and robbers seem to inhabit a separate world. They cooperate, they speak the same language, and they behave as if they need each other in order to clearly maintain their own identities.

During the course of any violent act, villain and victim are constantly exchanging information and mutually influencing the course of the attack. There has been for a long time a saying that the person murdered shares responsibility for the event with the murderer. This goes very much against our sense of justice.

Certainly this is not always the case, and we think at once of the little old lady who means no harm and is mugged by a crazed addict. The responsibility here does not appear to be interactive. The mugger could have taken on any victim, and the little old lady surely did not deserve the violence or "do her share" in bringing it about.

This argument only holds, however, when we think of the little old lady as an individual victim. She is also a "class victim," just as an individual policeman or a captured enemy flier is often a "class victim." She suffers because she is an immediately available symbol of a society that tells the addict, loudly and vehemently, that he has absolutely no right to live his life his own way—that is, with the drug he craves.

He attacks the woman not as a person but as an assumed representative of the class of "haves" who enjoy special privilege and protection from the hardships of life, a target that will provide him both with the funds to live his life and with an outlet for his fury at being deprived. In that sense, the act is based on a shared responsibility of the villain (the addict) and the victim (a society which denies drugs), even though the little old lady is an innocent bystander.

The Law

The villain-victim model contains some peculiar contradictions in relation to what constitutes an "excuse" for having committed a violent act.

Under the law, a murderer can obtain a reduced sentence if he can prove he committed the crime on impulse. Premeditation, on the other hand, is thought to deserve the worst possible punishment. This means that people who consider the consequences of an antisocial act before acting are presumed to be much worse than those who are mysteriously compelled "by their emotions" to act in the same way. In the days when the devil was thought to possess the soul of the impulsive lawbreaker, this may have made some sense; but in terms of the principles of interactive behavior, this view is absurd.

The person who accepts responsibility for his own illegal action is held to be more of a threat to society than the person who behaves irresponsibly. In fact, the impulse murderer is likely to be a person who has embraced irresponsible behavior as part of his style. He is more likely to be a repeater than the individual who carefully considers the options available to him and takes responsibility for whatever choice he then makes.

This odd misunderstanding in the law—that the impulse-ridden person is less guilty and should receive a lesser punishment than his more rational brother—is not only theoretically unsound but also pragmatically unjustified. The "impulse" criminal claims he was driven by circumstances to seek relief from tension, which "justifies" his violence.

The courts seem to be saying, "If a person won't accept responsibility for his own actions, then he can't be held responsible for them by society." This sounds very much like a recommendation that we all forfeit self-awareness because this is an excellent way to escape severe punishment whenever our behavior becomes destructive.

Once we look at violent behavior as an interaction, some of the apparent differences between the considered (premeditated) act and the impulsive act begin to fade. In both cases, the aggressor chooses what he will do in accordance with the probable consequences of his act on others. Both are stimulated or triggered by some circumstance involving other people, and both are subject to some interactive control.

Furthermore, there is no such thing as "pure thought" or "pure impulse." Thinking about a crime can trigger impulses; the impulse may even be motivated by the idea of the great sense of relief that will undoubtedly follow—that is, by a premeditation.

A notable difference between considered violence and impulsive violence is evident when we look for ways to prevent it. The "thoughtful" aggressor must learn how to stop himself from thinking dangerously aggressive thoughts (which he is perfectly capable of doing), whereas the impulsive aggressor must learn how to stop allowing himself to be propelled into a state of rage (which he is perfectly capable of doing). Both are in the same position, however. Both bear the responsibility for changing that part of their interactive styles which they know is likely to lead directly to criminally violent action.

It is clear that criminal law is based on a false premise as to what constitutes responsibility. The control of violence is vested in laws based on a "villain-victim" philosophy, an irrational philosophy that rewards those who refuse to think about their own behavior and clearly fosters the very conduct it is presumably so concerned about.

By Reason of Insanity

The same dilemma (Is premeditated violence worse than unaware or impulsive violence?) surfaces again in the matter of a defendant's motivation: did he know right from wrong? Did he consciously make a "wrong" choice—or was he insane at the time of the crime?

The question of whether a human being can distinguish right from wrong in a general sense is a remarkably complex problem. It goes back to the Garden of Eden, where Eve and Adam defied God by eating the fruit of "the tree of knowledge of good and evil." It is in fact an area, if not an arena, in which psychological knowledge and the law meet head-on.

The law, like God, never questions its own definition of "right" and "wrong." But it readily excuses an accused person who generally does not appreciate the meaning of legally "wrong" conduct.

The rationale is: He is insane if he cannot make this general distinction, and it would be inhumane to punish someone who is thus "not responsible for his own behavior." Instead of being jailed, he is referred for psychiatric treatment.

This sounds like an enlightened law. The trouble is that the law, being an old and traditional institution, has not kept up with the psychological understanding of human conduct: psychologically, defense "by reason of insanity" is double-talk. Were such reasoning applied consistently, the inability to discriminate between right and wrong should always be an airtight defense, and many if not most of those serving time today would be freed.

We all have a number of blind spots, particularly under stressful or threatening circumstances. In all "crimes of passion," including most murders, the criminal could easily be labeled "temporarily insane" at the moment of the crime; clearly, his usual ability to make moral discriminations was not functioning at that moment. Or we might say he was convinced of his immediate personal rightness even though his act happens to be legally wrong. So why should he not be entitled to a defense of insanity?

For centuries, behavior that was not understood was called insane behavior. But since Freud (perhaps since Dostoyevsky), we do not speak of "insane behavior" without acknowledging that every one of us engages in some bizarre behavior—acts we freely label "insane" when performed by someone in a mental institution. Furthermore, we now recognize that such behavior appears to be meaningful once we understand the subject's psychological makeup and the pressures he was under at the time.

We can no longer relegate "insane behavior" exclusively to people detained in mental hospitals. We could easily relabel it "coping behavior," and we admit, if we are honest, that we, too, engage in thoroughly irrational behavior at times. Perhaps we have little more than discretion and good luck to thank for the fact that they and not we bear the labels "crazy" and "mad."

All of us have hang-ups left over from infancy: behavior we learned long ago and have never fully given up, feelings and attitudes and actions that distort our values and enable us to see "right" where everyone else sees "wrong." Whenever this particular pattern is reactivated, we are certainly not competent to distinguish right from wrong.

Why shouldn't an embezzler be entitled to claim temporary insanity during that strange, atypical period in which he, an otherwise "honest citizen," was embezzling? Why shouldn't an impulsive lover escape being sued for child support by pleading that he had no way of distinguishing right from wrong at the moment he was impregnating the woman?

The diagnosis "insane" is reserved for people who don't fit, or who don't fit in. On the other hand, the label serves as an ideal cop-out for anyone who wants to be relieved of responsibility. Many difficult but common human problems are now dignified by being labeled psychiatric diseases over which the patient presumably has no control. The patient is in fact relieved of all responsibility; he is identified as a flawed object who is available for treatment and thereby comfortably relieved of his humanity—his free choice, his self-determination.

The arbitrary nature of the diagnosis ("insane") is underscored by the "insane" experiment of Dr. David Rosenhan, professor of psychology and professor of law at Stanford University. He and seven colleagues applied for admission to mental hospitals, were diagnosed as insane because they said they were worried about their mental health, and were treated for as long as seven weeks before being released. During their hospitalization, they behaved normally. The only people who suspected they were "pseudo crazies" were some of their fellow patients. Rosenhan's conclusion: "We cannot distinguish the sane from the insane in psychiatric hospitals."

The contradiction between law and psychology does not suggest a universal plea of innocence. But unconscious motivation *is* a fact of life that the law of the land in no way acknowledges. The law holds the defendant totally responsible for his conscious motivations, but allows him to disown his own unconscious motivations—and disclaim responsibility for his acts—by protesting that he was insane at the time.

According to the myth of Oedipus, Oedipus, who had been abandoned at birth, unknowingly killed his father and married his mother. Was he guilty of patricide and incest? A modern court of law would absolve him since he did not know that Laius and Jocasta were his parents. Oedipus himself, however, accepted responsibility for his deed and, by implication, for being unconsciously motivated to do what he did.

It is clear that every society attempts to ensure its own survival by prosecuting individuals who violate its customs and belief systems. But should conscious motivation even be taken into account—especially when unconscious motivation is not? The only clear criterion for "violation" is the observable consequence of the individual's acts. Such a criterion means that the individual is held responsible for what he does, whatever his conscious and unconscious alibis may be.

Sorry About That: "Accidental" Murder

A white-collar worker recently killed his son by accidentally locking the boy in a freezer. The man was adjudged innocent of any crime since the tragedy was observed to have been an accident.

This person had been involved in similar violent accidents before. As a child he had killed a cat by accidentally dropping acid on it. He almost drowned his brother by accidentally shoving him into a well. He accidentally left a cocked bear trap in the pantry and the trap sprung shut on his father's foot. All this may not have been consciously intended, but it was probably unconsciously motivated.

It seems that if the law is to protect society, the distinction between conscious and unconscious motivation has to be reassessed. The only way to do this properly is to base legal judgments on the consequences of a defendant's acts, giving due attention to the frequency with which similar acts occur.

We have learned to listen to the consequences of a friend's behavior when we wish to identify his unconscious motivations. If our courts looked at crime from the point of view of consequences, all of us would be strongly motivated to accept responsibility for what happens as a result of our actions, regardless of whether or not we were "insane" or drunk or "just not thinking" at the time. Ignorance of the consequences should be no more valid a defense than ignorance of the law.

The man who locked his son in a freezer is an extreme example of what can happen when we disregard unconscious motivation. Everyday examples are milder but plentiful. Someone who is always surrounded by angry people explains it away by saying we all live in an unfriendly world. A husband bitterly blames his wife for nagging whenever he shows up. In both cases, the situation would be greatly improved if the subject could be induced to consider the consequences of his typical behavior and ask what contribution he may be making to the discomfort he is complaining about.

Institutionalized Violence

Violence in human affairs is definitely not "negative" per se. It is "good" or "bad" according to the century and culture, the subculture, and the occasion. American kids are truly horrified—and delighted—by Little Red Riding Hood and the Three Little Pigs and Hansel and Gretel; when they grow up they graduate to Count Dracula and Godzilla and Hitchcock.

Of course, there is also "honorable violence," which occurs spontaneously when we find ourselves on the side of violence, whatever its nature. We feel righteous rather than horrified. The issue may be reprisals in a family feud or the bombing of an enemy village. The principals may be union martyrs or company scabs. They may be kamikaze pilots on their sacred missions or they may be Americans strafing Tokyo suburbs.

"Honorable violence" is commonly institutionalized, in which case it is usually carried out by agents of official institutions and their supporters—by employees or government agencies, by members of special-interest groups, by many teachers and parents, and by police in the normal course of their assumed duties and by soldiers in times of martial law or military occupation. These agents easily deny that they used violence, or, if confronted with evidence to the contrary, that they had any such intentions.

Institutionalized violence is usually subtle, and it can be expressed in such a manner that the source is almost unrecognizable, as in the violation of individual rights, particularly the right to privacy, the misuse of government power, the secret use of unlawful means to achieve ends that may be thoroughly worthwhile, the extortion of money in exchange for political favors, and deliberate deception by elected and appointed officials.

All of these violations of our Constitution are nonetheless practiced with impunity for the most part. They cause despair and hatred among people, generations, classes, races, and they bear the seeds of revolution. When the culprit is a high government official, this one man, armed with political power, can do more violence to his people than a thousand desperate criminals.

The use of such subtle violence has developed slowly, step by step, and does not look like overt violence to any but total strangers and the immediate victims. Usually it is carried out anonymously—that is, the real author of the action is seldom identifiable. Even when he is occasionally identified, as in the Watergate exposé or the My Lai massacre, he claims that he was himself deceived, that the real responsibility rests elsewhere, or that the action, though reprehensible, was justified by the ends it was intended to achieve.

We seem cheerfully to accept the attendant fraud, and we applaud the anonymous voice in television's *Mission: Impossible*, which gravely states (a moment before it self-destructs), "As usual, Mr. Phelps, should you or any of your Iron Force be caught or killed, the Secretary will disavow any knowledge of your actions."

Individual styles, like national styles, portray very accurately the individual's peculiar preferences and compromises, but they must be evaluated within the frame of a given society. What behaviors are deemed acceptable? What do we have to do to be labeled "violent"? What can we get by with and still be called only "self-assertive"?

When the individual happens to be politically powerful, these semantic trivialities may be a matter of life or death to thousands of other human beings. A ruler may appear mild—even warm and concerned—but with a nod or a smile he can deprive many thousands of their rights and property. With an appeal to some concept such as "national character" or "national security," he can deprive hundreds of thousands of their lives. Germany under Hitler was able to kill Jews and other undesirable "nonhumans" because the German people accepted biased definitions of words like "necessity" and "human" and "violence."

If all people by the name of Smith were to be declared nonhuman, and if it were really "the thing to do" to beat up on nonhumans, then many of us non-Smiths would act out our feelings about "outsiders," and Smiths would be our target. We would respond not to the individual person but to the "Smith image," the socially acceptable scapegoat.

The Smiths of the world may not have been at fault themselves, but they are living in a society that needs scapegoats, and they have contributed to the conscience of that society. Also, they respond as scapegoats or victims are expected to respond, thereby reinforcing the expectations of their persecutors and their prosecutors. (The Jews of Warsaw foiled their persecutors when they refused to behave like victims but behaved, instead, like soldiers.)

Why does violence thrive in spite of the overt opposition of the law, the church, the school, the family, and all other "good" institutions? Several conclusions emerge.

Violence is an interactive process, and human beings appear to enjoy their roles both as villains and as victims. But violence can also be expressed in a multitude of other ways, from very subtle verbal innuendoes to carefully organized acts of massive aggression.

The human species apparently gets too much from violence to ever succeed in outlawing it. Violent behavior is a powerful means of manipulating others on many levels, unconsciously as well as consciously, and we are not about to give up such powers.

It is not easy to curb behavior which is "natural" to the species, and analyzing only the perpetrator's motives will not enlighten us very much. Progress in this area hinges on recognizing the interactive nature of violence and aggression.

The key lies in the proposition, "What if they gave a war and nobody came?" On a more everyday scale we would say, what if someone makes an aggressive lunge and nobody responds? If this occurs consistently, the aggression cannot satisfy the aggressor; it fails to elicit the horror or intimidation or resistance that it had dependably elicited in the past. This is why passive resistance may work when nothing else does. It is why the flower children survived as long as they did.

16

A New Way of Seeing: Can Society Change Itself?

Do the principles that allow us to change individual behavior have any bearing on society as a whole?

While the application of these principles to broader social problems is speculative at the moment, we can ask the questions and suggest a few promising answers.

But first let's look at the central assumptions of our "communications analysis" model and the principles by which individual behavior can be changed in terms of large groups and the mechanisms of social change:

The model is based on the assumption that we must be able to predict and in some measure control the immediate environment if we are to survive psychologically. This we accomplish largely by unaware "manipulation" of other people. The central mechanism involved is a barrage of seemingly innocuous cues so subtle that we control without knowing it.

We have a deep instinctual need to be involved with others, whether lovingly or hatefully, and these unconscious pressures keep us continually engaged with people. Our most cherished needs tend to be hidden, and we often work hard, without awareness, for goals we claim we don't want.

Unconscious control creates serious problems because those responsible don't know they are controlled—or, for that matter, that they are controlling. We can change the unconscious manipulative behavior of another person, perhaps a group of people, but to do so we need information that can only come from listening in a particular way.

This kind of listening requires emotional disengagement and careful attention to the consequences of the behavior we are observing (not what a person or a group says it wants but what it actually gets). This means listening for the entire pattern in which a specific problem behavior is embedded. It demands an appreciation of the fact that discordant needs and the compromises that follow from them are not so much a problem as they are a solution to existing, mutually exclusive pressures.

Other "rules" for effective listening include: Don't listen for what you want to hear; don't take first impressions seriously; never accept secondhand reports when direct listening is possible; and do ask what a person allows himself to do by using "feelings" as an alibi.

The secret of changing behavior is to realize that we can change people only by motivating them to make them change themselves. This can be accomplished by giving an unexpected response to their accustomed messages in order to generate uncertainty and a search for new options. Finally, the people we want to change have to be free to reprogram themselves and reorder their priorities, and they should be supported in doing so.

Obviously, our ability to motivate such change in other people requires that we first handle our own feelings and relinquish some of the familiar rewards that an established relationship has been bringing us.

How to Move a Mountain

Will these principles work with more than two people? Can one person ever, without using force or propaganda, change the behavior of an entire group?

We do have some prima facie evidence that this can happen in some group situations. In group therapy, for example, each individual has a unique style with which he attempts to affect the behavior of the entire group. Without realizing what he is doing, he resorts to "techniques" such as silence or unhappy facial and postural expressions, or perhaps an enumeration of his sufferings.

Some are so successful that the whole group begins to act in a new way, often by supporting and encouraging a member who had scarcely been noticed before. Some resort to violence or to argument. Others make use of their sense of moral sensitivity or moral outrage. All such communications are attempts to engage the group in the individual's personal web of emotional behavior, and the particular method used reflects the individual's typical style.

We once worked with a group of prisoners, all of whom were deeply suspicious of the therapist. They wondered if he were more than just an extension of the warden. However, one of the prisoners had a natural style that permitted him to sense the demands of this group, and he saw himself as a co-leader.

He took the initiative by talking about the death of his father, his own guilt in the tragedy, the fact that he had been regularly sent out to find the man when he was off on a drunk and that when he failed in his search one day, the father froze to death in the gutter.

These communications were intense and moving, and this prisoner became immediately the center of the group. His self-disclosure was contagious. The other men, sensing his relief and recognizing his leadership, began to talk about their own guilt and their own intense home experiences. The co-leader clearly set the emotional climate for the group, and his style drew deep personal responses from the others.

It so happens—as this persuasive prisoner later confessed in private—that his father was still very much alive. He had invented his "guilt" for effect. But it was not a plot or a conscious intent to deceive; it was his way of doing things, and it illustrates the power of an individual to dramatically change the behavior of a group.

An even more impressive example occurred in a German concert hall during the Hitler regime. The conductor, Franz von Hoesslin, who was married to a Jew, was told he had to choose between separating from his wife and leaving the country. He chose to leave.

In his last concert in 1935, he conducted the Ninth Symphony by Beethoven. The work was played beautifully, and the choral finale—Schiller's "Ode to Joy"—was memorable for its theme, "All mankind will become brothers" (*Alle Menschen werden Brueder*). After the performance von Hoesslin came on stage and simply and shyly announced that this was his last concert.

The tumultuous applause was interrupted when a citizen walked up onto the stage and with great feeling repeated the phrase, "*Alle Menschen werden Brueder.*" He then suggested that the audience line up and sign a referendum to keep von Hoesslin in Germany—with the implication that he would remain with his wife.

At this time there were no demonstrations in Germany, for they were discouraged by force and by the threat of internment in a concentration camp. The suggestion to collect signatures was a truly daring demand. Yet a substantial segment of the audience, still immersed in the emotional climate of applause, lined up and one by one signed the declaration.

Suddenly several Storm Troopers stood and yelled at the audience, "Jew lovers!" and there were echoes all over the music hall. "*Judenfreund!*" The man on the stage repeated, with tremendous volume, "*Alle Menschen werden Brueder,*" and for a few seconds silence reigned.

People continued to line up and to sign the petition in spite of the threat of concentration camps, loss of jobs, and social repression. The Storm Troopers were bodily ejected from the hall. People who had not dared to utter a whimper of protest now spoke up. They were engaged in the truth of what it means when all men are brothers.

One man succeeded in bringing about a profound change in the behavior of a large group. He did so spontaneously, but he nevertheless employed the principles we are familiar with for changing the unaware behavior of others. He listened accurately to the consequences of von Hoesslin's behavior and to the emotional potential of the audience. He then delivered a strong unexpected response—a defiant and upsetting act that disoriented everyone and opened them up to new behavior. He then allowed them a free choice as to what action they might choose to take.

Throughout history the powerful individuals have been those able to use similar cues for their own ("good" or "bad") ends. The Roman conquerors, by showing their battle scars to the electorate, created an emotional climate that brought them enthusiastic political support.

Franklin Roosevelt, during a critical election campaign, stood up from his wheelchair to demonstrate his personal strength. Hitler, by way of his own passionate involvement in what he was saying, convinced his followers that Germany had been deeply wronged by the Treaty of Versailles and had forfeited its national honor. Goebbels berated his audience as "ignorant masses" and yet was answered with thunderous applause.

Societies do change all the time, and sometimes even in a spectacular manner, but the direction of the change is more often than not unplanned and unpredictable. Frequently, it is instigated by an unexpected change in the environment, or by a change in technology, one central to the society's fundamental values or to its physical survival.

Famine or the coming of an ice age will force an entire society to develop new techniques and customs in order to cope with changed living conditions. The invention of the wheel, the internal combustion engine, and the flying machine caused men to modify their traditions and change their living habits in a way they could never have done by conscious design.

The environmental change, or the profound technical innovation, served as an unexpected response to the entire society; behavior that had worked for centuries suddenly proved to be ineffective or unrewarding, and a new way had to be found.

The principles involved in changing an individual may clarify what happens when broad social change is prompted by unpredicted events in the physical or social environment. Unconscious motivational forces are likely to be present, much as they are in the case of individual change.

We shall look briefly at three areas: television entertainment, the rationale for the Vietnam War, and changing life-styles in the United States. This perspective may provide clues as to how recent changes have come about, what the motivational forces have been, and how a society might think about planning for beneficial change in the future.

TV: The Hidden Message

The conscious message that commercial television delivers to its nationwide audience is, We want nothing more than to please you, educate you, and entertain you, and of course induce you to buy certain products and services. If these were the only characteristics of television, the medium surely would not have the effect it does have on the behavior of the American public (we are speaking of more than our buying habits, obviously).

Television, unfortunately, is a profoundly covert medium. It delivers a number of potent messages of which its practitioners, sponsors, and devotees are perfectly unaware—messages about affluence, one-way communication, and guns, for example.

In its dramas, in its advertisements, and even in its news stories, television teaches us that affluence is not only desirable but is to be had for the asking (as in giveaway shows). Affluence is presented as a totally rewarding indulgence that attracts beautiful women and handsome men and provides a bright spectrum of exciting recreations.

Furthermore, since television bills itself as "typically American," we all get the message that affluence is everyone's birthright. Most of the people watching television are not affluent, however, so what is drummed into their heads is the message that they are in fact denied the "good life" to which they are rightfully entitled.

People who would have been more or less content with their status twenty-five years ago see the pictures and sounds of affluence in their homes hour after hour. They are urged to rush out and buy the luxuries they cannot possibly afford, and it makes them feel they are deprived, second-class citizens.

Another "hidden" message that comes constantly from the tube is that there is no redress. There is no opportunity to answer back or to complain. We are continually bombarded with stimuli urging us to respond, but our immediate responses have no effect on anyone. Nobody out there on the other side of the little screen cares.

Children are given constant and consistent training in the experience of being talked to without concern, or with patently phony concern. In fact, the new generation of children exposed to *Sesame Street* demands constant and rapid stimulation in whatever may be offered to them as "education." Not surprisingly, they find school boring.

Television does what drugs do. Drugs—soft or hard, prescription stimulants or street acid—allow the passive subject to be turned on or soothed without responsibility, without the risk of dealing with reality or with other people. They provide an effortless massage of one's feelings without contact or consequence.

Television is a one-way trip. No channel is provided by which we might ask, How come everybody but me gets to taste the good life? We are asked—or compelled—to accept that the big, affluent world out there *does* it to us and *sells* it to us and we have nothing whatever to say about it.

The result of such one-way communication for many viewers is a pervading sense of nonconsequence, powerlessness, and isolation. They are cast in passive roles and left with no options. If they react with helpless anger, we should scarcely be surprised.

It would seem that an antidote for such training in powerlessness should require some kind of activity from which we can get a solid reaction that tells us our existence has some meaning, some impact on the world.

But the only concrete hope that medium holds out for the down-trodden—by way of yet another unconscious message—is totally nega-tive: a foolproof way for an underdog to make his presence vividly apparent and to have an unforgettable impact on society right here in his own hometown, or for that matter in Bermuda or Paris or Hong Kong. Television repeats again and again and again the message that *the gun* is the answer. The gun will make the weak strong, render the meek coura-geous, bring riches to the poor.

The overt message is that the bad guys get it in the end, but the covert information, the information that sticks, is that the gun is an equalizer, a magical wand that can change our lives, particularly if we are ugly or very small or impotent or feel we have been wronged and tread upon. The gun is presented—unconsciously for the most part—as the answer to one-way communication and to the flaunting of unattainable affluence. And the gunman always lives the more exciting life. Even his death is not to be taken too seriously.

A further message is that, in the face of violence, society is enor-mously vulnerable. Television has not only shown us how easy it is to poison water supplies, blow up power stations, hijack planes, and disrupt communications networks; it has even gone on to make these powerful acts of violence appear to be a lot simpler than they usually are in fact.

These violent stylistic "entertainments" frighten people but also give them a sense of power such as they had never possessed before. The common man, reduced to a cipher with no voice and no right to talk back, discovers that the monolithic, unhearing power structure is indeed vulnerable; it is not as powerful and unreachable as he had imagined all these years.

A case in point is the recent sentencing of two teen-agers who had held twenty-five people hostage for seven hours in a suburban Sacramento, California, bank. They had taped shotguns to the heads of three hostages and demanded a one-million-dollar ransom. They were sentenced to life imprisonment shortly before Christmas 1974, by Superior Court Judge Mark Brandler, who said the crime was patterned after a caper on a television show aired two weeks previously.

Before surrendering, the young kidnapers had demanded (and were given) an opportunity to plead their case on television—an ironic reversal of the usual one-way flow of communication in the medium.

Television violence does not often motivate crime so directly. What it does do is to communicate a largely unaware emotional climate, which covertly moves viewers toward pressing the establishment for their share of power. Unfortunately, the only means for realizing personal power that television consistently emphasizes is violence. What television consciously tells us we should rely upon (due process) is very different from what it depicts as being the way that works (the fastest gun).

At stake is the behavior of a great many members of our society—how they think, talk, and act about regaining a sense of personal consequence and a fair share of power and affluence. This behavior is being changed by the discordant and largely unconscious messages we are getting from whatever group is responsible for the program content of television.

These messages are delivered in the form of an endless barrage of seemingly innocuous cues. The medium will not change of its own accord, even if it consciously hates guns and violence, for it is not aware of its own unconscious message and doesn't wish to be made aware of it.

The current state of affairs is also perpetuated by the fact that the discordance of television's double message in regard to violence is not so much a problem for the medium as it is a solution to an earlier problem. The earlier problem was, How can we stay with gun stories (which sell) and still believe honestly that television is unquestionably a great boon to all mankind?

Is there any way that viewers as a group can change the programming behavior of TV producers as a group? There is only one way this could be done, according to our theory, and that is to deliver to the medium an unexpected, or asocial, response to its gun message, a response so uncomfortable that television will set about to change itself.

The obvious (and most unlikely) unexpected response is for viewers to destroy the ratings of pro-gun programs by not watching, or to hit sponsors with boycotts and sustained protests. One reason that this is so unlikely is that viewers are richly attracted by the implied message, namely that there may soon be a time when they can partake of the unrealistic affluence so flagrantly paraded in their homes.

How Not to Listen: Vietnam

The history of American involvement in Vietnam provides a clear parallel to the personal experience of a man who ignores the consequences of poor judgment and focuses instead on the problem of justifying himself. The man compounds his mistakes with further acts designed to prove himself right and thus delivers a series of increasingly discordant messages. He refuses to check with reality and to hear the advice that could rescue him.

The avowed purpose of the United States was to combat the influence of the communists in Southeast Asia. Policymakers argued that if we did not "save" South Vietnam from communism, neighboring nations would also "fall" like dominoes. We were saving the country, even if we had to physically destroy it in order to do so.

When our considerable efforts proved inconclusive, some of our hidden motivations came to the surface. We now had to win this "non-war" in order to support our friends and maintain the confidence of our allies. Our own honor became more important than the political freedom of the Vietnamese.

When massive bombing proved to be an ineffective technique in the jungles, we responded to this information by dropping twice as many bombs. The only consequences we dared look at were things like counting the number of enemy dead each day to "prove" we were winning, and even in this activity a large head count became more important than objective reporting of the facts.

We got to be so out of touch with reality that we actually achieved what we claimed to be fighting *against,* and we remained the only people in the world who could not or would not see it. We would not face the actual consequences of our actions, and we thus permitted ourselves to give the communists the very things they most wanted: we greatly strengthened the resolve of North Vietnam and solidly unified its citizenry; we bled the economy of the United States by fueling a major war effort on the opposite side of the earth; we ensured worldwide sympathy for our dogged little opponent; we accomplished a disastrous political split among our own people.

Seen in this perspective, the massacre at My Lai was just one more bonus for the communists. The United States in effect committed treason against itself (by providing aid and comfort to the enemy) while patting itself on the back.

The parallel with self-defeating behavior in an individual is remarkable. Our most cherished needs were hidden and we were busy achieving goals we claimed we did not want. We couldn't find our way out of our worsening dilemma because we were not aware that we were ourselves responsible for it.

We were obsessed with "target behavior" (head counts and bomb counts) and failed to notice the fixed-action pattern of our overall involvement. We failed to hear the discord we were continually communicating to the world and to our own people.

We listened only for what we wanted to hear. We never considered asking what real-life consequences our rationalizations and our patriotic feelings *led to* because we were so concerned about justifying what we *wanted* to do.

Changing the Establishment

Sexual mores in the United States have changed radically during the past fifteen or twenty years. Not only are young people adopting a new morality almost as a matter of course, but many of their parents are moving in the same direction.

Such a dramatic change in the living and loving habits of a substantial percentage of the population cannot be explained simply by the invention of a more convenient contraceptive. Our society has been changing itself, and the change appears to be not only spreading but lasting.

We like to call it a "sexual revolution," but sexual behavior is only part of a much larger pattern and is not likely to have changed without the other changes that are occurring along with it.

The new pattern involves a reassessment of professional commitment—of our entire work ethic; it involves a breaking down of the old male and female role stereotypes and of discrimination on the basis of age. It recognizes the rights of women and accepts generally many things (cohabitation of unmarried partners and homosexuality, for example) that were previously tolerated only among a few fringe elements of society.

It does embrace a revolution in sexual behavior, but it is more fundamentally a revolution of individualism, a new definition of a human being's rights to choose his work and choose his pleasure, free of stereotypical role expectations and with a minimum of censure and social pressure.

In many ways, the changed social behavior of large groups in our society parallels the change of an individual who consciously or unconsciously creates a new environment for himself. In both cases, the change appears disruptive to many people caught in the periphery of what's going on, but it is neither capricious nor destructive. It has come about as the result of very careful listening to the consequences of the old way.

Using every means at its disposal—books, newspapers, television, musicals, records, films, concerts, word of mouth—society has looked at itself and told itself about itself, often in very critical tones. The criticisms are usually well founded, sometimes devastating, and together they amount to an unexpected response so uncomfortable that the culture has to begin looking for better ways of handling some of its daily problems of living.

New ways and bold experiments fare better when undertaken in a supportive environment, as we would expect, and it was a lot easier to make a new life-style stick in California than in Mississippi. Also, such changes are much easier for the young than for their parents, because older men and women have invested tremendous funds of energy, emotion, and money in the more conservative style they adopted long ago from their own parents.

The traditional, established ways are still supported by people who have a vested interest in them or who cannot themselves face the prospect of changing: namely, the "establishment." The messages of the establishment are necessarily filled with discordance; the establishment is strong and effective precisely because it has found workable compromise solutions for most of the complex problems that threaten society.

When the discordance became too great to be easily rationalized, it became obvious to many of us, particularly to children who were lectured in honesty by dishonest adults and told to be loving by stiff-lipped disciplinarians. The discordance became traumatic when the establishment overreacted to minor innovations such as rock music and long hair, treating these with more contempt than it ever showed for racial discrimination, armed intervention in other nations' internal affairs, industrial profiteering, or blatant political dishonesty.

The establishment of any era inevitably classifies new customs and new values as serious problems when in fact they are solutions—brand-new compromises for existing problems the establishment finds too uncomfortable to look at closely. As with changes in an individual, old habits persist and persevere, for they are familiar, reassuring, and were in their time workable solutions to some distressing problem.

But just as an individual has a personality—certain consistencies of style that determine what experiences he will tolerate—so an establishment also has its stylistic characteristics. Many "establishments" in history were incapable of accepting any change whatever; they were not geared to accommodate a changing reality. Revolutions typically occur when the establishment takes a "let-them-eat-cake" view of life, where changes in the environment—realities such as starvation, for example—are denied.

It appears that the establishment in our country has a more "giving" style. There is a growing recognition among Americans that authority (central authority in particular) can make serious mistakes in both judgment and deed. This feeling is expressed by members of the establishment as well as by the self-styled "free spirits" who protest current policies or initiate new modes of conduct. The nation's style of reluctantly accepting change allows us to learn from some of our mistakes and makes overt revolution less likely.

Society does not make a habit of listening to itself, but it always pricks up its ears when internal discordance becomes too loud to ignore or when painful organs within it deliver distressingly unexpected responses to the whole body. We then search for a better way of coping and look upon innovation and experiment with more tolerance. Each "new morality" or "new freedom" becomes a candidate for popular acceptance once it has shed its excesses; that is, it may well become the new "establishment" before long.

In America, the people were able eventually to listen for the consequences of their own behavior in Vietnam because their national style permitted such listening and self-criticism—something which was surely not permitted, for instance, in Germany in the late thirties. As a result of careful listening, we look for and eventually discover other options—

more accurate labels for old concepts and behaviors that are more in line with our current needs.

Such an attitude, such a style, allows us to experiment with new ways of dressing, relating, working, and believing, without having to worry about being tarred and feathered. Our current style, which encourages us to doubt people in authority, is never specifically taught but is covertly present everywhere.

Creative Responses

Although it does not look as if a society can deliberately change its own behavior or traditions in a predetermined direction, individuals can change in major ways and today a great many of them are doing so.

The individual change in each case stems from inescapable necessity or from a creative response to a difficult situation. The usual response to an interpersonal problem or a threatening situation is to react in the same familiar way that has perpetuated similar problems in the past, or to make a declaration of good intention.

Good intentions, unfortunately, are neither creative nor helpful, although they may serve to protect the speaker from routine criticism. They imply the acceptance of responsibility but are in practice only gestures in that direction. A parent's good intentions are not enough to repair a badly damaged family communications network, and a television executive's good intentions do not often improve the quality of TV programming.

What does make a difference is a response that ignores what is expected and addresses itself directly to the real issue, which is often hidden. It is action that acknowledges the obvious expectations but suggests an answer to the unconscious dilemma.

The creative response is not routine and it does not concern itself with declared intentions. It is a direct reaction to the observable consequences of whatever actions have been taken so far, and it assumes that the actor has created these consequences, whether he is consciously aware of what he is doing or not.

The creative response is most of all disengaged. It refuses to be conned or pressured, to be sucked into following an old script. It refuses to follow precedents. It exercises an absolute veto insofar as it refuses to participate automatically in an established pattern.

According to a newspaper report, a young man went into a grocery store, pulled out a gun, and told the elderly woman at the cashier's desk to "stick 'em up and hand over the money!" The woman smiled at the bandit and said, in a kindly voice. "How much do you really need, son?" The man lowered his gun and said meekly, "Two dollars, ma'am." He took the two dollars handed to him and left.

We are all run by patterns, and we can change them if we care enough. Human beings do not inevitably ossify with age, but remain flexible most of their lives and are able to change at any age, given the proper incentives or training.

We believe it is realistically possible to regain our smothered freedom of informed decision and choice. We should be and can be free to decide to what ends, by what means, and by whom our personal behavior is to be controlled.

We do have free choice and we do make choices. Usually, our choices are made by default, but we can reach out and choose clearly at any time. We can change patterns that aren't working. We can do this if we listen well, if we have the guts to deliver a hard response when one is called for, and if we have the humanity to allow the other person to find his own way. We all stand to gain in personal freedom and in dignity of our own making.

Index